Sweet
and
Delicious
Wishes

What readers are saying about
Magnetizing Your Heart's Desire

Written with profound love and clarity!

Sharon Warren has given us all a great gift for this millennium! *Magnetizing Your Heart's Desire* shall be joyfully introduced at ALL of our events. It is written with profound love and clarity. Thank you, Sharon!

Lee Carroll & Jan Tober, World Renowned Authors and Lecturers of the Kryon and Indigo Children books.

TIMELY! EMPOWERING!

Through true accounts and personal experience, *Magnetizing Your Heart's Desire* illustrates how the events of our outer world clearly reflect our inner dialogue of thought and emotion. Long after her book has been read, Sharon Warren's words remain with us, echoed as the miracles that offer themselves in each moment of our lives.

Gregg Braden, Author, International Seminar Presenter
The Isaiah Effect, Decoding The Lost Science of Prayer & Prophecy

Everyone should read this book!

"If you want to learn about the laws of manifestation—read this book! In a beautiful, simple and powerful way, Sharon Warren teaches us all the spiritual principles necessary to create our lives with heart and meaning."

Carolyn Conger, PhD, International Seminar leader

Do Miracles Still Happen? You Bet! Read this book!

Do miracles still happen? You bet! Read Sharon Warren's book, *Magnetizing Your Heart's Desire*, live her principles and you'll experience miracles in your own life. Within days, the course of my life and my family's was changed for the better because of this book. I've been wearing the magnets in an elegant locket around my neck just to remind myself of the true inner power she has taught me I possess. Some call it faith, Sharon calls it the Law of Attraction, whatever the words, this is the same stuff that parted the Red Sea!

Tamera Smith Allred is an author, award-winning newspaper columnist and reporter, and a Pulitzer Prize nominee

Extraordinarily Valuable Book!

"An extraordinarily valuable book for those who are on the path of self realization and transformation."

W. Brugh Joy, M.D., Author of *Joy's Way*,
A Map For The Transformational Journey

The book we've all been waiting for!

This is the book we all have been waiting for! Everything we will ever need to know about growth, self-help and spiritual development is packed into these pages. Easy to read, easy to understand, filled with fun and practical wisdom, *Magnetizing Your Heart's Desire* will change you inside and out, now and forever!

Mimi Greek, Arizona, Award winning author:
MasterMind DreamMakers, In Love, In Power & In Joy

We can't keep it on our bookshelf!

I don't actually read words—I go by FEELINGS and this book is an INCREDIBLE FEEL every time it is in my hands. We can't keep it on our bookshelf because it sells so quickly!

Judy Manganiello, Owner,
A Peace of the Universe Bookstore, Scottsdale, AZ

I couldn't put this book down!

I was unable to put your book down until I had finished it! *Magnetizing Your Heart's Desire* is like finding the light switch in a room after stumbling around in the dark. Thank you so very much for enlightening my life!

Darlene Erickson, Minnesota

A Real Treasure!

Sharon Warren has presented a direct, simple yet insightful vision of one of the fundamental forces of our universe (electromagnetic attraction). Practical in her approach, Ms. Warren addresses how this knowledge of electromagnetic attraction can be used in daily life. For beginners in metaphysics, this book is a real treasure. And for advanced students, this book is a great reminder of the energetics underlying our actions and our desires.

Tom Kenyon, M.A., author of Brain States, Intntl. Seminar Presenter

I've ordered 90 copies so far!

So far, I have ordered 90 copies of *Magnetizing Your Heart's Desire*! I have given copies to my children, my staff and my friends because it is such an outstanding book that changes lives. I want the best in life and Sharon Warren has clarified and simplified how to live a JOYFUL life. The magnets are ingenious and so are the fun and inspired teachings!

Laurie Hostetler, The Kerr House, Ohio

♥ ♥

A Rare Book That Could Actually Change Your Life!

Featured Book Selection, May, 2003 at OfSpirit.com

Leaving the hype for books that need it, I'm going to be straight and to the point: *Magnetizing Your Heart's Desire* is one of those rare books that could actually change your life. Of course, you have to read it and utilize the insightful wisdom it conveys in order to expect any change…or do you?

To tell you the truth, I honestly believe that the mere act of reading this book will affect how you think…which will automatically incite changes to your life force energy…which will then set off a chain reaction of vibrational attraction to create the exact vision you have for your life. Phew! And since you are creating whatever it is that you are thinking about at this very moment—be it something you desire or something you fear—then I recommend you get a copy of this book fast to learn the proper way of aligning your thoughts so you will get what you want rather than what you don't want out of life.

I have to comment on the surprising bonuses that come with this book: cool magnets that demonstrate the power of attraction, a gorgeous hardcover with full color graphics (not a paper book jacket), heavy crisp quality paper, fun graphics and playful text layout, and a pretty purple ribbon for a bookmark. This is not an inexpensive book to publish. Yet, the expense and energy put into the creation of this book turn it into much more than a read; it makes reading it an experience!
—Bob Olson, OfSpirit.com editor, 2003

AN IMMEDIATE ZING IN MY HEART AND SOUL!

Well, my friends, I rarely come across a book that is an immediate zing in my heart and soul! Sharon Warren's *Magnetizing Your Heart's Desire* is an amazing book that will "EMPOWER" YOU beyond what you could ever imagine. This book covers everything! It has many very specific tools on how to truly magnetize all your deeply held heart's desires in your life. I absolutely adore this outstanding book! It is so comprehensive and fun. The rare-earth magnets are brilliant and a joy to use to understand the Law of Attraction. I am fascinated using the Creation Box and how powerful it is. This book teaches how to magnetize all your heart's desires. I have featured Sharon's book in my product catalog, as well as on my web site at MPowerTV.com. It truly contains fresh, life changing tools in every chapter and I want to share this inspired book with everyone who is excited to live on purpose.

Michele Blood, MPowerTV.com & Musivation Intnl., LaJolla, CA., 2003

POWERFUL AND FUN!!

I love the way Sharon weaves humor and stories along with her incredibly powerful (and simple!) ways in every chapter to create what we want in our lives. By using these tools, I created the *very best and highest* paying job I have ever had. Thank you, Sharon, for helping me manifest my heart's desires and laughing all the way to the bank!! You and your book are awesome! I threw the "other" books away and use only yours.

Dallas, Gold Canyon, AZ. 2003

Empowering ! I magnetized a $5 Million Dollar Home!

I am a living example of how Warren's teachings work and empower us with easy tools, practical skills and inspiration. I am a true believer and immediately magnetized my heart's desires! I removed myself from a toxic relationship, wrote down my heart's desire and faithfully visualized a home for seven days.

I quickly and easily manifested living in a magnificent *$5 MILLION DOLLAR HOME on two acres in a gated community* for six months without incurring a cent of rent!! This estate is truly a sanctuary where I am living in the lap of luxury with all services provided. I am safe, secure and living like a queen. The law of attraction in action tools in this book magnetized my heart's desire quickly and it is a dream-come-true!

My copy of *Magnetizing Your Heart's Desire* lives by my bedside, marked with colorful highlights and my personal margin notations. I read and re-read it. After meeting Ms. Warren, I find her to be playful, fun, insightful and spiritual, and as uplifting as her book. Thank you so much, Sharon Warren, for one of the most life-changing books I have ever read!

Lorraine, Paradise Valley, AZ, August, 2003

A Life Changing Book!

This book is for those looking for change in their life...for the better! I am impressed with how easy this book is to understand, but detailed enough to give you the thought processes to totally turn your life around to positive wanting. This book has changed my life!

A Reader from Colorado Springs, CO. – 2003

See more testimonials in the back of this book.

Magnetizing Your Heart's Desire

Name it and Claim it!

Sharon Warren

Sharon A. Warren, M.A.

Amazing Grace Unlimited Press

Magnetizing Your Heart's Desire
By Sharon A. Warren, M.A.

First Edition published in November, 1999
Second Edition published in November, 2002
Third Edition published in January, 2004

Published by
Amazing Grace Unlimited Press
Phone: (480) 816-9930 (M-F 9 a.m.–4 p.m. MST)
Fax orders: (480) 816-9960
E-mail: iam@amazinggracenow.com
www.amazinggracenow.com
www.magnetizingyourheartsdesire.com (Sharon's *Flowing Your Energy* columns online)
www.lawofattractioninaction.com
www.sharonwarren.com

Interior Design: The Printed Page, Phoenix, Arizona using Corel Ventura™ Publisher

ISBN: 0-9674990-1-1
LCCN: 99-96403

Printed in Korea through DaehanPrinting.

Contents

Safety Warnings Regarding the Use of Magnets

THESE MAGNETS ARE VERY POWERFUL. They should be treated responsibly and with respect. **Keep them under adult supervision at all times**. These magnets **SHOULD NOT** be in the proximity of pacemakers, watches, credit cards with magnetic strips, computers and computer disks, televisions and stereo equipment, nor audio and video tapes. Children love to invent games with magnets with an assortment of steel washers, paper clips, nuts and bolts, etc. **Due to the size of these magnets, they are not appropriate for children under 10 years of age. Be sure to monitor any children who may play with them**. You can demonstrate attracting or repelling forces through a wooden desktop or magazine. You can also use them to find lost articles that are magnetic (like picking up nails when hanging pictures, etc).

When I wrote this book last year, the larger set of magnets which are described herein had been originally used by my husband in the food industry. I utilized that set of magnets in classes for demonstration purposes for years. That size is 2" high by 7/8" diameter, however, they were too large to easily package with this book. In 1999, I discovered the availability of rare earth magnets. While these magnets are smaller in size (1" high x 1/4" diameter), they are equally powerful to demonstrate the principle of repelling and attracting. They are also an ideal packaging size to accompany this book. Magnets are available on the order form in the back of this book if you wish to have additional sets.

I am grateful that we "magnetized" the **Arizona Industries for the Blind** to package this product. My dear friend, Carolyn Henderson, is legally blind and I have been inspired for years by her wonderful attitude in spite of her physical challenges. She lives a victorious life and was instrumental in the final editing of this book. It was a sweet vibrational match to attract AIB for packaging the magnets and helping physically challenged people move towards greater self-sufficiency.

Acknowledgments, Applause & Appreciation

I celebrate and joyfully dedicate this book to the following people for whom I am profoundly grateful in the alchemy of my life:

To Abraham and the inspired teachings co-created exuberantly and exquisitely through Jerry and Esther Hicks. And, my deep gratitude to Patricia Mulreany for her delicious co-creation with Abraham-Satarcia and our uplifting times together.

My divine partner, beloved husband, and fellow adventurer, Duaine Warren, who abundantly supported and totally encouraged following my bliss in pursuing my dream of writing, *Magnetizing Your Heart's Desire*. I love you eternally for all that you are and do—and especially for your wit and sense of humor which helped enormously through the "dry" spells.

Germaine Cabe, whom I fondly and aptly named, St. Germaine. Precious friend, enthusiastic cheerleader and divine counselor, who held the vision and was always available as a shiny accomplice in magnetizing miracles with constant support, time, humor, vibrancy, superb editing skills and endless supply of in-the-moment-on-demand creative graphics.

Troy Warren, our beloved son, who was the first recipient of the "hands-on" magnets and our exhilarating experiences to evolve as Deliberate Creators. And to my precious, yummy grandchildren, Alexis, Schuyler (Skye) and Chelsea, who constantly teach me about the magic of love, innocence, play and fun.

Donald Curtis, my dear father, and Betty Babbitt, who proved through the teachings in this book that "you can teach an old dog new tricks" by their courage, willingness and commitment to learn and grow in becoming Deliberate Creators! And, my dear mother, Margaret Curtis, who shared her love and presence from the invisible realms of the non-physical and gave me the gift of life and laughter.

Tom and Pam Kenyon and the Bali Tribe participants for our sacred journey, which was the initiation and divine orchestration for this book being born; Gregg Braden, dear friend and fellow Cancerian; Mimi Greek, for introducing me to Abraham's teachings; Carolyn and Cork Henderson, Ann Kurchack and Shawn Swain, who were devoted allies and dearest friends that generously provided valuable feedback and were so supportive and excited in this birthing process.

My dear forever soul sisters, Joanne Snow, Laurie Hostetler, Joyous Lesperance, Shirley Fredrick, Mary Lou Shambaugh, and Robin Mullin, who are always sweet, succulent supporters in all our juicy co-creations and loving, fun adventures. And, angel Monica Kane, for her computer expertise and assistance in sustaining my MacIntosh to complete this book, as well as our mutual camaraderie and passion for angels.

To all my beloved mentors and teachers, both physical and non-physical, who have divinely guided me, I am eternally grateful. Like the words shared in one of my favorite songs, Amazing Grace, "When we've been there ten thousand years, bright shining as the sun, we've no less days to sing God's praise, than when we'd first begun."

Lisa Liddy, (printedpage@cox.net), an impeccable, professional book designer and typesetter, who magnificently assisted as a midwife to birth my book into this polished, professional reality. I had God bumps and tears upon seeing my manuscript for the first time…a moment I will always hold dear. Lisa truly goes the extra mile and is devotion in motion in her dedication to excellence and detail.

Marcia Schaefer, who scouted and blazed the book production trail ahead of me—a wondrous, sharing companion of all her book's resources, as well as a superb coach.

My heartfelt appreciation to Dan Sherman, a human being disguised as an angel, whose contribution was amazing grace.

My greatest gratitude and love to Jan Tober and Lee Carroll for their ongoing support and the inspired and shiny contribution they are making to the world through their Kryon and Indigo children work.

**According to author, Janice Graham,
poet Jimmy Santiago Baca has alluded to writing as,
"A sparkling fountain of energy that fills your spirit."
I wholeheartedly agree!**

Sharon A. Warren,
Fountain Hills, Arizona
1999

I celebrate and joyfully dedicate this book to all shining souls who are open, ready and excited to create miracles and magic as Deliberate Creators in magnetizing your heart's desires through the Law of Attraction in Action.

Since I have been teaching for 30 years, I have a multitude of notes and files. Some stories were shared by students and friends who had personal stories or resources, many of which are not signed nor dated. Every effort has been made to trace all present copyright holders of the materials shared in this book, whether companies or individuals. Any omission is unintentional and I will be pleased to correct, add and acknowledge any resources or people in future editions of this book and workshops. Your assistance is appreciated.

I would very much enjoy hearing from you and also love to know what really worked well for you in magnetizing your outcome. My hope is that you find value and inspiration in all aspects of your life in magnetizing your heart's desires.

Introduction

"Each soul comes to this Earth with gifts."

"The road to your soul is through the heart."

...Gary Zukav, The Seat of the Soul

The Magnets

You may be wondering why this book includes a set of magnets. Magnets demonstrate how energy flows. Like a set of magnets, when you focus your energies, you can magnetize your heart's desires. When you are focused as a Deliberate Creator, you are excited and exuberant. Things are really thriving and cookin' in your life and you have a passion for becoming more of who you really are. You are creating and vibrating joy, love, delicious well being, yummy friends and relationships, inspiration, having great fun and a darn good time knowing you are the Divine Attractor. You dearly appreciate and are divinely enthusiastic about your life. As you will see, the magnets demonstrate this dramatically when they are moving toward each other through positive attraction, attention and direction. You are aware of your gifts and abundantly sharing

↑↖↗↙↘←→↓ ↓→←↘↙↗↖↑	De-magnetized
↑↑↑↑↑↑↑↑↑↑ ↑↑↑↑↑↑↑↑↑↑	Magnetized
→→→→→→ →→→→→→	Congruent

1

them. You have an instant understanding of how the energy of the "outer" magnets are a mirror for your inner thoughts and vibrations when your energy is focused and lined up. It is the Law of Attraction in Action.

Conversely, when your life is riddled with fears and you don't make conscious choices to create your reality, your life looks like the "de-magnetized" illustration. The energy is not focused in any consistent direction. It is scattered and randomly moving in many different directions. When your life is "demagnetized," you are not living your life on purpose. When you turn one magnet around from one end to the other, you will see how they repel and resist. You cannot get them "aligned" or connected. This is what happens when you push against life with thoughts and vibrations such as anger, struggle, anxieties, frustration, money worries, not being "good enough," unforgiving, blaming, criticizing, and complaining. We are all magnetizing events into our lives through the Law of Attraction either consciously or unconsciously.

The Best Way to Predict Your Future Is to Create It!

The magnets reflect whether you are magnetizing and moving toward your heart's desires or whether you are in resistance. You can push against and resist what is happening in your life or you can consciously choose to participate joyously as a Deliberate Creator. Life treats you the way you treat yourself. This is a "hands-on" book. Using the magnets as a tool will assist you in seeing how you set energies into motion through your positive or negative emotions. You will learn how to magnetize your heart's desires and activate the special gifts you were born to share and celebrate.

"May you live in interesting times..."

...A Chinese Proverb

This book actually was birthed as a result of a journey to Bali in 1997. My husband, Duaine, and I had planned a metaphysical group trip to Bali co-created with our colleagues, Tom and Pam Kenyon, for a total of 28 people. My master's degree is in *Sacred Sites, Art & Architecture* and my husband and I have traveled successfully the world over both alone and with groups for many years. Participants always rendezvous in a designated city so we can all travel together overseas. However, this was the first time we had such group "misadventures" of this nature.

Our participants' travel "misadventures" included planes with engine problems; flights that were delayed or canceled; weather problems in Chicago resulting in the entire airport shutting down in August; and four people had to stay there overnight and missed their flight to Los Angeles and Bali; two participants' travel itineraries didn't match their actual tickets when they checked in so they missed their Alaskan flights to Los Angeles and our outbound flight to Bali; one person's luggage didn't arrive for the overseas flight, and we even had a "lost" passenger from Alaska who arrived in Bali a day early without any itinerary of where to stay. Upon our arrival in Bali, another passenger discovered the return portion of her U.S. ticket was missing from her airline folder. "Shift" happens! We went with the flow—bumpy beginning that it was! The Chinese proverb quoted earlier is also known as the Chinese "curse" and so our trip became very "interesting" right out of the gate.

Little did I dream that these "misadventures" and "challenges" in travel plans would turn into the book you now hold in your hands. Contrast was definitely afoot. It became an exquisite "set up" for what would unfold in how I ultimately magnetized new personal understandings and insights about life's "opportunities"—formerly known as "problems" (depending on one's perspective). We can see things as an "upset," or as a mirror which reflects a "set up" for our personal growth and unfoldment. The choice is always ours.

One of the first things we observed in Denpasar (Bali) as we traveled through the city were all the sacred statues decorated and adorned with BLACK and WHITE fabric. We immediately asked our driver why the statues were adorned in this way and he said it had to do with the light and the dark forces—my first subtle clue for "**contrast**."

In our group, we had one well to do couple who were what could kindly be called "high maintenance." They complained, criticized, judged and compared anything and everything the entire trip. Nothing ever seemed to be good enough and they verbalized it to anyone who would listen. Later I realized how all of this fit in my personal growth and the important part that **contrast** played in shifting in my awareness. The high maintenance couple missed most of the magic of being in "paradise."

Fabric adorning statues and homes in *Bali (1997)*

They were so busy "shoulding"—while the rest of our tribe was grateful, fulfilled and totally in awe of the beauty and inspiration we were experiencing. In retrospect, I realized how it was all divinely designed, as each person and situation was essential in the interplay of light and dark forces being exquisitely orchestrated as "contrast."

Had I other than experienced the light and dark aspects being splayed out, I wouldn't have had the heightened understanding of how "contrast" can serve us. It literally became the inspiration for this book. Contrast presents different perspectives through a mirror of "opposites" and new decisions and choices are then born with greater clarity.

The black and white illustration above could also represent the Game Board of Life or a Chess Board. There will always be polarity in life to provide contrast. It's then your "move" as a player on life's game board to flow energy and vibrate with your heart's desire. You have a voice, as a Deliberate Creator, in making new choices in the Game of Life. You become more skilled by knowing what feeeels good and focusing on what you want. How you feel is always your point of attraction.

We lived in Indiana for 23 years. As a former Hoosier, I was very familiar with the Indy 500 car races and the black and white flag symbolism. It means "contrast" or slow down. In other words, be aware of what you are feeling. Most of us are aware in basic physics that like attracts like. Good feels good and bad feels bad so the Universe is giving you clues to which energy you are vibrating. Choose what empowers you and feeeels good because that is your signal for the Law of Attraction in Action. The power and speed of magnetizing your heart's desires is always through your pure, positive, passionate, penetrating emotions. Your thoughts and emotions feed, vibrate, pulsate and radiate in every area of your life—negatively or positively.

A woman I read about named Frances Messier, in a brief synopsis of her trip to Greece, noted that on a hilltop at Delphi, where one looks across olive trees to the sea, there is a circular pavement centered with a medallion. Around the medallion are five words:

Beauty–Truth–Love–Justice–Choice

The word **CHOICE** is rarely found in lists with those other qualities, although choice determines how much of the other four we have.

This book is dedicated to the value of **CONTRAST**. It will demonstrate and illustrate how to magnetize your heart's desires easily, effortlessly and quickly. You will learn the value of contrast in making higher choices and new visions for your joyful decisions with delicious outcomes. You will be delighted, ignited and excited to see how you can learn to magnetize your heart's desires through the Law of Attraction by using these magnets as a "hands-on barometer" for how you are flowing your energy.

The Law of Attraction Flows Through the Power of Your Choices and the Clarity of Your Focus.

The Law of Attraction in Action

Go confidently in the direction of your dreams! Live the life you've always imagined!

…Henry David Thoreau

These magnets are a wonderful mirror for your life. How would it feel if you were willing to make any life situation be easy in your imagination? Take a moment to visualize going confidently and joyfully toward your dreams and the life you have always imagined instead of being "side-tracked" and immersed in worry and anxieties. Struggle is a strain. Ease energizes and is liberating when you are aligned and moving toward your outcomes. Let the magnets demonstrate how focused energy "matches" and moves you immediately toward your heart's desires. Will Rogers said, "Even if you're on the right track, you'll get run over if you just sit there." You are constantly giving birth to your creations every day through your dominant thoughts and intentions and even attracting the things you do not want through your creative powers.

Magnetic Attraction in Action
Playing With Your Magnets is Fun!

Let these magnets be a life-changing concept. Hold them in your hands and let them show you how you attract or repel your heart's desires with every thought. You are literally creating a new world consciously and deliberately, in this very moment, by using these magnets as a profound tool to demonstrate the Law of Attraction. These magnets are your "vibrational meter" to measure and receive instant feedback on

6

how your thoughts attract, create and expand constantly through the LAW OF ATTRACTION, both positively and negatively.

I invite you to play with the magnets now and have fun. Feel and see how they work. Turn the magnets around from one end to the other end so you understand the energy of attracting and repelling magnetically using the two magnets. Notice the difference in how easy it is to create (attract) when you have an instant energy match magnetically and how difficult it is when you have to struggle (repel=push against) when one magnet is turned around to the opposite end and is a "mismatch" with lots of resistance. You cannot get it to touch the other magnet no matter how much you may attempt to by "trying" or forcing it. Notice the magnetic ease and speed of attracting when the energy is properly "lined up," as well as the struggle that results in "pushing against" when one magnet is turned around to the other end.

This book could easily have been entitled, **I CREATE** because we literally do create or discreate with every thought—deliberately or by default. You will know when you are creating deliberately because you feel joyous, loving, exuberant and harmonious. You feel a strong sense of freedom and play, abundance and excitement for your creations and your passions. **Life will be saying YES to you** when you are deliberately creating, attracting, vibrating and manifesting your heart's desires on purpose.

A Fun Fishy Creation & Demonstration Story

A humorous example of instant manifesting is a true story shared by my dear friend, Germaine Cabe. Her husband, Steve, like my husband, Duaine, has been somewhat skeptical and a "doubting Thomas" in the past. This is a true story:

> "My husband and friends have become very good-natured with their tongue-in-cheek about my constantly saying, 'Just ask the Universe.' At least now, they have stopped rolling their eyes and crossing their arms when I either request something from the Universe or give thanks to the Universe when my various desires and outcomes manifest. I was out of the country

when this 'creation' occurred so I know the Universe was clearly showing them how perfectly it all works, even when I'm not around to do the asking and intending on their behalf.

My husband and our two close friends, John and Michelle, rented a rowboat and went trout fishing. Michelle got a good bite and excitely reeled in her catch. She got it up close to the boat, but since they had no fishing net, the slippery trout managed to jump right out of her hands. They mourned the loss of the trout and set about with determination to catch another one.

Minutes later, John felt a tug on his line and hollered, 'I've got one!' He reeled in fish #2 and the same scenario was repeated. He got the fish up to the side of the boat, had no net to bring it in, fish got away. John swore under his breath and grunted, 'THAT'S IT! THE FIRST THING I'M DOING WHEN WE GET OFF THIS BOAT IS GOING DOWN TO THE COUNTRY STORE AND BUY A FISHING NET! THIS IS RIDICULOUS! We'll never catch anything this way!!'

Powerful In The Moment Declaration "Nets" Magical Manifestation

Five minutes later, John said, 'Hey, I got something...no, wait...I think my line is just hung up on a log. It doesn't feel like a fish—not enough action.' He tugged and reeled away. Then he felt the tension ease and started to bring in the mysterious object. Can you imagine it was a FISHING NET?! A very nice fishing net, looking no worse for wear after being submerged for who knows how long. The threesome broke out into laughter, raised their beers to the sky and shouted, 'THANK YOU UNIVERSE!' A strong desire with no resistance. An instant manifestation in magnetizing their heart's desire! I really think they are starting to believe and see how this 'Universe stuff' works."

What a wondrous and fun example of THE LAW OF ATTRACTION IN ACTION! Also, notice that when they received their desire, they remembered to say thank you!!!

Achieving Vibrational Harmony

These magnets are a dramatic mirror of what happens when you achieve vibrational harmony with your heart's desire. Germaine's inspiring fish net story exquisitely illustrates that when your heart's desire and your vibration are aligned, magic happens. That is because you are connected to your Source and your Stream Of Well Being without resistance. What looks like "magic" is simply the right use of energy. When you are connected to your Stream of Well Being, you will be vibrating on purpose.

Every moment we are awake or conscious, we are outputting a vibration and the Universe accepts that as our point of attraction and matches it through the **LAW OF ATTRACTION**. Some of you are aware of affirmations and use them frequently. However, often you don't receive the results of your intentions because the words are spoken "routinely." Many of us unknowingly send vibrations and signals that contradict our desires. An example Abraham[1] has often used is: "I'd like a new red car"…which is your heart's desire, followed by "and I can't afford it" or "it's too expensive," which is then in direct opposition and cancels out what you say you desire. So, where is the vibrational match?! Whenever you are "contradicting" your heart's desire, you have resistance (such as I can't afford). You are then vibrating "lack." The Universe accepts that as your signal and will respond and match it accordingly through the Law of Attraction in Action.

Take the magnets in your hands again and state your personal heart's desire for a __(your choice)__ (a new red car or whatever) which is a vibrational match. Notice how the magnets are powerfully drawn together in the same direction once you have identified your intention. That's a vibrational match! Good job! Piece of cake!!! Now, the Universe must deliver to you that which is pulsating and radiating from your vibration because it is in harmony with your decision and your point of attraction. **That's the Law of Attraction in ACTION!** You can see how exciting and fulfilling it is when you have a powerful match dramatically demonstrated by these magnets. Your energy is pure, positive and

---

1   Abraham. See appendix.

pulsing with the vibration of your heart's desire and you can easily see the magnetic results.

A Chinese proverb says it very succinctly:

"If you keep going in the direction you're going, you'll end up where you're headed."

Another way I've heard something similar is:

"It's easier to ride a horse in the direction he's headed."

In fact, it always makes me laugh out loud when I think of riding a horse any other way. It's so obvious. And yet our beliefs often throw sand and resistance on our stated intentions and affirmations by offering a contradictory statement like "but I can't afford it"—or "it's too expensive." It's like riding a horse backwards.

Now take your magnets in your hands again and turn one magnet around so you are using the opposite end. You will notice what happens to the magnets when you make up your own statement which you are aware would contradict your heart's desire. See how the magnets actually repel one another! That is creation by "default" which pushes it away. Most people don't make it through a whole sentence without contradicting their intentions, so which intent is the Universe going to respond to? Obviously, one statement cancels out the other so nothing happens and now you can understand why. The magnets give you the bigger picture of the negative and positive polarities. Now you can see and demonstrate how you induct and "conduct" the energy toward or away from your heart's desires. Which energy feels better when you play with these magnets? That is the one you always will attract!

Get Your Energy Going All In One Direction

Once you have identified your heart's desire and experience it energetically and emotionally, you feeeel a YES, YES, YES! You will know by your elation and enthusiasm when you have achieved a vibrational match. If you are coming from neediness or lack and notice you are filled with contradictory statements, you will eventually learn to see and feel the incongruity of saying, "I can't afford" and upgrade it to, "Well, I don't know how the Universe can create this although I believe it can." You will see your energy wave beginning to flow in the right direction to magnetize your heart's desires.

"A belief is only a thought that you keep thinking."

…Abraham

Start aligning your words and feelings so you are consciously aware when you are **deliberately creating** and when you are creating by **default**. As you begin to see your vibrational matches, it's a fresh and exhilarating awareness which accelerates your personal growth. You will also begin to recognize your vibrational output. Use the magnets to deliberately begin again whenever you need a visual reflection for creation with a fresh start. Allow yourself to know and feel when you are in alignment with your heart's desire. Remember your intentions are negated through contradictory statements or beliefs. Negative emotions and thoughts attract the "opposite" rather than the vibrational offering and outpouring which is a match to your true desire. You may be amused and amazed at how frequently you "catch" yourself in contradictions and observe which direction your energy is flowing. It takes practice, willingness and clarity to upgrade your words, actions and especially your feeeeelings to match your decisions.

The Law Of Attraction In Action State It and Create It!

I've come to appreciate how important CONTRAST is, because out of diversity, an opportunity is born for fresh CHOICES. Choice is then followed by a NEW DECISION, which is necessary as a Deliberate Creator. And being in a deliberate state of I CREATE is a very powerful place indeed. You will notice new CLARITY is born out of contrast. Contrast doesn't mean booga-booga or challenge or conflict. It simply brings more awareness and light so you can choose once again as a divine CREATOR.

Vibrational Matches

Abraham says: "What you are getting always matches what you are vibrating and what you are vibrating always matches what you are getting, without exception. They are always the same." For example, have you reached the place at some time in your life when you were shouting, "No, I'm mad as hell and I'm not going to take this anymore!" This has become a well-known phrase since the movie, *Network*, with Peter Finch, was released.

Out of your "NO" springs clarity of what your YES is moving toward, and you feel powerful in your decision, even though at the time, it may feel like you are swinging between two trapezes without a net. You have clearly come to a decision of what you are NOT going to take or do anymore even though the energy may be "contradicted" in the moment. That's when you begin to have clarity and line the energy up deliberately. It may take days, weeks or months to come into alignment with the energy of knowing your heart's desire. When it happens, you will feel and think the YES emotionally in every cell of your body! It is similar to dominoes being lined up. Suddenly you touch one and everything falls into place. Energetically, you will then have evidence which reflects your alignment of vibrating on purpose.

As you experienced the magnets repelling one another, you could easily see how they demonstrated "pushing against." Resistance is the only thing which keeps you from your Stream of Well Being, which is always flowing as pure, natural, pulsating, powerful and positive energy. You will always know what you are vibrating by the way you feeeeel.

It is all how we choose to experience contrast. If we experience life as a "reactor" and as an "upset," we will have serious stress and restrict the flow of our heart's desires. We are then literally stepping on our own "hose" and contracting or pinching off our Stream of Well Being. In my classes years ago, I metaphorically used an analogy of an ordinary garden hose. If you step on it when watering your garden, then the water and flow would obviously be restricted. It would not be obstructed from the "Source" where it originates at the faucet or spigot. It would be hindered by your cutting off the flow and stepping on your own hose. Most times, the crimping of the flow is unconscious. When we understand we are "**CREATORS**" with **CHOICE**, we see life as a "set up" exquisitely and divinely prescribed for us in all its contrast and diversity. We can bless the stress and transform it creatively for our personal evolution.

Are you a CREATOR

Allowing the Stream of Your Delicious Well-Being
(or)

A REACTOR

Notice it is the same identical letters transposed causing "resistance," that results in "habitual reactions" and thought patterns and emotional "ruts and grooves."

You can see life as a **Set Up** for your growth and evolution
(or)

An **Upset**

where you have stress,
turmoil and resistance
(again, notice the identical words are reversed)

As Richard Bach said in his book, *ILLUSIONS, The Adventures Of A Reluctant Messiah*, "Every problem has a gift for you in its hands...you seek problems because you need their gifts." From a higher perspective, I believe our soul sees contrast as a "set up" to become more conscious and to awaken us to the greater realities and possibilities which exist within us. Problems are our evolutionary drivers which prompt us to new, fresh desires and decisions. As a friend of ours always says in any "crisis," "Oh God, I gotta grow again."

Problems As Our Evolutionary Drivers

You have two choices: You can "go through them" or you can "grow through them." If you go through them as an upset, you will probably repeat the crisis in another way until you get the life-lesson or message. When you "grow" through your "set ups," you spiral up in the Game of Life knowing you are the CREATOR who creates your reality. It's only ignorance that allows people to settle for less. When you are filled with self-pity, anger and resentments, you are stepping on your own hose.

**Notice in the sea of contrast whether you are "going with the flow"
as a DELIBERATE CREATOR creating**

(or)

**"Pushing the river"
as a REACTOR re-acting
which equals = resistance and pushing against.**

When contrast arises, ask what is your heart's desire? Then, you can choose once again to be a Deliberate Creator and make a new decision. Follow your bliss and align with your Stream of Well Being for your highest outcome.

Abraham has said three things are always true of resistance:

- ♥ Resistance is the only thing which keeps you from your natural well-being.

- ♥ Negative emotion is always present as your indicator of resistance.

- ♥ Resistance always means you are pushing against something.

**Resistance is using contrast to decide what you don't want.
You don't stay there—it's only an opportunity and
a signal to <u>make a new decision</u> in the diversity of contrast.**

Magnets Graphically Demonstrate Resistance

Now take your magnets into your hands and again experience what it feels like to be in resistance "magnetically" as a vibration so you truly understand this concept. If the magnets are in the attraction mode, turn one magnet around to the opposite end. Feel how the magnets are now distanced or pushing against each other. This is what happens when you are reacting and upset. The magnets now clearly demonstrate how we actually "repel" energetically, rather than create our desired outcomes. Is this an amazing demonstration of the Vibration of Resistance?! Can you actually get them together by pushing or forcing them when one end of your magnet is in the resistance position? No, they will not get remotely close to a match, as they are spiraling and vibrating resistance around each other without ever being able to come together. This is because the energy is not flowing easily and forcing it won't make a match.

When you are connected to your heart's desires with pure, clear, positive energy, there is a magical match of your outcomes coming together magnetically because there is no resistance. The Law of Attraction expresses both negatively and positively without judgement. It simply is the "law" in action. What you think about and vibrate expands both appropriately—or inappropriately (if you are in resistance). The Law of Attraction is impersonal and neutral. You are always creating through your vibrational signal and offering.

Allowing is using contrast to decide what you do desire

As you begin to observe yourself, you will know whether you are "matching" or "mismatching." When you have vibrational matches you will know by the way you feel when it clicks into place, just like the magnets strong attraction and pull. It's a match—an "ah-hah"—a zinger—a YES, YES, YES! Appreciate yourself and how you can magnetize your physical manifestations and go for the gusto!! You can put your toe in with meager results or jump in enthusiastically with both feet to magnetize your heart's desires. Be consistent in your vibrational offerings. When you are aware of how your thoughts and energies feel, then you begin recognizing whether you are allowing and/or resisting, in being a Creator or Reactor.

Goosing Up Your Imagination

Abraham has talked about Esther Hicks[2] making candy. For instance, when you cook candy on the stove, the recipe doesn't say how many minutes to boil it. The recipe does say cook it to the soft ball stage, and then dribble it into a clear glass of cold water, and if it's not done, it will simply dissolve or make the water cloudy. And if it is almost done, it will form a clump you can test for the right consistency. Stir constantly with your positive thoughts and feelings so you are flowing direction toward

2   See Resources, page 228 for Esther Hicks and Abraham.

your "confections." And that's the way Abraham suggests we use physical manifestation. Test for the consistency of your vibration! Don't be afraid of making a mistake! Jump in wholeheartedly and realize, "What I'm getting is what I'm vibrating. Hmm—what I'm getting right now is other than what is pleasing me in every way. Hmmm—I think I could use more visualization and less observation." Time to "goose up" your imagination and play down your observation. Always offer thoughts, words and feeeeelings which are a vibrational match to what you now desire. Keep the heat on until it comes to your desired consistency and outcome.

"What you are speaks so loudly I can hardly hear what you are saying."

…Ralph Waldo Emerson

In the mid-70's, my husband and I attended an Alpha Awareness training for five nights with the founder, Verle Minto, which was an excellent course for personal growth. One of the first processes given was to cancel out all negative words every time you heard yourself saying them. An example would be "I hate," or "I am so sick and tired" or "he's a pain in the neck" or "you'll be shooting yourself in the foot if…" or "it's too good to be true." This was then immediately followed by saying "cancel/cancel" so that you overrode and cleared what you had just said to avoid becoming ill or having a stiff neck (or hemorrhoids, if you happen to think someone was a pain in the butt, or kidney problems if they "pissed" you off). I've also had people say "I just love you to death" or "I'm just dying to meet you" and I suggest that they "love me to life" or be "excited to meet me" for obvious reasons. How often have you heard "I'm anxious" to see you when what they really meant to vibrate is "I'm excited to be with you." Why have "anxiety" when you can vibrate excitement and enthusiasm! How many times have you heard someone saying "Doesn't that just slay you?" or "That is killing me." Notice what you are attracting and creating (consciously and unconsciously).

The emphasis in this particular course was on spoken words, more than thoughts, as if our thoughts weren't quite as important. In actuality, what matters is the awareness that you are radiating and vibrating constantly by what you are **feeeeeling**—whether it is your thoughts, words or beliefs. We have come to personally understand canceling a word verbally doesn't cancel it out your vibration if you are still **feeling** any contradictory energy or any resistance.

Most of us are aware of having a soul or a non-physical counterpart. In order to be connected to our Higher Self or Inner Being, our physical vibration must be very similar or aligned to the vibration of our Inner Being. How would we know that's true? When you are appreciating, loving, joyous, complimenting, laughing, and feeeeling good, you are in harmony with the vibration of your Higher Self. You feel exuberant and uplifted. When you are speaking or thinking words of criticism, judgement, anger, comparison, competing, focusing upon lack or fear, power, control or "withholding" issues, then your vibration is very different from your real Being. Whenever you experience an absence of love, or you feel negative emotions, you have only to summon the desired creative energy (your heart's desires) and become aware of your Stream of Well-being and re-connect to Source!

Your Vibrations Summon Your Destiny

I invite you to be consciously aware of what is pulsating and vibrating within you and radiating from you—through your words, thoughts, feelings and actions. What we ultimately seek is our connectedness with the loving presence of our Inner Being who adores us. When you feel really good, uplifted and fulfilled, you know you are vibrating in harmony and on purpose with whom you really are by being aligned with your heart's desires. Your personal magnetics, or what is sometimes called "magnetism" or charisma, are your vibrations attracting your destiny. As you come to understand the inner connectedness with your Stream of Well Being, what you summon and vibrate through your delicious desires will be fulfilled. You can now become a Deliberate Creator through your expectations and eagerness to flow energy toward your heart's desires.

> **"You cannot improve your life by pushing against what you do not want. The more you are in conscious connection pulsating and resonating pure, positive energy with Source, the more vibrational matches you create and attract."**
>
> ...Abraham

When I was going through my class files from the past, I found a story I had shared as a real-life teaching illustration of being either creators or reactors. In 1987, there was an article in the *Science Of Mind Magazine* entitled, "Don't Curse The Roaches" where a contributor, Frances Hammond, shared her experience in how things changed dramatically when she stopped reacting.

Don't Curse The Roaches

Frances had moved into a beautiful, affordable and conveniently located waterfront apartment. One defect, however, became increasingly noticeable as the days passed—roaches! Lots of roaches! She called the manager to ask for additional exterminating services and was told she had to expect roaches when you live on the water. Management did monthly spraying and that was it. She said the foul smell of the spray drove her out of the apartment, but it acted like vitamins for the roaches. They seemed to double in number and vigor. She was furious with management. She put out roach traps to no avail. Various powders had no effect. Neighbors complained too. The roaches soiled everything, eating scrapbooks, cookbooks, even hardback books on the living room shelves. Frances found roaches sitting on her toothbrush. Even when she slept, she was jerked to wakefulness by a roach crawling over her face. Anger was building in her every day. The climax came at noon one day when she saw a roach sitting right on top of her fresh tuna fish salad. Beating her fists on the counter in rage and frustration, she cried out involuntarily, "God do something! I can't stand this any longer!"

She threw out her lunch and sat down by the living room window. Her eyes rested on the deep blue water, the green trees and the blue sky. She was moved to murmur, "Thank you, God, for the beauty that is mine." Peace came over her and she recalled these words:

**"Don't curse the darkness;
instead, light a candle."**

That meant: don't look at the problem; give thanks that you already have the solution and believe that you have it. Don't curse the roaches. The next time a roach came into Frances sight, her anger flared. As she killed the insect, she remembered her new approach, which prompted her to say (between clenched teeth), "Thank you, God, for my roach-free home." Over and over, every time she saw roaches or their soil, she repeated her affirmation. Gradually, it broke her anger habit. As weeks went by, she faced the pests feeling she was already free of them in the Mind of God. It took weeks to restore inner peace after such strong resentment. In the library three months after she had begun her affirmations, she was prompted to leaf through back issues of some periodicals. She saw a headline about a roach trap which was highly rated for situations like hers.

The next day's newspaper carried a one dollar off coupon for that very product, which she immediately purchased. She again gave thanks for her roach-free home. Installing the traps presented some complications. She quietly repeated her affirmation of thanks. Within four days, she had a roach-free home in complete manifestation.

Frances' greatest discovery, however, was not the product itself. These roach traps, in fact, had been on the market for years, even when she was cursing the roaches. Help had been there all those months, but she had been too angry and resentful to attract it. And so, her greatest discovery was that she had to change her thoughts and vibration before she could change her circumstances.

This story of contrast is such a wonderful illustration of the Law of Attraction in Action! The more Frances pushed against what she didn't want by reacting, the more roaches appeared in her reality. The more she resented the roaches, she "re-sent" her negative emotions over and over, which resulted in creating more roaches by "default." She got more of what she didn't want! She magnetized and matched them crawling into everything! I am sure most people can identify with how distressing this situation would be.

When Frances had enough "contrast," she called upon the most infinite force in the Universe by saying, "God, do something!!", which instantly magnetized a **fresh new vibration** into her life. She asked for and received solutions which began to flow toward her immediately. She "remembered" to give thanks and metaphorically lit a candle. It literally brought more light into her heart and higher choices into her life situation. She changed her mind about cursing the roaches. That decision then automatically commanded a fresh vibrational signal being broadcast for a "roach-free home." She had new clarity and flowed and summoned energy toward what she did want! She now vibrated a new sense of well-being because in her consciousness she was already free of them. Naturally, the whole Universe then conspired on her behalf so she would be in the right place at the right time with the right publications and products. Frances even magnetized a coupon to make this endeavor more affordable! Solutions and people and help abounded all around her to magnetize her outcome. You will always know more about what you want when you have the contrast of what you don't want. Once you make a new decision and commitment, you are then deliberately creating from a fresh place and magnetizing the outcome already being fulfilled.

When you are vibrating on purpose as a Deliberate Creator, it is so exciting, exhilarating, fulfilling and lifechanging to come to understand…

It's The Law of Attraction in Action!

2
The Art of Magnetizing and Manifesting

Webster's Dictionary defines magnets in the following way:

> **Magnet (mag'nit)**: Any piece of iron or steel that has the property of attracting iron or steel which may be naturally present or artificially induced; a person or thing that attracts.

> **Magnetic (mag-net'ik)**: That which is or can be magnetized; powerfully attractive; said of a person, personality.

I invite you to allow your first alignment in magnetizing to be simple, fun and easy so you are attracting effortlessly and quickly. If it feels like struggle, then you will magnetize "struggle" and repel rather than attract your heart's desires.

First, imagine you are connecting magnetically with your Source, God Force, Superconsciousness, Higher Self or Inner Being, Spirit, Love, The Universe, All That Is or whatever you perceive this energy to be. Feel that a blending and merging is occurring by inviting, remembering, and attracting this union magnetically. Become aware of your breathing, and as you now inhale, be excited and delighted and imagine yourself receiving a specific heart's desire. When exhaling, release your intention into the world where your deliberate creation is then vibrating as your "outcome already fulfilled." Allow it to be natural and touch the deepest, most joyful places within so you feel the ecstasy of having your wishes granted now in your imagination.

For instance, if you choose to have more money, know there are principles of universal energies magnetically inducted through first **feeling abundant**. Accept and know you deserve your heart's desire. Appreciate having the vibration to attract more "green energy" (money) and give thanks that the money is already here. In other words, **have an attitude of gratitude** continuously, in spite of what the appearances may be in the moment. Stay out of the "how" and just know in your heart you are attracting your desires so that you are in vibrational harmony with your creation.

When I was much younger, there was a parable in the Book of Matthew that always seemed unfair and hard to understand: "To him that has, more will be given and he will have great plenty; but to him that has not, even the little he has will be taken away." It seemed so harsh until I came to understand that Jesus was talking about consciousness. **To those who have a consciousness of plenty, more will be given and they will have even greater riches in their lives**. To those who have not, who have a narrow or "limited" consciousness, then the little they have will be taken away.

What are you expressing and experiencing in your life right now? From a consciousness of abundance or from a consciousness of lack? Is your life rich, full and prosperous? Or do you affirm, nurse, curse, and rehearse with a litany of complaints all day long, which then means your problems will stay with you or build up even more through your constantly talking about them. Naturally, blame, justification and explanation will diminish and restrict your life.

What you think about EXPAND S

In another parable it is said, "You can't put new wine into an old wineskin." Again, this is speaking of consciousness—the new "ascended" wine can't be poured into a narrow, constipated vessel because that consciousness is unable to be filled and stretched to new levels of being, allowing and receiving. We literally demonstrate every moment at the level where our consciousness is vibrating. Jesus was the new wine, the new consciousness who brought the vibration of love, rather than an eye for an eye and a tooth for a tooth. My funky sense of humor says there must have been a lot of blind and toothless people in the Old Testament days based on the verses describing those parables.

An Attitude of GRATITUDE

Many people have financial issues and follow the path of least resistance by "paying" their bills rather than having an attitude of gratitude. How many people do you know who love to pay their bills? **The LAW of ATTRACTION in ACTION** is: Choose to write your checks with an attitude of gratitude so instead of "paying" bills as an obligation or duty, be grateful to have the funds and bless the money and checks and see your funds multiplied. Remember, what you think about expands!

I used to write G.M. (God's Money) on the upper left hand corner of our checks. I intuitively knew the Law of Attraction. I knew if we constantly magnetized and blessed our abundance by keeping it in circulation and allowing it to flow joyfully into and through our lives, it would expand! This was also long before the days of carbon-copy check registers and so if I forgot to enter the amount in the check register, I would then put G.O.K. Duaine said, "I now know what G.M. stands for…but what in the world does G.O.K. mean?" And I said, "**G**od **O**nly **K**nows!" One has to have a sense of humor in expanding consciousness!

The next time you have bills for the phone, electricity, water, rent or mortgage, instead of seeing the utility or banks taking your money away—or feeling you have to "pay" your bills, I invite you to sit down and enjoy the process. Have an attitude of gratitude and give thanks for the abundance flowing through you now and continuously so you are vibrating prosperity rather than lack of money.

Giving is an attitude of gratitude and it multiplies!
Paying is a mentality of taking away and of subtraction.

That is why "to him that has given, more will be added," as we are each a core consciousness pulsating, radiating and vibrating. To him that has "paid," the little he has is subtracted and more is taken away. If you "pay" your bills out of a sense of obligation, then you will feel there is never enough. When you joyously bless your money flowing abundantly and have an attitude of gratitude, it will return to you multiplied and expanded.

Which Reality Do You Choose to Participate In?

Sometimes we hear people say, "I can't afford this," or "It's too expensive," which of course then becomes a self-fulfilling prophecy of limitation. Remember to hold only the thoughts and vibrations that reflect the world you choose to participate in. The Universe is always ready when you are ready and it is standing by, waiting for you to choose and commit to your heart's desires. Remember, abundance is not something you create, but that which you ATTRACT AND ACCEPT. You can flow energy toward the joyful experiences that you desire, which attracts the money magnetically.

What are you now ready to ask for intensely and receive expansively? Take five or ten minutes daily to specifically identify, imagine, envision and feeeel excited about your highest outcomes. Have clarity on why your heart desires these experiences. Talk to others who are genuinely excited about your deliberate creations and who enthusiastically support your endeavors. Tell the Universe why you want to have it! Be joyful about your intentions and let the aura around you sparkle and sizzle with your magnetic vibration. Write a vivid poem or script out your desires as a chapter from *This Is My Life* to set your tone and let your heart sing. Let your vibration ring with the beauty of your creations manifesting now. You are rewarded to the level of your expectancy. Have fun with all of this and know it is holy to be humorous! See your dreams through fresh eyes and let it be a surprise how the Universe delivers it. Be eager as you write and imagine what you are deliciously experiencing as you envision your outcome being fulfilled. Give thanks, believe and know you deserve to have your wishes granted now and continuously.

Your Magic Genie

Imagine a magic genie appears in front of you right now who says, "I will grant you three wishes. Your wish is my command. Ponder a few moments and then write your three wishes in the margin of your book or in the Notes pages in the back of the book. What are you choosing to magnetize now—in this very instant?

Great! You have now declared your dreams to the Universe. You are now on the royal road to your three wishes gestating and coming to fruition! Did you feel an inner glow of excitement as you reveled in your energy flowing with the visions of your decisions! When was the last time you felt this exhilarated? As you generate enthusiasm for your heart's desires, you are connected to your Stream of Well Being. You may modify the wishes later as you fine tune your desires. You are the mapmaker and the visionary. You are the Deliberate Creator. You are the receiver. What have you been waiting for? Know that you are the magnetic human compass and you point and direct the way by summoning and flowing the energy. Point the compass needle in the meaningful and magical directions you choose to go. You will be flooded with more light and serendipitous routes, which lead to a whole download of scrumptious information to create your outcomes fulfilled. Consciousness and energy vibrate at certain frequencies. As you feel and resonate with your outcomes fulfilled emotionally, it accelerates and steps up to a higher vibration because you have clarified your heart's desires.

Fun Guidelines for Enlightenment

There is a wonderful being, Steve Bhaerman, who writes jokes and scripts known as "Swami Beyondananda." My favorite is entitled, "Guidelines for Enlightenment," and one line is, "The most powerful tool on the planet today is Tell-A-Vision. That is where I tell my vision to you, and you tell a vision to me. That way, if we don't like the programming we are getting, we can simply change the channel." And personally to that I would add, we all have the remote control in our hands. It's called choice and making a decision for your vision!

Another guideline I love is: "Be a fundamentalist—make sure the FUN always comes before the mental list. Realize that life is a situation comedy that will never be canceled. A laugh track has been provided and the reason why we are put in the material world is to get more material. Have a good laugh at least twice a day and that will ensure hilarity." When was the last time you had a good belly laugh? Have fun with your visions. Be of good cheer! Be prepared for magic in the moment and miracles on demand.

While having fun contemplating what my three wishes would be, I realized that one of them was, "**I AM the Magic Genie Who Grants the Wishes Fulfilled**." Indeed we each are our own Deliberate Creator, a.k.a. The Magic Genie! The Universe totally supports and cooperates as you say YES to your outcomes fulfilled.

As I think and vibrate, so I AM. I create, attract, expand, and manifest now and continuously according to my vibrational output.

The way you accept what you receive and how you spend money reflects how you are magnetizing the Law of Attraction as a Deliberate Creator. As you come from clarity, joy, and renewal you are making new contributions in your consciousness and depositing magnetic energy to play in higher realms and claiming your wildest imaginings. Money is a wonderful byproduct of following your bliss. When you do what you love, abundance will follow in the form of "green energy" (money). Be creative and feel your aliveness and zest in initiating new, upgraded realities about money. Each of us "broadcasts" our signal all day long in attracting either lack or abundance. Every time you say "I can't afford," you expand your lack and it becomes a declarative statement to the Universe. You will then notice not having enough because it becomes a self-fulfilling prophecy.

There is a wonderful anecdote in the book, *Creating Affluence*, by author Deepak Chopra, M.D. He was involved with a group discussing a world peace project when someone asked his teacher, "Where is all the money going to come from?" [for this project]. And his teacher replied, without hesitation, **"From wherever it is at the moment."** There is infinite abundance available, and when we are willing to receive and invite prosperity on all levels, it becomes our reality as Deliberate Creators. Prosperity abounds! Abundance abounds! Well being abounds!

26

The Investment That Always Pays Off

Neville, an author who is deceased, wrote books our family loved. His stories are filled with wisdom and creative insights in imagining from your "outcome fulfilled." He states in one of his books that his wife awakened from a profound sleep and heard a voice of authority say, "You must stop spending your thoughts, your time and your money. Everything in life is an investment." The dictionary defines "spend" as: to waste or squander or to lay out without hope of return. Invest means to lay out for a purpose from which a profit is expected. I often told my students at Indiana-Purdue University, "Stop sitting on your assets and invest in yourselves!" I can relate to his wife's dream for whatever you choose to "invest" in will be magnetized into your daily life and into your future.

Neville was an early pioneer in the art of thinking and investing in what he called the "end" process by imagining from your fulfilled outcome. He felt the wise person magnetized their aspirations and dreams by already feeling, thinking and being in their outcome (even when logic and reason may deny it). When you are confident in creating your reality in your imagination from your outcome fulfilled, then you are investing in yourself and that is the asset that always pays off. Remain loyal to the unseen reality as though it were already true, for indeed it is.

You now have a skeletal framework for understanding magnetism to demonstrate how it works by attracting substances that match them— **like attracts like**. When I was a child, I used to have miniature Scottie dogs on oblong magnets. One was black and the other was white— again contrast. We could make them attract, repel, spin or move any way we desired as we played with them. It was fun to pick up paper clips, iron nails or anything they would "attract."

You can now easily see how your thoughts magnetically attract as you begin to fine tune and master what you choose to attract. Your feelings energize your thoughts and propel them from your Inner Being to your outer reality. The stronger or more emotional your feelings are, the more accelerated the process of vibrational attraction becomes.

Magnetic Energy in Your Hands

Another way to demonstrate magnetic energy is to USE YOUR HANDS. Begin by clapping them together or rubbing them briskly against each other for at least 15 seconds or more. Then move your hands up in front of you with the palms facing one another. Observe what is happening with your hands as you move them a few inches apart. Slowly move them back and forth or closer and farther apart in distance. The movement is similar to playing an accordion. Notice what you feel and what is happening between your hands. Most people will be aware of magnetic ATTRACTION or RESISTANCE between their hands as they "play" with the energy. Just as the battery in your car has negative and positive cables (poles), so do you as a human. You are a battery of water cells which radiates a current of energy. Have fun as you play with this concept to understand the metaphor of how energy works in your life.

Are You Appreciating or Depreciating?

Appreciation could be defined as recognizing and being grateful for all the blessings you do have in your life. Depreciating is when you lower, reduce or don't recognize the value of what you have. If you belittle, disparage and complain, you will reinforce not having enough. I know people who constantly "depreciate" by complaining, criticizing and comparing. There is a restaurant in Scottsdale that has a sign, "**NO SNIVELING**." It's good advice because whining blocks your flow. You will never have enough until you feel the "enoughness" inside of you. In the movie, *Water World*, there is a line by Kevin Costner where he says, "It's like a turd that won't flush." It may be a crude remark, but the more you talk about the "feces" of your life by constantly depreciating it or other people, you will be filled with resentment and keep re-sending the same signal. You block your flow because you're stepping on your own hose. Or, as a friend says, "It's like a cow stepping on its own tit." It may not be a very classy expression, but it's a great metaphor.

> **"If the only prayer you ever say in your entire life is THANK YOU, it will be enough."**
> ...Meister Eckhart

Gratitude is a feeling of being grateful, appreciative and profoundly thankful for what is working in your life in both giving and receiving. Having an attitude of gratitude always reinforces the Law of Attraction in Action and creates things flowing freely.

Joyfully or Forcefully?

If the subject of contrast, choice and being a Deliberate Creator is new to you and you are feeling somewhat in "whelm," take a deep breath! Ask for help in understanding and integrating (which means practice!) so you can revel, have fun and be inspired as you continue reading the upcoming creation "recipes." Allow it to be easy and playful! Use the magnets often as a mirror of how you choose to attract your outcomes—joyfully or forcefully?! If you feel discouraged or frustrated, that means resistance is present and it will expand. Longfellow said, "The lowest ebb is the turn of the tide." When you feel inspired and enthusiastic, you will vibrationally attract your deliberate creations.

Do you know it is "scientifically" impossible for the bumblebee to fly? According to recognized aerotechnical tests, bumblebees cannot fly because of the weight and shape of their bodies in relationship to the total wing area. However, the bumblebee doesn't know this, so they fly anyway!!

Some years ago at the conclusion of a spiritual workshop, the teacher asked each person to share brief comments about the weekend. One woman was very touched although on "overload" since this was her first experience of anything of this nature. She expressed how she felt like a "beginner" and how much she had yet to learn. I will always remember the teacher's laughter and re-assurance as he said, "You are in front of those who are coming behind you!" It's so true. As we evolve, there is always someone in front of us who is helping us go higher. We also assist those who are coming behind us and reach out our hands and hearts to eagerly invite them to create, grow and deliciously soar together.

Notice that contrast is diversity and variety as you will see in this beautiful sharing from Lin Yu Tang:

"Certainly no one can say that life on this planet is stale and monotonous...there is the alternation of night and day, and morning and sunset, and a cool evening following upon a hot day, and a silent and clear dawn presaging a busy morning, and there is nothing better than that.

There are cloudy days and misty days, alternating with clear and sunny days...there are spring showers and summer thunderstorms, and the dry crisp wind of autumn and the snow of winter.

There are magnificent redwood trees, fire-spouting volcanoes, wondrous caves, majestic peaks and undulating hills, placid lakes, winding rivers, and shady banks...the menu is practically endless to suit individual tastes. The only sensible thing to do is go and partake of the feast and not complain about the monotony of life."

Come, Partake of the Feast.
Appreciate the Diversity
Spread Before You of Your Heart's
Desires Being Fulfilled.
Be Magically Open and
"In The Moment"
With Your Wishes Granted
And Miracles On Demand
By Your Command
And So It Is!
And Forever Will Be!

3
All Thoughts are Energy

**"All Thoughts are Energy
All Energy Follows Thoughts
Where Your Attention Goes,
Your Power Flows"**

…Sharon Warren

**"We have the tool of thought within us to create
a thousand joys or a thousand ills."**

…James Allen

Electricity is a wonderful analogy in terms of consciousness for it is a power we are all familiar with. Often we take it for granted until we have a power outage and are without it even for a short time. Just as the Law of Attraction is neutral, so is electricity. It doesn't care if you plug into it or even what you plug into it. If you turned on your radio or TV or VCR and it had "static," you would not blame the source of power, which is the electricity being generated to your home. Electricity is impersonal and is simply the mechanism through which it flows to your appliance. You would know that the TV, radio or VCR was faulty, not the source of electricity.

In the mid-70's I had a dream and I was awakened with one key word—**TRANSDUCER**. It was flashing like a bright light in my brain. I asked my husband what a transducer was since I was unfamiliar with the term. He said it meant various devices that transmit energy from one system to another or sometimes transducers are used to convert energy. I wondered then if "transduced" was a metaphor energetically of my "dream state and Inner Being" vibrationally transmitted to my "physical self."

Later I read that in working with electricity, there are certain materials that "**conduct**" the electrical current freely, while others act as "resistors." If you desired to use all available power, it would be routed through a conducting material. If you desired to restrict the flow of power, you would route it through a resistor. This is a very similar principle to the magnets you are now using to demonstrate attracting (conducting) or repelling (resisting). When you are flowing energy easily, you are conducting it with little or no resistance. When you are reacting to a life situation, you have resistance and the flow is restricted.

You can easily see how you will create and attract very different results depending on how you are using consciousness to flow energy. The same analogy is valid for magnets and electricity, as well as being applied to demonstrate the Law of Attraction in Action. Our thoughts are like electro-magnetic energy and we have the choice of either being conductors or resistors. There is only one pure power energy flowing through us and the originating source itself is neutral. It is your choice how you choose to flow your power—as a Creator or reactor.

Your power ends where your fears begin.

If you are experiencing hate, resentment, anger, illness and distress then you will have "static" in your life. The church I was raised in as a child talked about fear and God and they don't even belong in the same sentence as they are totally different vibrations. Fear comes from lack—period! We are each the "vessel" or electro-magnetic instrument for the Law of Attraction. As you release resistance, you then allow power to flow through you as a Creator channeling it toward your heart's desires. You also have equal opportunity, choice, and free will to distort, short-circuit, or contaminate this pure energy. Heaven or hell, poverty or prosperity, creator or reactor are all states of consciousness. Did you know the word "devil" is simply <u>lived</u> spelled backwards and "evil" is <u>live</u> reversed? It's all a matter of where you focus. What we consider a negative life situation is simply energy in need of transformation. The energy itself is impersonal. We are each "wired" for our divinity and creativity and we can let our light shine at whatever brilliance we choose to vibrate and radiate. We each have access to the same Stream of Well Being and Source.

You Will Never Have Any More Power Than You Have at this Moment In Time

Your power is simply waiting for you to direct it. As you sow, so you reap. As you ask, it is given. What are you sowing and what are you reaping? What are you asking for and what are you receiving? Are you the vibration that conducts or are you experiencing lots of resistance in your life? Are you a victim, reactor, or blamer? When you become aware of any resistance which the Universe mirrors back through your life circumstances, you can choose to direct and re-route your power as a DELIBERATE CREATOR. All the energy that has always been there will come roaring into your life full speed ahead. As you become more aware potentially of what you are, you don't acquire more power; you just become aware of all that energy within you waiting to be released. You are a whole, complete person right now. You may not be aware of it just yet. That's why your evolutionary journey is so exciting. The Universe will be totally supportive and cooperative whether you choose to react or create. That's why it is important to understand that all thoughts are energy and all energy follows thought.

"Do not pray for dreams equal to your powers. Pray for powers equal to your dreams."

…Phillip Brooks

It's up to you to make conscious, clear, joyful choices as you become more aware of following your heart. You will discover that people treat you the way you treat yourself! Whether you attract happy people or those who push your buttons will tell you what you are most often attracting through your thoughts—consciously and unconsciously. I'm not talking simply about positive thinking. When you understand the Law of Attraction and how every thought you think expands, it will transform your life. I have often said, "I am excited about becoming more of who I am," because it is so enriching and life-affirming. I will never have any more power than I have at this moment in time. I am committed to becoming more aware every day of flowing energy wisely toward my heart's desires. My latest personal Arizona license plate boldly proclaims CREATOR, which is, in essence, who we really are.

Heaven or Hell?
You Create the Experience

One of the best definitions I've read of hell was from the best-selling book, *Conversations With God—Book I*, by Neale Donald Walsch. When he asked God in his dialogue, "What Is Hell?" God replied, "It is the experience of the worst possible outcome of your choices, decisions, and creations. It is the pain you suffer through wrong thinking. Yet even the term 'wrong thinking' is a misnomer, because there is no such thing as that which is wrong. Hell is the opposite of joy. It is unfulfillment. It is knowing Who and What You Are, and failing to experience that. It is being less. That is hell, but it does not exist as this place you have fantasized, where you burn in some everlasting fire. What purpose could I have in that? You, yourself, create the experience."

Vibrating On Purpose

We have the awesome choice and responsibility (meaning our ability to respond) to live our vibration on purpose. And every day we have the reflection of whether we are living our life "backward" or living, harmonizing, creating and vibrating on purpose. When life seems difficult and filled with contrast, it's the Universe giving us a cosmic nudge to pay attention. It is a tap on the shoulder to become more conscious of what we are attracting. It's so easy or convenient to get into the blame game, which leads to a whole chain of blame and results in avoidance by not taking responsibility for what was created. Other people may say it is "God's will." I know when I bless the stress, it's to have another perception, to touch into a deeper place within me to see how it all fits in my spiritual growth and evolution. If you ignore the "stress" or "static" and

you gunnysack it, then simply know, it will get BIGGER

because what you think about and focus upon vibrates and expands.

If you ignore the gentle cosmic nudges from the Universe, it may become a cosmic shove to really pay attention. It usually results in a ruder Wake-Up Call with the Cosmic Alarm Clock going off in your face so you can't possibly miss it! Often it becomes a full-blown crisis because you ignored the earlier nudges. It is your responsibility and privilege to plug into the power which is always available to you at whatever "current" you are ready to attract.

Coming Attractions in Action
The Whole Picture

There is a story in India about six blind men and an elephant. Not being able to actually see the elephant, the only way they could perceive what an elephant looked like was by touching it. Each one approached the elephant and felt it.

The first blind person, grabbed the tail and said, "An elephant is like a broom."

The second blind person grabbed the leg and said, " An elephant is like a pillar."

The third blind person, touching the trunk said, "An elephant is like a hissing snake."

The fourth blind person, touching the ear and said, "An elephant is like a fan."

The fifth blind person touched the tusk and said, "An elephant is like a spear."

The sixth blind person touched the side and said, "An elephant is like a brick wall."

All of the blind persons were correct, yet the truth is that their interpretations all varied according to their experience and perceptions. None of them had the whole picture or full reality of what an elephant is. I remember appreciating the line in the movie, *Absence Of Malice*, when as a reporter, actress Sally Field said, "It's accurate, but it's not the truth." Each of the blind men understood the part he had touched and yet none understood the whole reality. I believe we are here to become more of what we are; to come to love, understand and appreciate our wholeness;

to integrate and bring more light to our blind spots; and to become more aware of the vastness and magnificence of our being.

A westernized version of this metaphor would be a seventh blind person who touched the heart center of the elephant and felt the pulse and vibration of love. This person would call the others to do the same, and they would all be uplifted and unified in the radiance and luminosity of love. If we are not happy within ourselves, we are not going to find it outside of ourselves, except perhaps fleetingly. People often want to find love and happiness outside of themselves without taking their "blinders" off to bring more self-love and light into their lives by being a Deliberate Creator. When you become the person you would like to attract as a divine partner, he or she will show up faster than you can click your ruby slippers.

Exuding Light

There's a wonderful joke about the minister of a rural church deep in the Ozarks who suggested to his parishioners that they purchase a new chandelier. It was put to a vote and the members voted it down.

"Why do you oppose the purchase of a chandelier?" asked the preacher.

"Well," said one of the flock, "first we can't spell it, so how can we order it?"

"Second, even if we did get it, no one can play it; and third, what we really need is more light!"

You see, the light we are seeking is within each of us—it's life, it's light, it's love. As we become more aware of these energies and nurture them, we then radiate and magnetically attract our heart's desires as vibrational matches.

I have taught many dream workshops and classes through the years and one of the elements I always discuss is Carl Jung's psychological material concerning the "shadow." My definition of the "shadow" is simply "blocked light." Jung said, "There is no light without shadow and no psychic wholeness without imperfection. To round itself out, life calls not for perfection, but for completeness."

Light is Active

Author Lee Carroll in the *Kryon Quarterly* wrote, "Light is active and dark is passive." As an example, it was illustrated in the following way: "There are two rooms. One is painted white and is flooded with bright light. There is another room right next to it that is painted black and has no light whatsoever. Say you are standing in the light room and the door opens, revealing the entrance to the adjacent dark room. Notice the dark from the other room does not suddenly flow in! There is no encroachment or blackness into the white room that you are in. Now let's say you are standing in the dark room. When the door opens, the light from the white room suddenly flows into the dark room and it is no longer dark. Light has completely taken over and the darkness is no longer complete."

The article continues, "This is the way your self-discovery and enlightenment works. Light is active since it represents truth. Darkness, or the 'dark side' is defined as the absence of light. The 'shadow' is actually the intellect without love. When you begin to carry more light, the darkness is overwhelmed. As you exude light, others will see it."

Intention is Vibration

The point is whenever you have "contrast" in your lives—and sometimes your contrast is more potent or dramatic than other times— you then come to a quicker decision of what it is you desire. That is the first step in bringing more "light" and focusing on what you desire. Right now you may not be vibrating even close to your awareness of what you choose to create, but you will learn to through choice and your willingness to be a Deliberate Creator.

There is a story about the Irish horse derby. A man who was new at horse racing and betting decided he would go down to the stables and look at the horses. He saw an Irish priest making different gestures over this one horse, and so at race time, he watched. Sure enough, this horse came in first. So the man thought he'd better watch the priest one more time, and sure enough, again the priest was doing some fancy hand work. Again, this horse took first place. So, thinking the third time would be a charm, he watched the Irish priest and his hand movements and then bet all his money on that horse. And the horses were off! Midway through, the horse suddenly fell over dead in his tracks with his feet sticking up in the air. The man was so disgusted at this turn of events, he went down and confronted the priest indignantly at his loss of money for betting on this horse. And the priest replied, "That's the trouble with some of you people, you don't know the difference between a blessing and last rites!"

Have clarity about your heart's desires and what you are "betting on" so you clearly understand what you are signaling and attracting! Your intentions are your vibrations. The "recipe" to identify your heart's desire and then focus only on your intended creation is simple. Be aware that it is not always easy because you have had lots of experience with detouring into fear and negativity. It takes practice and repeated experiences to learn how to flow energy creatively. Lots of energy and lots of practice. Don't deviate back into any of the difficulties because you want to radiate a fresh start. That new vibrational signal is the point of magnetic attraction for the Universe to accept your creations and intentions. If you focus on the problems, your problems are expanded. That then results in "miscreating" with more contrast. **Intention is vibration and creates new energy because it is a clean slate upon which you write daily through the power of your intent.**

Margin of Greatness

My husband, who is an avid baseball fan, used to motivate his employees with this story he read somewhere. In professional baseball, most batters hit for an average of .250, which means that they get one hit for every four times at bat. That is considered a respectable average, and if that hitter is also a good fielder, he can expect to enjoy a good career in the major leagues. Anyone who hits .300—three hits out of 10 at bats—is considered a star. By the end of the season, there are only perhaps about a dozen players, out of hundreds in the leagues, who have maintained a .300 average. Those hitters are honored as the great ones! They get the contracts, the acclaim, and the commercials and the fans adoration.

What is the difference between the greats and the ordinary hitters? ONE HIT OUT OF TWENTY! A .250 hitter gets five hits out of 20, and a .300 hitter gets six hits out of 20! In the world of baseball, ONE MORE HIT OUT OF 20 IS THE MARGIN OF GREATNESS. Is that amazing? What a minuscule, slim margin for greatness! It really puts it into perspective that you can always do a little more than you think you can when you hold your vision and trust the process of becoming more of who you really are.

The slim margin between baseball's mediocrity and greatness in this story can also symbolize you as a Deliberate Creator in life. When you visualize and imagine your dreams being fulfilled through your joyous feelings and inspirations, you will see them actualized in your daily life. You are then vibrating on purpose and becoming more of who you are potentially. As you step up to the home plate of your life, your intentions are your vibrations. You will manifest more of your magnificence in every single arena in which you joyously vibrate with your career, your family, your relationships, your abundance and your heart's desires. You can always visualize a little more than you think you can. You can always imagine a little more than you think you can. If you experiment with this principle, you will know yourself at exhilarating new levels of flowing energy toward your margin of greatness with a wonderful sense of well being.

Lighten Up!

Here is a lighthearted and funny story I received from my dear friend, Joyous Lesperance.

> "As the foreman was inspecting workmen on the site, he was surprised to find one worker hanging from a rope in the middle of the room repeating, 'I'm a chandelier, I'm a chandelier.'"

> The foreman gives him a stern talking to as the other men watched and orders him back to work. During his next inspection of the same room, again the worker is hanging from the rope doing exactly what he was told not to. Furious at his disobedience, the foreman fires him on the spot. To his surprise, every worker in the room begins packing up their tools and leaving.

> He stops one worker and says, "Why are all of you leaving?" To which the reply was, "You don't expect us to work without light do you?"

LIGHTEN UP!!! When was the last time you laughed out loud? Roared with laughter? It is the divine elixir of JOY which enables us to giggle at ourselves, as well as being with others who are in the JOY vibration. A sense of humor lights up and lightens our daily life.

Vibrational Matches

The magnets are an inspiring teaching tool to demonstrate the Law of Attraction. They are an excellent demonstration of whether you are moving toward or away from your heart's desires. You can now easily understand how life energies naturally come together through the Law of Attraction when you are a Deliberate Creator. The Law of Assertion is what you experience when you are pushing against or in resistance, which only brings more contrast. When vibrationally you match the vibration of your own desire, there is no contradiction. There is no resistance because the energy is positive and pure. When that happens, the Universe must deliver to you that which is in vibrational harmony with your desire, because your decision is your point of attraction.

Most people don't make it through a whole sentence without contradiction. An example Abraham gives is: "I want more money—I am so tired of the struggle." The Universe can't respond to two different vibrations so nothing changes for you. We have to purify our vibrations, which means getting our energy focused and lined up for our heart's desires. Even when outer conditions appear to be disharmonious, you can still "believe" and "conceive" what will be achieved as you receive and allow your creation to manifest in your imagination. Focusing your imagination, combined with your vibrational alignment statements, is literally the art of magnetizing. Purity and clarity in your thoughts and desires is essential to your well being. Everything comes to us through our vibrational output.

Pulsing a Vibrational Signal

Abraham has said, "Every moment you are pulsing a vibration, and the entire Universe is accepting that as your point of attraction and is matching it. Once you've identified what you desire, then your work is to offer a vibration that matches it. You can tell by the way you feeeeel whether you are matching it or not. The important thing we will say to you is that no one, nothing, can deny your desire. ONLY YOU CAN DENY YOUR DESIRE through contradictory vibration."

Frank Sinatra's popular song entitled, *I Did It My Way*, is a grand vision for vibrating and visualizing for a few minutes while you are still in bed each morning HAVING IT YOUR WAY. When you are "prepaving" your day, imagine and have it your way! Envision yourself on the freeway, having it your way with smooth-flowing traffic, courteous drivers, people yielding to you to allow you to enter the lane you desire, green lights and safety for you and your passengers. I also "intend" safety and well being for my family. You are focusing your intent and flowing energy in pure, positive directions and riding the energy wave of saying YES to how you choose your day to unfold. Do it with each segment of your day. You are vibrating on purpose!

Energy Leaks

I believe it was author, Dan Millman, who first shared a wonderful story of a seeker calling to God on the mountain top.

"O' Great Creator, fill me with Thy Light."
Then from within a voice speaks...
"I am always filling you with light, but you keep leaking!"

When you keep observing "what is" by current "appearances" then you are offering a vibrational outpouring that is other than matching the vibration of your desire. You are then "leaking" your energy, and it dissipates your connection with your Stream of Well Being. When you learn to flow energy purely toward your heart's desires, experiencing it from your imagination and outcome fulfilled, you are then a Deliberate Creator who is in vibrational harmony with your creation. You must feel the power in your decision and not detour into observing any appearances of your "current outer reality" (what you don't want) because that contradicts the energy and results in canceling out your heart's desire through resistance.

Monitoring Your Circuits

It is vitally important that you feel good about your choices and decisions for then you are vibrating in harmony and you will begin to experience vibrational matches that are exhilarating. Years ago I read that the root of the word harmony (defined as a pleasing or orderly whole; congruity; melody) came from the word hormone which means to stimulate or excite, to stream or secrete. This is a vibrational match to what Abraham recently shared, "Every cell in your body has a direct relationship with Creative Life Force, and each cell is independently responding. When you feel JOY, all the circuits are open and the Life Force or God Force can be fully received. When you feel guilt, blame or anger, the circuits are hindered and your Life Force cannot flow effectively. Your life experience is about monitoring those circuits and keeping them as open as possible. The cells know what to do. They are summoning the energy."

Marshaling Your Energy + Intent = Magnetic Attractions and Outcomes Fulfilled

An example of matching and mismatching can be illustrated again by using your magnets. Most people who are metaphysically inclined already do believe they are creating their reality—especially when things are manifesting easily. The opposite is also true that when things are not easy. There is some kind of resistance, usually unconscious, and yet no one is doing it to you. The key is knowing that often it is unconscious. As you become aware of how you "miscreate," you then awaken to becoming more conscious. For instance, if you think something is hard to do, then you consent to that being true and struggle becomes your experience. How often do you hear others say, "It is so hard," or "Life is a bitch?" I respond by saying, "Yes, but I prefer it to the alternative, don't you?" Guess what expands and you get more of by putting those thoughts out there? Once you become aware that what you focus on expands, it is the turning point for understanding how to create deliberately.

**The rich person and the poor person are NOT different minds.
They are simply different users or perceivers
of the same mind and consciousness available to all of us.**

Neville shared an analogy in one of his books using a piece of steel as a magnet. The magnet you hold in your hand when "magnetized" doesn't differ in its substance from the "demagnetized" state, except in its arrangement and order of molecules. A single electron revolving in a specified orbit constitutes one unit of magnetism. When this is de-magnetized, the revolving electrons haven't stopped nor gone out of existence. There is simply a re-arrangement of the particles. If they are all mixed up in all directions, they are de-magnetized. When the particles are MARSHALED in ranks so a number of them face one direction, the substance is then a magnet.

You can now easily see how your thoughts and vibrations must be marshaled like these magnets you hold in your hands. Focusing your energies all in one direction creates a vibrational match when you combine your heart's desires in your imagination with your outcomes fulfilled. It's the Law of Attraction in Action. Health, wealth and genius do not occur by chance. They are manifested through your intentions and marshaled and "magnetically arranged" by your heartfelt feelings.

You "de-magnetize" and "rearrange" the particles in your vibration every time you detour into fear, lack or struggle. You are then "miscreating" rather than vibrationally matching your highest choice. By embodying and unifying your thoughts, words, feelings and actions, you are flowing magnetically—you are then the "flow-er" in the stream of creative energy and can bask in your delicious decisions and creations. It is fun to realize that the word "flow-er" also is "flower." Now that's also a vibrational match, for we are here to grow, bloom and flourish.

Sweet Succulent Imaginings
Have Confidence In Your Outcomes Fulfilled

When you go into a restaurant and the waiter or waitress is ready to take your order, do you say, "I don't want a cheeseburger" or "I don't want vegetable soup" or "I don't want an omelet." Of course not! You place your order for a steak, fries and salad with the clarity and confidence that the chef in the kitchen is going to create **exactly** what you ordered. You don't jump up every five minutes to see if the chef is fixing an order of something you didn't order or didn't want. You trust that your order is being fulfilled exactly the way you requested it. The same is true by focusing on your creations in your sweet succulent imaginings, your wildest dreams and your heart's desires. They are being fulfilled through the Law of Attraction in Action.

When you are really hungry, have you noticed how your appreciation enhances what you ordered and you are practically salivating waiting for it to be served?! You already anticipate how it is going to taste. That is the same excitement you generate and feel in your deliberate creations through the power of your imagination of how wonderful and yummy it feels, looks, tastes and smells! What are you saying to yourself, what are others saying to you in your creative experience—what is your vibrational offering in how fulfilling your desire feels?

Your Vibrational Output

What is your vibrational output including? Is it as good as it gets? Can it be better, purer, clearer, richer, juicier? Is it in sync with your most heart-felt desire? How delicious is it? How focused and connected are you in your Stream Of Well Being? Are you fully appreciating your succulent connection to Source? Are you praising, trusting and in total harmony with your beliefs? Are you feeling invincible? Triumphant? Are you a vibrational match to your Core Energy? Is your energy marshaled magnetically to manifest your heart's desires easily, effortlessly and quickly? Do you feel wondrous?! Excited?! Connected?! Focused?! Enthusiastic? Accelerated energetically? Exuberant?

The Law of "Trying" Vs. The Law of Attraction

If you have resistance, are you able to observe, recognize and choose again? Notice if you are into the "Law of Trying" rather than the "Law of Attraction." One word to eliminate from your vocabulary forever is the word try—either you do or you don't, you will or you won't—there is no TRYING! Can you withdraw your attention from "what is" momentarily and focus upon your highest choice? What is your goal other than "trying?"

"It is necessary, therefore, it is possible."

...G.A. Borghese

It's fascinating that the words "tried" and "tired" are an anagram of the same letters. Eliminate words forever like "TRY," "if only," and "it's impossible." Theodore Roethke said,

"What we need is more people who specialize in the impossible!"

Change the word impossible in your mind's eye to "I'm-possible!" It was a wise person who said that a mind expanded to the dimensions of a greater idea can never return to its original size. What you think, say and vibrate does make a difference! Being a Deliberate Creator does require experimenting in charting your course for new directions of discovery where you live in a vast new unlimited world of infinite fertile possibilities.

"We live at the edge of the miraculous."

…Henry Miller

I took my Mental Health university class to see, *The Empire Strikes Back*, many years ago. I saw this film in the theater six times before it came out on video. One of my favorite dialogues was between Yoda and Luke Skywalker when he was being taught the power of telekinesis to lift his spacecraft out of the fog. I will "fast forward" to where Luke is saying to Yoda, "I'll give it a try." And Yoda replies with one of my favorite lines, "No, try not! Do, or do not. There is no try!" Then Luke complains that he can't because the craft is too big and again we fast forward to Yoda's response with, "Size matters not…look at me…judge me by my size do you? My ally is The Force and a powerful ally it is. Life greets it and makes it flow. Its energy surrounds us and binds us. Luminous beings are we!" Other noteworthy lines in this same scene where powerful teachings occur when Luke says to Yoda, "You want the impossible!" and then when Yoda actually levitates the ship, Luke responds, "I don't believe it!" and Yoda says, "That is why you fail."

Commitment Enlists Providence

I also was working with a blind student at that time who received as much benefit from attending this film as those who could visually see this movie. He moved from being a shooting "victim," to creating a higher outcome. Deliberate Creators do not "try." When you express "try," it denies your ability to create and flow energy. It is so exhilarating to know you are the yeast and the leavening agent for rising to new dimensions in consciously creating your reality. Either you do or you do not! You always have energy to do what you love, and conversely, when you know yourself, you also have clarity on **not** doing what isn't in your flow without any excuses or apologies. For Proust, discovery consisted not in seeking new landscapes, but in having new eyes; and W.H. Murray said "Commitment seems to enlist providence."

I first heard this true story from my mentor, Dr. Brugh Joy, in 1980. His point was about the phenomenon of perceptions with the Indians and Magellan's ships. I'm sure most people will remember Magellan, who sailed around South America and landed there. He had three huge masted ships anchored out a distance in the sea. The natives couldn't see those ships because they were so far beyond anything they could ever imagine, and they had no reference point for sailing vessels of this magnitude. The natives could see the small boats that Magellan's crew used to row up to shore. The traders that the Spanish used to come ashore were similar to the natives' own canoes. However, the natives absolutely could not see the big ships. When they looked out upon the waters, they saw a clear horizon with nothing upon it and kept saying, "I can't see it."

Then, the native shamans appeared and said, "If you look out there on the horizon and envision this boat, it is about this big and this long and this high." So the natives strained and looked again and again, and finally one of the natives said, "Does it have a red flag?" and their shaman said, "Yes!" They were sensing a possibility and concept for something for which they had no previous framework or reference point. Once one of them saw the red flag, they filled in the gaps. This amazing historical story was allegedly found in a diary in Magellan's own handwriting. This is a wonderful demonstration of how when our perceptions change, gradually everything becomes clearer and filled with new possibilities.

Hold the Vision

When Lazaris, a metaphysical teacher, shared this same Magellan story later on an audio tape, it was in the context that whenever you feel no hope, or there's no change in your life or your world seems to be falling apart and all you see is an empty unbroken horizon, know that the beautiful still exists and there's still a life to be celebrated even when you can't feel or see it. As you hold the vision and trust the process by summoning and flowing energy toward what you want, your perceptions will shift and soon you'll be seeing things differently. Know that focusing on what you want is a process; you don't suddenly get it overnight. The more you practice creating deliberately, the vibration of summoning energy for your heart's desires will begin to feel more and more familiar. You have to tweak it a bit here and fine-tune it a bit there to see how the Law of Attraction in Action actually responds to your fresh start. Each day is a clean slate to practice anew! You will begin to see things differently as you flow pure, positive energy beyond what you have done before. This is not new knowledge. You are becoming more of what you already are. It's a fresh inner knowing and a clearer way of seeing and being. And it is absolutely exhilarating when you feel your connection and notice what you think about attracts and expands. You always have a choice of remembering and connecting with your Stream of Well Being or not. You have free will and choice as a Deliberate Creator and attractor; or you can be a reactor and resist and push against, which will bring more of the same because like attracts like.

A Celebration of Imagination

"Imagination is taking an image and adding power to it."

Have you ever asked yourself what imagination is? On a recent tape, Abraham superbly outlined what it means by saying:

"Imagination is taking an image and adding power to it. When you take images and focus your creative attention upon it, you hold yourself in vibrational harmony with the image. Now you and the image are vibrating at the same [ratio] and the Universe will find things that match it to bring to you. If you are only briefly identifying the image of what you want, and mostly observing it is not here, then the Universe is matching the image that is dominant within you."

In the book, *The Ecstatic Journey*, the author, Sophy Burnham, was asking questions in meditation and one day an answer came back: pray. She thought about that for a moment and then said, "Why should I pray? You already know what I want. What's the point?" Instantly three answers came back to her telepathically: "So we will know what you want, in order that we might give you what you need; because when you pray, for a few moments you surrender—it may be only 15 seconds out of 15 minutes of attempted prayer. But in that moment of surrender, you open a window through which we can enter to deliver the desires of your heart;" and Sophy said she could not have expected, even in her wildest imaginings, the final answer; "Because your prayers energize our work."

What We Resist, Persists

If you talk incessantly about your problems, or how much you dislike your job or co-workers, or how hard your life is, or how many hours you have to work, or are often critical of your mate, family or co-workers, it focuses and expands and becomes your point of attracting more of what you don't want. By hating or intensely disliking anyone or anything, you generate the vibration of more hate or distaste through the Law of Attraction. Take time to re-focus and choose once again for your highest outcome as a Deliberate Creator.

The Oyster and the Pearl

An oyster takes a grain of sand (irritation) and makes of it a pearl. Our lives provide a constant opportunity as Deliberate Creators to learn that every limitation, every gritty grain of sand, everything that irritates us can be transformed if we would own and embrace the situation as our own magnetic "Attraction in Action." We have the power to manifest the beauty of the pearl through summoning and flowing energy as the masterful creators we are. We become the vibration we choose to attract for our own string of pearls.

When you focus on what you love to attract, by feeling and imagining your outcomes fulfilled, you then draw it to you magnetically. So often we think about what we don't want and the thing we fear comes upon us. Again, remember all thoughts are energy and all energy follows thought.

Variety Is The Spice Of Life And You Choose A Slice Or The Whole Enchilada

According to Abraham, "There is a big mix out there, and there's lots of different things going on, and there is not just one way which is intended to be the "right" way. Just like there's not just one color or one flower or one vegetable or one fingerprint. There is not one that is to be the right one over all others. Variety is what fosters creativity. And so you say, 'Okay, I accept that there's lot of variety, but I don't like to eat cucumbers.' That's okay, but don't ask for them to be eliminated and don't condemn those who eat them. Don't stand on street corners waving signs trying to outlaw the things you don't like. Don't ruin your life by pushing against. Instead say, 'I choose this. This is what pleases me."

"You are the Imagineer… Imagineering Your Heart's Desires in Every Aspect of Your Life!"

…Sharon Warren

For instance, the more you feel, think and imagine prosperity or attracting your beloved or any of your heart's desires, the more you are deliberately expanding and creating your reality. You will draw it to you magnetically more rapidly because you are feeding that energy. If you focus on lack, or not having your divine partner, you then repel the very thing you desire. Don't flagellate yourself if you detour into "negative" or resistant thoughts—that simply gives them more fuel and power. Just notice them, smile and say, "thank you for sharing," and replace them with thoughts and feelings of your highest choice and your wonderful outcomes fulfilled.

For example, when you find yourself saying "I can't afford," replace it with "I choose to easily afford" or "I can easily afford" and give thanks it is already here. Abundance or whatever you desire is simply attracted by the right use of your focused energy. Realize that being prosperous brings more choices and you are engineering your reality through your imagination—imagineering. It is already on its way through the power and intention of your thoughts, feelings and vibration. Visualize it flowing to you effortlessly. This takes practice, so when you find thoughts "wandering," re-focus and be as patient as you would be with your children when they don't know any better. You simply re-commit by taking responsibility for your thoughts or feelings and think about what brings you joy. If you won the Powerball or Lotto, what would you spend it on? That would prime the pump because you would be flowing energy abundantly, enthusiastically, lavishly and opulently. You are on the leading edge when you are a Deliberate Creator flowing energy toward your intentions joyfully. You then set your own vibrational tone which magnetizes and attracts your heart's desires.

"Devine" Attractions

When we lived in Indiana I met Dan Cheeseman. He wrote an article on how he had been choosing to attract prosperity wherein he saw himself as a grand-prize winner in a sweepstakes. The "ah-hah" occurred one morning in meditation when it came to him that this was not something he had to go out and do, but something he could draw to himself. He realized he needed to work on "receiving." Abundance is not something you simply create, but that you ACCEPT and we are each rewarded to our level of expectancy.

So, Dan started to "expect" receiving a winning announcement in the mail. One day his mail carrier brought a certified letter to him and Dan learned the Smirnoff Vodka had picked his entry. Dan had a School of Healing Arts and was an advocate of natural healing. The Universe sure has a sense of humor for Dan to then win a liquor sweepstakes.

In his article, Dan said he hadn't sent in many entries, nor done lots of affirmations for this contest, so the sheer number of entries was not a factor. He felt it was his attitude while doing it. In my opinion, Dan attracted this through his vibration. He made a decision and aligned with his heart's desires.

Smirnoff Vodka decided they wanted to present the check to him in person. Dan received a phone call and a voice said, "This is Mr. Divine from Smirnoff Inc. and we would like to set up a banquet to present the check for $10,000. The name **Mr. Divine** astonished Dan because the affirmation he had been doing was, "We open to the divine riches of the Universe and to divine abundance." As it turns out, when they met Mr. Divine, it is spelled with an "e." When the check was presented to Dan, it was from Heublein, Inc. Underneath was a sub-heading of "*Spirits Group*." So, Dan was presented with a check from Mr. Devine from Spirits Group. When Dan told Mr. Devine that he taught natural healing, Mr. Devine replied, "Smirnoff's is well-known for being the purest spirit."

This delicious story clearly reflects that ALL THOUGHTS ARE ENERGY AND ALL ENERGY FOLLOWS THOUGHT. Dan flowed focused energy and magnetized his heart's desire, plus Spirit had delicious fun "playing" in this process.

"Circumstances do not make the man— they reveal him."

…James Allen

Circum means around and *stance* means stand. Circumstances are the conditions that stand around us when we magnetize our heart's desires through our core beliefs and vibration. Another way of expressing it is, "By your fruits you will know them." The "them" is your thoughts and vibrations and the fruits are the events and conditions in your lives. I believe it was a Unity minister who said if you want to know the nature of someone's thought patterns, just look at the condition in their lives. And if you want to know what is personally going on in your sub-conscious, you don't have to go to a psychic. Just look at the condition of your home, your car, your job, your health, your relationships with your family and friends, and even your animals…is the dog snarling at you or the cat hissing at you or people honking at you? They are the "photographs" of what is going on in your "inner" life, thoughts and beliefs.

A Fresh Start

"The present moment is a powerful Goddess."

…Goethe

One day recently my bicycle odometer would not record the miles. I persisted in re-setting it, and again, it kept reading 0.0 even though it should have been recording miles. I finally realized the Universe was providing a playful metaphor that I always have a FRESH START, especially when I have zero or little resistance. I appreciate knowing I have the opportunity to create a fresh start or clean slate at any moment in time by simply paying attention.

**Your Experience Is Always
The Sum Total of the Content
Of Your Vibration!!
Each Day is a Fresh Start,
A Clean Slate,
And a New Beginning!
Imagine and Feed the Energy Wave
For Your Fresh Start Now!**

**Fresh Start
Fresh Start
Fresh Start
Fresh Start
Fresh Start
Fresh Start
Fresh Start
Fresh Start
From Your Heart**

4
Creation Is About Attraction

In an article in a former publication called *The Leading Edge*, Abraham speaks about creation and vibrations. He says that whatever you are thinking or talking about or looking at is your offering as a vibrational signal. Your vibrational signal is your point of attraction. Creation is not about standing here without something, and looking over there and seeing something you desire, and then somehow figuring out how to get it to come over here. Creation is achieving, through the power of visualization, a vibration right here where you stand. The Law of Attraction takes care of the rest. The vibrational match then comes to you. You cannot stand in the absence of something you desire and ever get it. You have to vibrate as if it already is or it will not come to you.

The more you allow your energy to flow with strong emotions to magnetize your heart's desires, your feelings and vibration have increased power to attract. If you have thoughts of "can't," then create another thought of why "you can." Imagine receiving your outcome, and feel how vivid it becomes when you are clear and unwavering in your focus. Remember, all thoughts are energy and all energy follows thought. Are you creating deliberately or "miscreating" through default by thinking about what you don't want? Are you matching or mismatching?

Excluding is Including

When Abraham speaks about inclusion and exclusion, the "excluding" aspect is a new insight or "ah hah" for most people. The word inclusion means things you want to include in your experience, like joyous people and kindred spirits, your divine partner, beautiful things you'd like to enjoy, a delicious fulfilling career, wealth and plenty of time to enjoy it, health, vitality and well being. In other words, the things you desire now!

The energy of exclusion means things not desired. Things you would like to exclude from your experience might be sickness, violence, bad drivers, not having enough money. Exclusion equals things not wanted. This is one of the most important things to hear, as there is no such thing as exclusion and every time you attempt it, all you really do is include something you don't want in your vibration or is the opposite of what you do desire.

According to Abraham, everything is about inclusion. When you say YES to something, you are including something you desire into your experience. When you say NO to something, you're also including something you don't want into your experience. It is easy to muddy up your vibration and keep it from being pure for that reason. Every time you say no to anything, you are including something which is contradictory to your desire in your vibration. That's what keeps you from offering the pure signal that would bring you rapidly what you do desire.

One of the humorous analogies Abraham uses is about being at a "cookie counter." You easily understand inclusion at the cookie counter when you say, "I'll have one of those and I'll have one of those and I'll have one of those." Inclusion! "I'd like to include that one (chocolate chip) and that one (oatmeal raisin) and also that one (macadamia white chocolate)." We don't see you saying, "Ah, look at that one. How did that icky cookie get in there? Why would anybody want that one?" We do not hear you say, "We better do something about getting that peanut butter cookie out of there. If we don't nip it in the bud, you know what will happen. Pretty soon, those icky peanut butter ones will take over the whole counter. If we don't stop it now, they will spread and there won't be enough room for the ones we do like. So, we've got to stop them." You don't do that with cookies because you know how absurd it is. It is equally absurd to look into your physical environment and see anything that you do not want and believe that you must exclude it as if it is an unwanted cookie.

Abraham describes **EXCLUSION** as: "Whenever you give your attention to anything you do not want, you are not and cannot and will not ever exclude it. You are including it by your exclusion. And as you include it, you are not offering a pure vibration. If you are not offering a pure vibration, a vibration that is in harmony with your desire, it cannot become a vibrational match. It must be a match by Law of Attraction."

54

Whenever you are looking at your problems, you are vibrating there and they will build and stay with you because you are in resistance. Wherever your attention goes is where your energy flows. So any solution cannot come because you are focused on the problem. Abraham has said that your vibrational output is not so different from a radio signal (air waves) and the entire Universe responds to your vibrational output and matches it. Most people are not deliberate about what kind of signal they are transmitting. If you are observing something that makes your heart sing, the Universe delivers back a vibrational match. If you are observing something you don't like, the Universe delivers back to you a match to what you don't like. You then stay in the mode of exclusion and resistance (and most of the time you do it unconsciously until you learn to vibrate on purpose)!

Vibrational Mirrors

The poet, Edwin Markham, wisely wrote:
Gone is the city, gone the day,
yet still the story and the meaning stay;
Once where a prophet in the palm shade basked,
A traveler chanced at noon to rest.
"What sort of people may they be," he asked.
"In this proud city on the plains o'er there spread?"
"Well, friend, what sort of people from whence you came?"
"What sort?" the man scowled:
"Why, knaves, scoundrels and fools."
"You'll find the people here the same," the wise man said.
Another stranger in the dusk drew near:
And pausing, asked, "What kind of people live here
In your bright city where yon towers arise?"
"Well, friend, what sort of people from whence you came?"
"What sort?" the pilgrim smiled and said,
"Good, true and wise."
"You'll find the people here the same," the wise man said.

This story has been told in many guises and forms, and the first version I read originated as a great master from Athens with the same storyline. It is a beautiful metaphor for knowing that everyone we meet is our mirror. Wherever you go, you will encounter and find yourself. Often, without realizing it, your own mood is being mirrored back to you. Is it being mirrored gracefully or "disgracefully?" Easily or through struggle? Everyone you meet is your mirror and sometimes it is through the lens of everything you don't want or don't like.

Marilyn Ferguson expressed this idea well in her book, *The Aquarian Conspiracy*. "When life becomes a process, the old distinctions between winning and losing, success and failure, fade away. Everything, even a 'negative outcome,' has the potential to teach us and to further our quest. We are experimenting and exploring. In the wider paradigm there are no 'enemies,' only those useful, if irritating, people whose opposition calls attention to trouble spots like a magnifying mirror."

Mirror Mirror

What you see mirrored is a projection of yourself both positively or negatively. Sometimes it is a mirror of what you don't like. Often it is a mirror of things that need to be changed to a higher vision and energy flow of what you do desire. Attacking and judging anyone is a waste of energy. We can all get into the blame game of what "he said" or "she did" and we could even provide convincing "evidence" to support how "right" we are or how unjust the situation was. However, that energy doesn't empower anyone and keeps us stuck in projections and a chain of blame.

A wonderful example of mirrors is a hilarious story I received in an e-mail from my dear friend, Joanne Snow. I laughed out loud, as it is such an amusing "hands-on" illustration of how we create our reality through our thoughts. It beautifully reflects "contrast" and how we magnetize situations into our lives through the Law of Attraction for our growth.

Hit the Floor

A woman was having her hair done at a West Hempstead, New York, beauty parlor and she told this personal cautionary tale about racial prejudice. On a recent weekend in Atlantic City, she had won a large bucketful of quarters at a slot machine. She was taking a recess from the slots to have dinner with her husband in the hotel's dining room, but first she wanted to stash her bucket of winnings in her hotel room. She told her husband she would be right back and carried her heavy, coin-laden bucket to the elevators.

As she was about to enter the open elevator, she noticed two men already inside and they were both black. One of them was big…very big…and she instantly felt intimidated. She momentarily "froze" and her first thought was that she would be robbed. Her next instant thought was, "Don't be a bigot!" as they looked like perfectly nice gentlemen, even though in her eyes, one of them was awfully black. She knew this was a personal stereotype, but her fear immobilized her. She momentarily froze as she thought, "I know these two men are going to rob me!"

She stood and stared at the two men. She felt anxious, flustered and ashamed. She hoped they wouldn't be able to read her mind, but knew that they surely did because her hesitation in joining them on the elevator was all too obvious. Her face burned. She couldn't just stand rooted there, so with a mighty effort, she stepped forward and moved into the elevator. Avoiding eye contact, she turned around stiffly and faced the elevator doors as they closed. A second passed, then another, and then another. The elevator didn't move.

Panic consumed her. She thought, "My God, I'm trapped in this elevator and about to be robbed!" Her heart plummeted. She felt sweat dripping out of every pore. Then, one of the men said, **"Hit the floor!"**

Instinct told her to do what he said. The bucket of quarters flew upward as she released it, threw out her arms and collapsed on the elevator carpet. A shower of coins rained all around her. She prayed they would take her money and spare her—more seconds passed. Then, politely one of the men said to her, "Ma'am, if you will just tell us which floor you're going to, we'll push the button for you." The one who said it had trouble getting the words out as he was trying mightily to hold in his laughter. She lifted her head and looked up at the two men. They reached down to help her up. Confused, she struggled to her feet.

The average-sized black man genially said to her, "When I said, 'Hit the floor,' I meant that my friend should hit the elevator button for our floor. I didn't mean for you to hit the floor, ma'am."

The woman felt so embarrassed and knew she had made a spectacle of herself. She was too humiliated to speak. She wanted to offer an apology, but words failed her. How do you apologize to two perfectly respectable gentlemen for behaving as though they were robbing her? The three of them gathered up the strewn quarters and refilled her bucket. When the elevator arrived at her floor, they insisted on escorting her to her room. At her door, they bid her a good evening. As she went into her room, she could hear them laughing as they went back to the elevator.

The woman pulled herself together and went downstairs for dinner with her husband. The next morning, fresh flowers were delivered to her room—a dozen roses. Attached to each rose was a crisp $100 bill. A card read, "Thanks for the best laugh we've had in years!" It was signed, **Eddie Murphy and Bodyguard.**

A Course In Miracles says that there are basically two energies…love or fear. Attack and gossip and prejudice are coming from "fear." Blame and guilt cannot abide where love resides. So, we can choose love or fear—one or the other. We will always know what is being mirrored because fear and love cannot co-exist together. Abraham has said, "You cannot love your children and worry about them at the same time. Most people mistake worry for the emotion of love. They think worrying about somebody means you love them." The two energies cannot co-exist. It is a contradiction of terms. We are each the "Creative Cause" of the mirrors in our lives, and it is our choice to become the change we want to see happen. For instance, there is a difference between gossiping and genuinely seeking heart to heart counsel or sharing space with an intimate friend for clarity. You will always know by the vibration because one energy seeks to understand and learn by being open and teachable, while the other vibration is a projected energy which appears to criticize, justify, blame, condemn or get others to change. When that kind of conversation occurs, the whipped cream usually hits the fan. The situation will expand with more negativity because that is where the energy is focused.

You are the Point of Power... The Static or the Transformer

Think about how an electrical transformer turns energy into power that can be directed—pure, potential power that can be used constructively or destructively. It can be power that lights up a city or blows up a city, depending on how it is dispersed. Electricity surges and circulates throughout the walls and floors in your home constantly. The power and current of electricity is always available to you. Most people don't know how electricity really works. However, you do know that you first have to PLUG into it by using an appliance or turning on a switch that asks for energy and commands a designated current. Electricity sits idle until you turn it on deliberately. The current is then operating as the Law of Attraction in Action for unseen energy to flow. The law of electricity is constant and it is neutral—it doesn't care what you plug into it. If you put a finger into an electrical socket or outlet, you will instantly get a shock and an immediate understanding that electricity is always flowing and generating power no matter what you plug into it. It is impersonal.

Your divine power works in exactly the same way. It awaits your connection and activation to your Inner Being by summoning and flowing energy as a Deliberate Creator. This unseen current is always available through your divine circuitry and the Law of Attraction. Life doesn't care whether you activate your connection nor believe in creating on purpose or by default. If you want to be activated, then you must be the one to plug into your Source.

We have remote controls for television, VCR's and stereos simply by pressing a button to change stations or to adjust the volume, etc. So where are the wires that connect our remotes to the appliance? We know that the technology accomplishes it; however, it's invisible because we don't physically see the airwaves beaming out that send the signals to the TV. Our thoughts operate in the same way. Having aware-ness and focused thoughts is our vibrational signal beaming out the Law of Attraction in Action, which brings more and more of what we are thinking about, negative or positive. Like attracts like. Whatever we focus on expands. While there is a lapse in timing between our thoughts and manifestation, whatever we give our attention to will be our experi-ence. Positive emotions are a higher, faster, purer vibration while nega-tive emotions are a lower, slower vibrational frequency.

Good Moods & Bad Moods
High Moods & Low Moods
Positive Emotions & Negative Emotions

When you begin to understand your moods, as well as your emotions, you will see life very differently. Positive emotions and being in a higher mood creates, attracts, generates and magnetizes your heart's desires more quickly than when you are in a low mood.

If you are in a "low" or bad mood or feeling negative emotions, I invite you to type out or write on paper the words, "This too shall pass away." You will know that you are in some form of **resistance** focusing your energy on negative emotions or situations. When I taught at the univer-sity, I occasionally had students who were considering suicide. I would tell them that you never know when things are going to get better. Situ-ations look very different when you are experiencing depressed energy, (which often is masked anger) and that's all you see or feel. A wise person said, "I've lived many years and had many fears…most of which never happened." You lose personal power whenever you fear. Then you feel even more vulnerable.

There is a story about twins; one was an optimist, and the other a pessi-mist. The story illustrates how their vibrational habits matched their outcomes. One got more manure while the other looked for the pony in the manure pile. Each was reacting to habitual thinking patterns. The vibrational tone they offered dominated their experience. The simple key is to choose thoughts that feel good and notice how you are consis-tently flowing your energy.

When you realize the influence your low moods have over your daily experiences and interactions, look at the aspects of your life that are working and make you feel good. When I was a child, there was a song lyric that went, "You've got to accentuate the positive and eliminate the negative." This simply means that when positive energies are flowing, things will always be getting better. Do you know that even the happiest, most joyous people on the planet have their low moods! The secret is in knowing how to summon and flow energy so you begin to feel better. This does not mean that you will solve the problem or the condition that is bothering you in that moment; you simply need a strong desire to feel better. When you want to feel better, take a few minutes to summon new, positive energy through your strong desire. Your point of attention and attraction changes, and the whole Universe then responds to that vibration. Remember, ask and it is given! You don't have to prove your worthiness. Just ask and know it is being given. Don't say, "I don't know how" or "I don't have a clue how to do this," for that becomes your declarative statement to the Universe and holds you in the reality or mood that you don't desire. Focus upon your desire to feel better. Life isn't a spectator sport. Become the change you want to see happen and summon positive energies that make you feel good.

Are You an Alternating or Direct Current?

You've probably heard electricity referred to as A.C. or D.C. current. A.C. stands for an alternating current, which reverses its direction periodically. It's a great analogy for life. When you aren't plugged into your Stream of Well Being consistently, you are an Alternate Creator. You engage an alternate current that attracts resistance, usually because you are giving your attention to lack or struggle. It then contradicts and dis-creates your heart's desires, which means temporary reversals until you pay attention to the flow you desire. D.C. electricity stands for a direct current, which flows in one direction. D.C. can also be an abbreviation for Deliberate Creator! When you appreciate and flow your energy creatively and focus on connecting with your Stream of Well Being, you are magnetizing pure, positive, passionate, pulsating, powerful energy. You acknowledge that you are an extension of this vibration of Pure Energy and Direct Current. Whatever you give your attention to, through your intentions, flows to and through you magnetically.

The Law of Attraction is constant, and it is always your free will and choice to be in or out of the Stream of Well Being. You are the channel or funnel to receive this outpouring of divine energy enthusiastically or not to receive it at all. You are the catalyst to your connection as a Deliberate Creator! Disconnection takes place whenever you are "reacting" or angry, critical and blaming. When this happens, you flow energy in opposition of what you say you desire. This is stepping on your own hose. Nothing is more important than that you feel good, which means flowing energy toward your HEART'S DESIRES and being in alignment with your outcomes. When you are basking and acknowledging what is flowing well, you are in vibrational harmony. Your guidance systems always let you know how you are flowing energy through your emotions. Are you an A.C. or D.C.? If you are an Alternate Creator, you will stink up your vibration. Alternate Creators are usually on the "pity pot" complaining, comparing, criticizing or attracting one crisis after another. As a Deliberate Creator, you are an uplifter who flows and receives a direct current consistently and feels infinite JOY and APPRECIATION for being tuned in, tapped in and turned on. Ecstasy is a new "current" when you consciously generate and direct your life as a D.D.C.—a Divine, Deliberate Creator!

You are the Point of Light

You are always the point of transformation, which channels your energy and directs your power and flow. When "mirrors" occur where you feel "resistance" wondering how you attracted "that" person or event, then notice which energy wave are you riding. It takes courage to commit to and to be aware of what you clearly choose to magnetize. When I first became consciously committed and involved in "becoming more of what I am," it was about as stable as a baby coming down the birth canal and just about as uncomfortable too! When you initially commit to your personal growth, it is like a newborn baby. It is a life-long process of learning what feeds you and serves you in your highest good. You first take baby steps and eventually learn to walk, then run and eventually you SOAR knowing in every cell of your being that you are a Deliberate Creator. Be gentle with yourself and remember to keep your sense of humor.

In 1995, my Lincoln went through a car wash with the car antennae inadvertently left up, which resulted in it being bent. I did have to laugh as I have a zany sense of humor and it sure looked funny in that moment. Of course, a bent aerial produced "static" on my radio because it wasn't getting a clear, pure signal. Very often in our lives, even though our Inner Being is standing by "beaming us up," we aren't listening to the signals because we aren't consciously connected to our Stream of Well Being. When we drive through the mountains here, often the radio stations become out of range and we lose the signal being broadcast. Source is beaming signals all of the time, but it is up to us to tune in and be on the right frequency band by fine-tuning to a clearer signal until we are re-connected. Feedback can come through intuition, a sudden impulse or inspiration, and even contrast or static to make a new, clear stronger decision. You are the receiver-amplifier who sets the dial to your "sound of music" or the "song in your heart" of what you choose to experience.

17 Seconds from Your True Heart's Desire

How are You Vibrating Relative to the Things You Desire?

Abraham has said how surprised most of us are to discover that, in most cases, we are not even close to vibrationally matching the things we desire. Because, if we were, the things we desire would be flowing into our experience. And yet, with very little effort of offering a pure vibration, we are much closer than we believe or realize.

Abraham teaches that if you hold a thought for **17 seconds** without contradicting it, another thought like it of the same vibration and same tone will come to it by Law of Attraction. And at precisely the 17-second point, these two thoughts will join one another. They coalesce. And when they do, there is an Energy that is expended. It's like a combustion point. And when these two thoughts join, they combust. You feel enthusiasm bubbling within you. In that 17 seconds, these two thoughts join and become one bigger, more evolved, faster vibrating thought. If you can stay focused upon the subject you have chosen for another 17 seconds, at the moment you cross the 34 second mark—that's just 2 x 17—this more-evolved thought will attract unto it. They then do the same thing—they coalesce and combust. These two thoughts become one, resulting in a higher, faster and purer vibration. If you can maintain your attention to the now more evolved thought, at the 51 second mark, (3 x 17), there is another coalescing, another joining of thought and another combustion point. If you can hold that more evolved thought for yet another 17 seconds, the same things happens and when you cross the 68 second mark, you have a combustion big enough to affect physical manifestation.

Leaving the Heat On

Abraham has said when you align your energies with the Energies that create worlds, when you are not contradicting your core desires, amazing things happen. To most of us, 17 seconds doesn't sound like much, and yet at eight seconds, most of us begin our "contradictory vibrations" and don't make it through a whole sentence without contradicting the vibration of our desire. Examples Abraham has shared are, "I desire more money...because I am so tired of the struggle"—that was just a couple seconds when the two thoughts canceled each other out. Or, "I want so much to be well...I'm frightened of this illness." I like his analogy of making tea where you say, I want a cup of hot tea and you turn the fire on under the teakettle. Just before it boils, you turn it off. Then you turn it on again, and just before it boils, you turn it off. For years now you've been trying to get hot tea. Just leave it on—just leave it on a little longer til it boils. That's the same recipe for the 17 seconds of pure thought to reach the combustion point. The reason it has been difficult to offer a pure vibration, without contradicting it, is because we're objective and weigh the pro's and con's, the pluses and minuses.

Contrast prods us into great clarity. Contrast (diversity) is essential to decision, and once your decision is made, then focus your full attention upon your decision and do your best to achieve a vibrational match to your outcome. The Universe then goes to work in helping you achieve whatever it is you are desiring. The reason you don't know the Universe is responsive to your vibration is what was explained earlier as "I want a new red car...but it is too expensive." The Universe responds to both vibrations, which are obviously contradictions and they cancel each other out or significantly dilute your decision.

Directing Energy + Focused Thoughts Magnetizes Your Heart's Desires Now!

According to Abraham when you begin to offer your vibration purely, and you see how the Universe responds, two wonderful things happen. The first is you show yourself you have the ability to hold your mind on something for 17 seconds. If you can do it for the first 17 seconds, you can do it for the second and third and fourth segments (34, 51 and 68 seconds). This gives the Universe the opportunity to show you that it is absolutely responsive to your vibration. You're going to learn that you are a beaming energy that is being responded to, and it will give you a sense of control. It will give you a sense of being the DELIBERATE CREATOR that you really are, meaning you are the focuser of energy. If you don't have the ability to hold a thought, then you cannot be a Deliberate Creator. You came forth to direct Energy and by directing Energy, you must hold the thought. And you will know if you are holding a thought by being sensitive to the way you feel, because you will actually feel the fluctuation of the vibrations within you. It is your emotional guidance system.

One superb analogy Abraham uses to illustrate being a Deliberate Creator. Imagine a quiet room fan and feel the stream of air blowing toward you. Now, stick a pencil in the fan. It would create quite a ruckus and play havoc with the air stream. **That pencil in the fan is exactly what negative emotion is. When you introduce a slower, lower vibration to a higher, faster vibration, you can feel the fluctuation in energy**. A pencil in the fan may be an extreme example of a fluctuation of energy, although that is exactly what negative emotion is. When you have a desire and thoughts about something you really want, and then you introduce the thought or conclude "I can't have it," in the higher, faster frequency of your desire, that disappointment or negative emotion is your pencil in the fan. It's you, introducing and miscreating through default into a lower, slower vibration rather than staying in your higher purer vibration.

Have you been around people who are constantly worried and fearful and then noticed how you also detour into "lack" and "anxiety" because you were influenced by their negativity, which then amplified your own concerns. That's their pencil in the fan. It's the lower, slower vibration. And you just got "sprayed" by it. The media promotes fear about everything from the economy to crime to sickness when in fact there is abundance available at all times, and we create our own safety and health through our thoughts. The commercials are suggestive enough to make one ill with sneezing, coughing, itchy eyes, headaches, and other pains. They are appealing both unconsciously and blatantly to your fears. While others are "surviving," you have the choice to be

thriving regardless of what's going on externally. You

have choice!! You can expand and create new possibilities every day as you get in touch with your potential as a Deliberate Creator and have greater visions with fresh decisions. You are a magnet attracting through the vibration of your thoughts. Through the Law of Attraction in Action, you draw unto you that which you are thinking. Listen to your guidance system through your emotions and know a wiser and older you, your Inner Being is always present and is transmitting to you through your feelings when you are listening. This is how deliberate creations are launched. When you are eager and expectant about manifesting, it becomes your magnetic experience. That's the higher, faster, purer vibration! Trust your IMAGINATION and know it is your soul speaking to you. Be excited and delighted in your energy flowing positively.

Law of Attraction Abounds!

I had just finished this chapter on creation, when our dear friends, Carolyn and Cork Henderson from Fort Wayne called me. Carolyn came to my university class many years ago by herself, brave soul that she is. She has an "eye challenge" and is legally blind, so she cannot drive. She didn't know how she would get home that night because bus service wasn't available. She shared her situation and inquired if I could ask if anyone in the class lived close to her home. I was happy to do that and was touched that she would have the courage to come to a class with this unknown factor. We introduced Carolyn and Cork to the Abraham material in 1997, and they were very enthusiastic. They were inspired at being Deliberate Creators and began to have immediate evidence of their creations and magnetizing their heart's desires.

While visiting Cork's aunt and uncle in Florida, they received as a gift an envelope with a new, crisp $50 bill. They also had lots of fun playing on their relatives' new Casio keyboard. Later that day, when they were talking with Cork's niece, they learned of her car's mechanical problem. She appeared to have "lack" issues because she perceives life as a struggle. They gave his niece the $50 bill they had just received, which would seem like a $1,000 to her. She was very grateful and it felt so good to them to help her out. A few days after returning to Fort Wayne, an unexpected check came in the mail for $1,000. They were ecstatic! It felt to them like more **evidence** of flowing energy. Two weeks later, they received a new Casio keyboard in the mail from their aunt and uncle, who said they would like for them to have one of their very own. More evidence of how Law of Attraction abounds!!

A short time later, an exuberant Carolyn called us. They had just received a check in the mail for $3,000 from this same aunt and uncle. Included was a piece of paper that said, "Just because we wanted to." They had also attended a company party over the weekend where one employee privately asked the owner, "Are Carolyn and Cork loaded or wealthy?" and she replied, "Not that I know of." I told Carolyn, little does this woman know that your vibration is carrying a new powerful, delicious, FRESH energy that is emitting a signal of your Well Being, and the whole Universe is seeing you both differently!!!

"There is nothing more powerful than an idea whose time has come."

...Victor Hugo

Prosperity zoomed and roared into their life at abundant new levels of manifestation because they summoned the energy as Deliberate Creators with such gusto! They revved up their desires with zero resistance and the Universe delivered! It is so heartwarming to see this level of magnetizing so easily, effortlessly and purely. They didn't have a clue they would be receiving any of these gifts! And yet, their vibrational output was magnetizing vibrational matches quickly because of the joyous signal being transmitted. They accepted and allowed this new level of prosperity! It was a vibration whose time had come, as every cell in their being was summoning this new energy. They emotionally embodied being Deliberate Creators at a whole new level and flooded the airwaves with fresh well beingness through their vibrational signal.

The Universe orchestrates your heart's desires through the Law of Attraction in Action! The stronger, clearer and purer your desires become as Deliberate Creators, the quicker manifestations occurred.

You are the Creator, Creating Your Creations

On June 11, 1998, I had a private appointment with Patricia Mulreany. Patricia is an artist from Florida who meditates regularly. Her friend who had a critical life-threatening illness asked Patricia for help and guidance. In their mutual meditation regarding this health issue, Patricia had a very unexpected communication come through her. Very suddenly and unexpectedly, an energy appeared in Patricia's meditation in a blaze of flashing or blinking lights and announced, "We are Abraham and we would like to address that question." Patricia's signal and tone attracted the Abraham vibration in an unforeseen fashion through her purity and desire to assist her friend.

My appointment was an illuminating session with personalized interaction where I asked questions of a specific nature. Abraham delivered precise material on the topic of Deliberate Creation, which was profound. I share it here because it brilliantly encapsulates the steps involved in being a Deliberate Creator:

> We enjoy these one-on-one conversations very much because we get to chew with you on the nitty gritty of your everyday life. We would like to review the steps of Deliberate Creation, even though you already know them.

Step One of Deliberate Creation

The first step of deliberate creation is to know what you do **NOT** want. Contrast is very important to your physical life. Without up, there would not be down. Without dark, there would not be light. Contrast is what creates the physical world. It is only through contrast that you can make decisions and it is only through decisions that you can create.

Step One of creation is always knowing what you do **NOT** want. And from knowing what you don't want will burst forth the clarity of what you do desire. Never do you want wellness more than when you feel ill. Never do you want abundance more than when you feel poverty or lack. Deliberate Creation, Step One is knowing what you do *not* want. You begin to get clearer and clearer. You begin to think in the direction of what is desired.

Step Two of Deliberate Creation

With Step Two, you begin to think about what you do desire and you feed that energy. You feed that energy into what you desire to create. As you think about it, you reach into this vast sensorium[3] of thoughts and senses that you have created through your lifetime. Every experience you have ever had through your senses—sight, sound, taste, touch, smell—any emotion you have ever experienced exists forever. You have a vast sensorium, so your deliberate creations begin to get clearer and clearer about what you desire. You bring forth bits and pieces of senses to create an emotion, which creates a feeling and a response. And as this energy becomes familiar to you, the sensation and emotions becomes stronger and stronger.

Step Three of Deliberate Creation

In Step Three of Deliberate Creation, you create a vibrational match to what you desire through emotion. This is very important to know and

---

3   Sensorium was a new word to me. Webster's Dictionary says it is: (1) the seat of physical sensation in the gray matter of the brain, (2) the whole sensory apparatus of the body.

remember: **THE POWER AND THE SPEED OF ATTRACTION IS THROUGH YOUR EMOTIONS.** And you know, whenever you have been angry or frustrated with something that you shake. When you are excited, or you are anticipating something that is thrilling to you, you physically shake. That is the power of vibration and the power of emotion. So emotion is the key to the power and the speed of what it is you are desiring.

When you feel the emotion of it and you know you have clicked in, you feel the YES! YES! This is what I want! YES! This is what I desire, YES! And then you hold that vibration for 17 seconds, plus 17 seconds, plus 17 seconds, plus 17 seconds and you have created your launch! This older, wiser part of you is a wondrous guidance system from our perspective. It is a miraculous guidance system—it is perfection. This guidance system speaks to you at every moment through your emotions. Because the brain mechanism moves very, very quickly, it is almost impossible to think two thoughts at one time. It is not possible to think a thought and realize, "I am thinking a negative thought." Your Inner Being communicates with you through emotion in every moment.

Step Four of Deliberate Creation

Step Four of Deliberate Creation is not your work. The how, the when, and the where are the work of the Universe, the work of this powerful Force. How do you know when you are in the flow? EVIDENCE ABOUNDS! Step Four of Deliberate Creation is looking for evidence.

To give you an example of how the steps work, I will share my personal experience regarding writing this book. A half-hour before my appointment with Patricia, I had shown her the proto-type I had created of my book with the magnets. She was so delighted and excited and immediately began to play with the magnets. She expressed that it was the most amazing, brilliant and original idea she had ever seen and said, "Millions of copies will be sold of your book!" I then shared my concern with her regarding whether packaging the book and magnets together could affect store scanners at the point of sale. I discussed my concerns with Abraham-Satarcia regarding the magnets and scanners issue. The following material is what was shared:

Energy Wave Patterns
Which One Are You Riding?

Let us say there are two waves. There is one energy wave that says I want to create this book and I am concerned about these magnets and the scanners. I think magnets with the book are a great idea and I feel very, very uplifted and can flow positive energy toward it. But I wonder if the magnets might affect the scanners.

Then, there is another energy wave pattern that says this book is easy and effortless. This book with magnets is a wonderful idea and I know that there are answers on how to package these magnets. It is easy and it is going to be effortlessly magnetized and answers are going to be attracted. So, there is an energy pattern that you are feeding here. You can feed and energize those thoughts until they become a tidal wave. A tidal wave of energy that is manifested in physical form for packaging. As you know, you were born with an Inner Being. You came forth with an Inner Being, which is an older wiser part of you. There are many names for it. Some call it Soul or your Higher Self. We call it your Inner Being. Ask your Inner Being to assist you.

There are Only Two Feelings of Emotions
One Energy Feels Good and One Feels Bad

So, when you are thinking about this book of yours and you have thoughts like "I don't know how the magnets and store scanners are going to work and I don't know how we are doing to do it," then you begin to feel worry, and concern. Remember, from our perspective, there are only two feelings—one feels good and one feels bad [shared with emphasis]. When you are feeling bad, it is your inner guidance tapping you on the shoulder telling you that you are standing in Step One of Deliberate Creation. You are feeding energy into the wave pattern that you do **NOT** want to create. When you find yourself in Step One, do not spend one moment there. Do not spend one speck of a sec beating up on yourself for being back in Step One. Instead say: Thank you Guidance System. Bless you!

You will know by your inner guidance system when you're slipping into Step One of Deliberate Creation. You know exactly what to do about that. It takes you 17 seconds. It may take you a few minutes to say, "Oops, what is it that I do desire? I want this to be easy and effortless." If you are thinking about when, where and how—how are we going to fix this problem, you're back in Step One. That's not your work, because you see, after you have matched the vibration through your Inner Being—you have found a vibrational match and you hold that for 17 seconds, + 17 seconds, + 17 seconds.

Luminous Fibers

A Tidal Wave of Energy

From our perspective, every cell in your body has luminous fibers. If you are frustrated, sad or depressed, the luminous fibers are weak—they're limp. As you become clearer on Step Two of Deliberate Creation of what you desire through your emotions, you bring yourself to Step Three of Deliberate Creation and find the vibrational match to what it is that you want. The things you are saying YES to—those luminous fibers are shooting out into the Universe in a powerful fashion and they are connected to Source energy! This is the pure, positive, passionate, pulsating, penetrating energy that creates worlds! This is God Force. This is powerful energy and when you are connected to Source, these luminous fibers are shooting out in a powerful fashion! If you hold those luminous fibers out there for 17 seconds, an explosion—a combustion takes place and each one of those millions of luminous fibers bursts into ten more luminous fibers! And when you hold that feeling for 17 seconds and each one of those bursts forth into ten more!! It is always attracting more of what is. Feed that energy wave of what you want until it becomes a tidal wave.

As you can imagine, I was ecstatic and very inspired with this interaction. It was brilliantly delivered with bullet-like precision for emphasis and impact. There was an accelerated intensity of emotion, as if a combustion had taken place. I was relishing every moment. Emotionally, this is where the juice is. You will feel how amped up it becomes vibrationally in connecting to your Stream of Well Being!

Thoughts are Energy Patterns
Everything in the Universe is Energy!

From Abraham's perspective, as they view our physical world, they see our world and everything in our Universe as ENERGY. The way that energy manifests in physical form is through vibration. There are WAVES of ENERGY PATTERNS—millions and millions of energy patterns that vibrate and oscillate into physical form. And that is how we create our reality through the Law of Attraction.[4]

I have shared some yummy "hands-on" details, which are outlined very specifically in Chapter 13 on how to laser focus your intent and feed your heart's desires with creation "recipes" in having it your way.

"Every person, all the events in your life are there because you have drawn them there. What you choose to do with them is up to you."

...Richard Bach
Illusions, The Adventures Of A Reluctant Messiah

---

4   Abraham-Hicks also share the Steps of Deliberate Creation in their books, tapes and events.

Your Dream Team

A Ship in Port is Safe
But That Isn't What Ships are Built for

In the story of Don Quixote, Sancho Panza clings to a window sill all night long, afraid of falling. When daylight comes, he finds that all through those long, dark hours of the night his feet had been only inches from the ground. We often cling to the known, afraid to let go and move into the unknown…and trust the miracle of adventuring into new creative attitudes and exciting deliberate directions.

> There is the story of a man walking in the mountains who was too close to the edge of a cliff and fell off. As he was free-falling, he desperately grabbed the limb of a gnarly old, fragile tree on the side of this shear cliff. When he looked down, he could see it was about 1,000 feet to the canyon below. He hollers for help to no avail.
>
> Finally he yelled, "Is there anybody up there?"
> And a deep voice replied, "Yes, I'm here."
> "Who is it?" the man asked.
> "This is God," came the reply.
> "Can you give me a hand?" the man asked.
> "Of course," God replied, "Just let go"…
> Panicked, the man said, "What?!!! Whatdayamean let go?"
> God replied, "Let go—I will catch you."
> To which the man hollered, "Is anybody else up there?"

We will be held by everything we hold. As we let go and release our grip on old patterns, thoughtforms and beliefs (remember, a belief is simply a thought we keep thinking), we are no longer in their grip and they have no power over us. What we resist, persists! What we hang onto tightly, controls us. The great Tao master and author, Lao-tzu said, "Nothing in this world is as soft and yielding as water, yet for dissolving the hard and inflexible, nothing can surpass it. The soft overcomes the hard, the gentle overcomes the rigid. Everyone knows this is true, but few put it into practice." He also said, "The Tao flows everywhere…when you look for it, there is nothing to see. When you listen for it, there is nothing to hear. When you use it, it is inexhaustible."

In India, the way people catch monkeys is by putting nuts in a narrow-necked jar that is then attached by a chain to a tree. The monkeys come down out of the trees and, of course, head right for the nuts in the jars. The monkey catchers then throw burlap bags over the monkeys to capture them. This is easily accomplished because once a monkey has his hand in the jar, he makes a fist inside and won't let go. Even though the monkey could escape by releasing his grip, he continues to keep a tight fist around the nuts and is captured.

If you are feeling bound by circumstances in your life, to what or where are you hanging on? Where can you let go? How is it serving you? As you let go, it may initially feel shaky or like you are between two trapezes without a safety net. Yet it becomes empowering one step at a time. You are leaving your past behind you and headed for your future while making your decision in the now. The trinity of self-knowing and self-balancing becomes self-fulfilling as you claim and name your heart's desire in this moment.

Giving Up Or Letting Go?

Many years ago I met Richard and Mary Alice JaFollas at Unity Village. Following is a wonderful excerpt from their newsletter, *Life-Lines*, which is a superb metaphor in letting go. "There had been signs posted on the beach which warned swimmers of dangerous rip-tides and advised caution. Several rescues had already been made that day. It seems that the swimmers panicked when caught up by unfamiliar forces and in their futile struggle, they exhausted themselves. There is a tried and true method of surviving rip tides, which is common knowledge to most people who grow up by the sea. It is very easy: you simply relax, stop struggling and resisting, and go with the flow. You may get carried away from the shore a bit, but the current will invariably bring you back to the beach at a point a few hundreds yards from where you started. When you go with the flow, you can trust it to bring you safely back to shore."

When you imagine your outcomes fulfilled and then let go, you can trust your "wishes granted" will come back to you in amazing grace and divine timing.

There is a wonderful illustration of letting go combined with trusting the process and holding the vision. In this story of faith, the fields were parched and brown from lack of rain and the crops lay wilting. People were anxious and irritable as they searched the sky for any sign of relief. Days turned into arid weeks and still no rain came. The ministers and priests of the local churches called for an hour of prayer at the town square the following Saturday. They requested everyone bring an object of faith for inspiration.

At high noon, the townspeople turned out en masse, filling the square with hopeful hearts. The ministers were touched to see the variety of objects clutched in prayerful hands…holy books, crosses, rosaries. When the hour ended, as if on magical command, a soft rain began to fall. Cheers swept the crowd as they held their treasured objects high in gratitude and praise. From the middle of the crowd, one symbol of faith seemed to stand out above all others. **A small nine-year old child had brought an umbrella**.

Action is Only a Fraction of the Law of Attraction

When you allow your magnetizing and manifesting to be natural and easy and when you are feeling excited, clear and focused, then what you think and feel emotionally is what you will attract. Action is only a fraction of your creative outcomes. The way you FEEL is responsible for what you are receiving. Look for reasons to feel good, to be excited, ecstatic, exhilarated and exuberant.

Remember, what you think about expand**S**.

If your heart's desires are vague or unclear, then you will other than manifest them. The well known author, Norman Cousins, believed that part of the responsibility of creating health and humor are always within you, no matter how stressful things are.

> When he was in the hospital some years ago, a nurse came by with a specimen bottle and handed it to him while he was having breakfast. When she left the room momentarily, he took his apple juice, poured it into the specimen bottle and handed it back to her when she returned.

> She looked at it and said "My, we're a little cloudy today aren't we?"

> Norman took the bottle, took a swig from it and said, "By George, you're right—let's run it through again!"

So, if you find your intentions are "cloudy," by George, upgrade your energy and "up" your consciousness! Be CLEAR and FOCUS upon that which you are choosing to create and attract. And remember to lighten up, as humor expands your horizons and assists you in the big picture with joyousness and a light heart.

It's Difficult to See the Frame When You Are Part of the Picture!

It is not through action that you are creating your life, it is through your vibration. Someone said, "Angels can fly because they take themselves lightly." If your goal is to joyously co-create, then it is important you FEEL GOOD. You are the sculptor. You can mold and sculpt your creation with elation whether it be for your health, wealth, wisdom, or loving relationships. Delight in the deliciousness of being closer to your outcomes fulfilled and your wishes granted. We have become so goal oriented, and we often forget that the joy is in the journey, not just reaching the destination. The path to the temple IS the temple. Your moment-by-moment experience is your life's evolutionary path. I have a water mug that says "I AMAZE MYSELF," which is a constant source of enjoyment and I giggle whenever I use it. I love surprises—life is inviting and exciting when we have adventuresome attitudes. Take time to savor your experiences. My husband who is "retired" from a major corporation says he has so many projects and is so busy he will never die! What an attitude of eagerness and zest for living!

The following is a touching story that reflects how precious our moment-to-moment experiences are.

> A little boy with a timid voice and idolizing eyes greeted his father as he returned from work and asked his Daddy, "How much do you make in an hour?" Greatly surprised, but giving his boy a rather glaring look, the father said, "Look son, not even your mother knows what I make. Don't bother me now, I'm tired."
>
> "But Daddy, just tell me please! How much do you make an hour?" And as the little boy persisted, the father finally giving up said "$20 per hour."
>
> "Okay Daddy, could you loan me $10?" the boy asked. Showing his impatience and positively disturbed now, the father yelled, "So that was why you asked how much I earn— go to sleep and don't bother me anymore."
>
> Later the man felt guilty and wondered what his son wanted to buy with the $10. To ease his mind, he went to his son's room and asked if his son was asleep yet and he said, "No, why?" And the father said, "Here is the money you asked for earlier." "Oh thanks, Daddy," rejoiced the son, while putting his hand under his pillow and removing some money. "Now I have enough! Now I have twenty dollars!" the boy said to his father, who was gazing at his son, confused at what his son had just said. "Daddy, could you sell me one hour of your time?"

The joy is in the journey, moment to moment, and when we get to the pearly gates, we aren't going to wish we had worked more hours to buy more "things." It is being here heart to heart with your tribe. You may choose to spend more time with your family and connecting with kindred spirits in more meaningful ways to create relationships which are loving and joyous. Always do what feels good in being fulfilled and align with your highest outcomes. Some people do what feels "less bad" which is a real contrast to following your heart and trusting your gut.

You Cannot Discover New Oceans Unless You Have the Courage To Lose Sight of the Shore.

I have talked about letting go. Often it is expressed as "Let go and let God," which seems then a contradiction of the saying, "God helps those who help themselves." Paradoxically, we can embrace both, as again we have contrast through diversity. When we imagine our outcomes fulfilled, when we are energized and ecstatic and aligned with our heart's desires, then we can literally let go and delegate it to Source.

Sometimes saying "Let go and let God" can sound so "wimpy" and passive. That's why it is important to be a co-creator in the creation process. And, if you are already an excited Deliberate Creator who is vibrating on purpose, then you are revved up and operating from a higher level energetically. You already have magnetized the Law of Attraction In Action through your passion and clarity.

In ancient times, when mariners sailed the seas, they used the sun and the stars to chart their way, as well as a compass. If it was cloudy, they had to rely solely on their compass. You also have a compass within you called your INNER GUIDANCE and your INNER BEING. As you become aware of your inner compass, it signals to you through your emotions when you are in your Stream Of Well Being, or when you are off your true course which means storms are brewing. All you have to do is ask yourself, "**How do I feel?**" From the steps of Deliberate Creation outlined in Chapter 4, you now know there are only two feelings of emotion…one feels good and one feels bad, which is your guidance system giving you instant feedback. Now you can quickly notice which energy wave you are riding and the speed at which you are moving toward or away from your heart's desires.

Divert Your Course?

Whether the following story is true or not, it's a great metaphor. It is allegedly a transcript of an actual radio conversation of a U.S. Naval ship with Canadian authorities off the coast of New Foundland in October, 1995:

> **Americans**: "Please divert your course 15 degrees to the north to avoid a collision."

> **Canadians**: "Recommend you divert YOUR course 15 degrees to the south to avoid a collision."

> **Americans**: "This is the Captain of a U.S. Navy ship. I say again, divert your course."

> **Canadians**: "No, I say again, you divert your course."

> **Americans**: "This is the aircraft carrier Lincoln, the second largest ship in the United States Atlantic fleet. We are accompanied by three destroyers, three cruisers and numerous support vessels. I demand that you change your course 15 degrees north, that's ONE FIVE DEGREES NORTH, or countermeasures will be undertaken to ensure the safety of this ship."

> **Canadians**: We are a LIGHTHOUSE…Your call.

It's Your Call!

Just as your set of magnets attract or repel, so does your inner compass point you in the direction of being a Deliberate Creator so you can summon your greatest love and passion. You have only to set your course toward your heart's desires. Do not allow others to chart your course for you. Name your yacht or ship and climb aboard now. You are Captain Creation at the helm of your ship joyfully and deliberately following the power and guidance within you. Source is always your co-pilot. Have courage, trust, and hold your vision forward as you lose sight of the shore (your past) with a fresh start and infinite splendid possibilities ahead. Know that the Lighthouse is within you. Ask the Universe to assist you in smooth sailing, with a safe journey and joyous creative adventures and companions. It's your call!

If the journey occasionally gets rocky, think of the poetic saying, "Should you shield canyons from the windstorms, you would never see the beauty of her carvings." What we praise grows, and what we condemn, withers and dies so set your sails for a brave new momentous world in consciousness! Be willing to let go of the past and let your imagination soar! Claim it and name it! Set sail and break out the champagne. You have ignited MAGIC! Bon Voyage!!

Author and inventor, Buckminster Fuller, said commitment is…"kind of mystical. The minute you begin to do what you want to do, it's really a different kind of life." Once you have made your decision to chart your own course by being a Deliberate Creator it is as if a whole Stream of Well Being and synchronicities come into play to orchestrate events better than you dreamed possible.

My dear friend, Joanne Snow, sent me a wonderful heart graphic:

A Memo From God
Good Morning! This is God. I will be handling all of your problems today! I will not need your help, so have a good day!

Abraham has said, "It's all in the molding of the energy, the defining of the idea, the considering of the issues, the attracting of the data, the gathering of more information, the clarifying of the desire and the contrast that helps make it sharper. You are the creators, but your life is about the **creation process**, not just the creation. However, if it weren't for the creation, you wouldn't be involved in the process. So your life is desire summoning energy through you. You are part of the flowing of this energy and you naturally feel enthusiastic when you are being a Deliberate Offerer. Think and flow, think and flow, think and flow."

Very recently, Abraham said in a Maui forum: "If we were standing in your physical shoes, when we awaken in the morning, once we are conscious and back in our body and comfortable, we suggest you sit with a pencil and paper as if you were addressing someone who had the ability to orchestrate and deliver anything you could imagine, sort of like you have this staff who is at your beck and call. We would sit and jot down a few of the things we would like The Staff to work on today. We would say things like:

♥ **Bring me ideas**.
(I added: Bring me brilliant, creative, succulent ideas)

♥ **Help me rendezvous with other like-minded people**.
(I added kindred spirits who are in integrity, as we enthusiastically co-create together and are deliciously aligned).

♥ **Help me be aware of my power**.

♥ **Guide me to thoughts that are in harmony with my core desires**.

♥ **Bring me evidence of how this all works in comfortable, humorous and delicious ways**.

If you would make these statements and ponder them three days in a row, your life would be transformed because the Universe will knock itself out to supply your wishes. Because you have asked so recently, you will recognize these unusual things that will come to you. **DECIDE WHAT YOU WANT**. Most of you are so busy dealing with 'what is immediate' that you miss what is really important. Spending more time imagining, and less time in action as a doer will bring your heart's desires."[5]

---

5   You may move ahead anytime to Chapter 13 if you are excited for more details to begin your Creation Box, Creation Book or know more about specific rituals.

Going Higher With Your Desires

I still have a handout I used in teaching years ago. It is entitled "**My Board Of Directors**." You are the chairperson and have a 12-member board. You and your board meet at a round conference table with 13 chairs. Your board members can be people who influence your life, people you admire, mentors, your Higher Self, angels, your spiritual staff, or any enlightened beings you desire. Next, you consider the strengths and inspirations of having this "DREAM TEAM" as part of your advisers and how they uplift, fulfill and assist you in going higher with your desires. Reflect on what you could learn from them as you "imagine," interact and dialogue together.

My Board of Directors

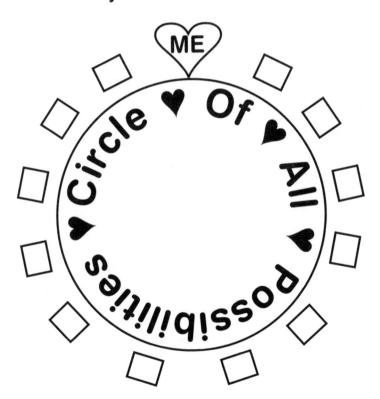

Dream Team Directors

What will you ask of them and what advice and feedback could they provide to assist you in fulfilling your outcomes? It's a powerful tool. Imagine people materializing for your corporate board meetings such as: Malcolm Forbes, Mother Theresa, Gandhi, Gibran, Napoleon Hill, Anne Morrow Lindberg, Archangel Michael, Helen Keller, Einstein, Carl Jung, Albert Schweitzer, Michelangelo, or Christ. Others who come to mind might include: Alan Greenspan, Warren Buffett, Bill Gates, the Dalai Lama, Ted Turner, Oprah Winfrey, Maya Angelou, Abraham, Dr. John Gray, Dr. Bernie Siegel, Jeff Bezos, Dr. Brugh Joy, Suze Orman, Dr. Deepak Chopra, Dr. Carolyn Myss, Alan Cohen, Gary Zukav, Iyanla Vanzant, Anthony Robbins, Dr. Wayne Dyer, Dr. Gladys MacGarey, Marianne Williamson, Louise Hay, Dr. Carolyn Conger, Neville, Sark, Robin Williams, Julia Cameron, Mark McGwire, Paul Newman, Dr. Phil McGraw, Jack Canfield, Dan Millman, Hilary Clinton, Nelson Mandela, your closest friends and key members of your family. Choose anyone whose wisdom and humor you appreciate. Choose people with vision who will assist you in your decisions as a Deliberate Creator.

The list of possibilities is infinite. Allow your imagination to explore what would most enhance your specific goals and why. You can also have different Boards of Directors for various projects to enhance the strengths needed at that moment. Take one member of the board and contemplate the important ingredients he or she brings to the corporate mix and how that person is most helpful. What are their individual characteristics, strengths and achievements which would reflect how this person could best serve you as the CEO of your company. How could each board member help you and what would you learn from them in the circle of all possibilities for your project? Are they people of integrity? Are they honest, fun, committed, bright, resourceful, compassionate, ingenious, successful, generous, inspired, and passionate in their endeavors, spiritual, serendipitous, as well as having street smarts? Do they carry the vibration of appreciation with consideration for others, as well as having a strong sense of self? Which of their attributes attract you? In your bylaws, activate the K.I.S.S. principle—Keep It Simple, Sweetheart! Let the Universe handle the details once you have done your deliberate creations.

For example, author Alan Cohen reports, "Malcolm Forbes, affectionately known as 'the happy millionaire,' enjoyed his money and his friends. He was known for throwing sprawling exotic galas, such as a multi-million-dollar soiree at a sheik's palace in the Middle East, to which he flew many of his friends for the celebration. When Forbes died, his will stipulated that he forgave all personal loans taken out by employees. Even from the grave, Forbes knew how to have fun with his money and used it to make himself and his friends happy!" Having someone on my Board of Directors who has a sense of playfulness and is joyously abundant would be a real bonus in not taking life too seriously . And, generosity is a wonderful attribute. As an example, Paul Newman donates the profits from his product food line to wonderful charitable causes. Consider how Ted Turner gave one billion dollars to the United Nations—now that is generosity on a whole new playing field. Have a sense of what kind of players you would like to have on your board and what expertise they bring to the table. Then write your mission statement.

Actor Robin Williams is on my Board of Directors because of his wonderful sense of humor. My husband and I were flying to England in 1994 and had the opportunity to meet Robin at the Los Angeles airport. He came into United Airlines Red Carpet Club where we were waiting for our flight and sat down on an adjoining sofa. My husband introduced us, and we had a delicious, fun conversation. We had seen *Mrs. Doubtfire* months earlier and Williams was just as funny in person as he was in that film. He had us laughing out loud for 20 minutes with his spontaneous humor. I would love to have someone as zany and sensitive as Robin is on my Board of Directors.

**"We cannot wait for the world to turn,
for times to change,
that we might change with them,
for the revolution to come
and carry us around its course.
We ourselves are the future,
we are the revolution."**

...Beatrice Bruteau

Have a sense of what kind of players you want on your board and what expertise they bring to the table. Once you have imagined your optimal vision and mission, you now have experts—your personal Dream Team—to help you facilitate and realize infinite potentials. You can also imagine or architecturally design an inspired and intimate conference space that reflects and supports the extraordinary global and strategic dialogues you will entertain around this table. It is a time of profound and succulent possibilities with revolutionary ideas being exchanged as you summon and flow the energy together. Do it now in your imagination. Let the magic begin and reverberate in your life.

Ask and it is Given...
In the Infinite Field of All Possibilities

Albert Schweitzer said, "**Sometimes our light goes out but is blown into flame by another human being.**" If needed, let your Dream Team spark and fan your flame of desires and inspire you to new potentials. Then, delegate your decisions, let go and consider it done. You can trust an opening occurs in the infinite field of all possibilities. You other than have to know "how." You will also learn to be a better "receiver" because the secret of success in pursuing your passion and heartfelt dreams is balancing energetically between giving and receiving.

As you learn to delegate, let go and trust, it will be as Mother Meera said, "**You are in a new world. Your old mind will not help you.**" Your former "patterns" (ruts) will no longer serve you when you choose to deliberately upgrade your life. You can now consciously choose to vibrate with your heart's desires and stay connected to your Stream of Well Being through the Law of Magnetic Attraction in Action! You will find your vibrational matches mirrored through rapid physical equivalents manifesting in the twinkling of an eye. You will experience the phenomenon of "acceleration" because things move toward each other at an increasing rate as you "up your consciousness."

It's so exhilarating when you recognize and remember the magnetics involved in the Law of Attraction in Action. Take short naps or meditate for a few minutes and you will be emulating creative geniuses like Einstein and Edison—they were well known for taking "cat naps" and turning within for guidance to relax and release the rational mind. Edison "failed" several thousand times before successfully creating the light bulb and receiving his "vibrational match" for the fruits of his endeavors. He trusted the process and held his vision steady—look how he changed the world and literally brought more LIGHT into our lives.

I love this short story by Portia Nelson, which clearly reflects a path of learning and provides feedback from every experience of contrast. She was asked in a seminar to write her autobiography. However, the participants were directed to do five short chapters on only one page. This is what she wrote:

(Chapter I):
> I walk down the street.
> There is a deep hole in the sidewalk.
> I fall in. I am lost—I am helpless.
> It isn't my fault.
> It takes forever to find a way out.

(Chapter II):
> I walk down the same street.
> There is a deep hole in the sidewalk.
> I pretend I don't see it.
> I fall in again. I can't believe I am in this same place.
> But, it isn't my fault.
> It still takes a long time to get out.

(Chapter III):
> I walk down the same street.
> There is a deep hole in the sidewalk.
> I see it is there.
> I still fall in—it's a habit...but, my eyes are open.
> I know where I am. It is my fault.
> I get out immediately.

(Chapter IV):
> I walk down the same street.
> There is a deep hole in the same sidewalk.
> I walk around it.

(Chapter V):
> I WALK DOWN ANOTHER STREET!

This inspiring short story of her life clearly shows her evolution from victimhood ("not my fault"=resistance) to taking responsibility in becoming a Deliberate Creator. By becoming more consciously and consistently aware, she learned to gloriously attract higher choices and outcomes in how she was flowing her energy.

Savor your delicious Dream Team. Feel the power of your own personal Board of Directors uplifting and guiding you.

Launch fresh rockets of desires and be inspired to infinite new possibilities and play in your very own field of dreams.

Feel, relish, relax, allow and appreciate all of your sweet, succulent outcomes flowing into your life now and continuously.

And so it is.

Synchronicity

And the Law of Attraction

Synchronicity is most often defined as a meaningful coincidence or significantly related patterns of chance. Even though the elements involved are not often obvious or causally connected, synchronistic events will have a meaningful relationship to one another. So much so, according to Dr. Carl Jung, the well-known author of many books on dreams, that something extraordinary or significant is brought about. He coined the term synchronicity, as well as what we today call introverts and extroverts. Jung said, "The phenomenon [of synchronicity] sounds mystical only because we do not understand it. But there are innumerable clues available given the right frame of mind—openness—the availability to synthesize the clues into a whole." Marilyn Ferguson was right on when she described synchronicity as, "A web of coincidence that seems to have a higher purpose or connectedness…"

Superficially, it may look like chance, but these events are often wild cards. When you look more deeply, they are meaningful arrangements in the Law of Attraction. They are often mirrors in your life which have strong parallels between your inner and outer life, which result in transformative experiences and serendipitous manifestations. Synchronicity can be the very person you were going to call today about an important matter when you intuitively drove to a restaurant and there she is by "chance." Synchronicity also seems to show up in your life when you need it. Or, the person who surfaced in your dream last night also literally showed up in real life the next day. Some people would call it "luck," although I personally don't feel things happen by random chance. Often friends will call me and say "The weirdest thing just happened," and I laugh because I know it is going to be serendipitous and synchronistic. What happened to you that you chalked up to coincidence? How did you meet your divine partner? What about the job or money that turned up at just the very moment you most needed it. There are times when you absolutely KNOW your experiences have been orchestrated by higher forces.

Frank Joseph's new book, *Synchronicity & You*, explores 17 categories that synchronicities fall into, some of which include telepathy, premonitions, dreams and every day coincidences. He feels that synchronicities are not random coincidences, but rather significant events that shape our experiences in the world around us. When we pay attention to them, they have purpose and meaning.

A Funny Thing Happened...

Tom Kenyon, our dear friend and colleague, shared a wonderful story about an event back in the 1970's.

> When Tom was working at a junk store in the Haight-Ashbury area of San Francisco, he went from week to week with just enough money to squeak by. For various reasons, Tom's employer forgot to renew his operating license, and the city shut him down for two weeks. Tom was without work, without any money and his rent was due.

> A week before this crisis, Tom had visited art stores to price art supplies and had a monetary figure in mind of what he would need. With only 12 hours left until rent was due, he hopped the train that went to the farthest western point of the city to watch the sunset. Tom said he was very melodramatic back then and he felt his life was coming to an end because his biggest fear was to be a street person with nowhere to live. He figured it was perfect to watch the sunset in his emotional state of despair.

> As Tom watched the sun setting into the Pacific Ocean, he sent out a prayer to the Universe for help. After his vigil, he returned to the train station to ride home. On the way back, a very strange feeling of peace came over him and he felt that everything would be alright.

Tom missed his stop and wound up several blocks away. Walking back to his apartment at night, he crossed a deserted street and something caught his eye. It was a metal money clip with no identification. It held just enough money, to the very dollar, to pay Tom's rent for the next month, as well as enough money left over for the art supplies he wanted. This is a perfect example of synchronicity and divine timing.

The *Arizona Republic* newspaper has a weekly column by Thomas Ropp, who writes about stories that are weird, offbeat, funny or simply defy the odds! Often they are profound and touching examples of how synchronicity works, although he does not call it by that name. This article, printed on July 6, 1998, entitled, *"Brought Together From Out of the Blue"* is a wondrous illustration of synchronicity and "walking down another street."

Out of the Blue

"Twelve years ago, Pam McCarville's boss gave her an open, round-trip airline ticket to California as a Christmas present. McCarville was reluctant to use the ticket. She had never been to California, didn't know anyone there and besides, was terrified to fly. Nonetheless, on the last possible weekend she could use the ticket, she packed just enough clothes for a few days and went to Sky Harbor to catch the next flight to Los Angeles. 'I had no idea where I was going and had absolutely no plans,' McCarville said. 'In Los Angeles, I took the first free hotel shuttle I came across at the airport.'

She ended up at a pricey hotel near Venice Beach. She needed a place to stay, but this was too expensive. Still, she went into the hotel's lounge and ordered a drink at the bar. McCarville said, 'The bartender brought my drink and advised me that a gentleman wanted to buy me a cocktail and offer me a chair at this table.' She declined. The bartender returned and told her the gentleman would buy her dinner if she would re-consider.

Pam said, 'This got me angry. I was going through a period in my life where I was fed up with men anyway. I asked the bartender where this 'gentleman's' table was and I wanted to tell him that 'no' meant 'no!' She turned from the bar, following the bartender's nod. Preparing for an ugly scene, McCarville's heart stopped when her eyes met the man's eyes. Her father, Ernie, was smiling at her from across the room. She had not seen him for many years. Their relationship had been strained since her parents' divorce and she blamed it on her father.

Cautiously, she joined him at his table. 'We ended up talking for hours. He explained and apologized. I understood and accepted. We went on to spend the most wonderful three days getting to know each other all over again.' What made this meeting even more unlikely is that Ernie, a manufacturer's representative on a business trip, was filling in for another employee. Her father said he lived in Missouri and his territory was in the Midwest and he never traveled to California.

Within a month of their meeting, Ernie called Pam to tell her that he had terminal cancer. She flew to Missouri that day and brought him back to Arizona, where she cared for him until he passed away a few weeks later. 'What brought us to the same hotel on the same day, I'll never know. But I've never doubted the existence of God since then,' said McCarville."

Give Reality a Rest

What do you think? Law of Attraction in Action? A divine appointment? Synchronicity afoot? Walking down another street? A "chance" Christmas present from a boss for an employee who was terrified to fly? What are the odds of this father traveling to California and ending up in this precise hotel lounge at the same moment his daughter reluctantly flew to Los Angeles and stopped at this hotel?

This was such an enchanting true story that I still get "God bumps" when I write about it. I truly believe these two people were magnetically pulled together by following their inner compass and guidance until they came into the vibrational sphere of each other through the Law of Attraction in Action, which defies any "logic" of how this magnificent physical manifestation unfolded. So, give reality a rest and flow your new focused energy towards your heartfelt desires. Make a decision right now to gloriously walk down the Street Of Your Dreams connected to your Stream of Well Being. The Universe always responds to your fresh new vibrational signal! Synchronicity is afoot when you ask and know it will be given; and when you knock, the door will open…if you are ever willing to walk through them where your well being and heart's desires abound! That's what ships are built for! They aren't meant to stay in port. Have fun as you explore, adventure and discover new inner and outer worlds. You are Captain Creation at the helm of your ship charting your destiny.

Whatever Floats Your Cork
and
Following Your Bliss

The author, Joseph Campbell, originally coined the phrase, **"Follow your bliss,"** which has a similar vibration and intent to Abraham's expression, **"Floating your cork."** The succulent quote from Campbell is:

> **When you follow your bliss,
> and by bliss I mean the deep sense of
> being in it…you follow that,
> and doors will open where you
> would not have thought there would be
> doors and…where there wouldn't be a
> door for anyone else.**

In Abraham-Hick's quarterly publication, there was an article entitled: *Whatever Floats Your Cork*. Here are some of the highlights:

You are Creators who came forth to identify new desires, not just to observe what already is. You came forth to experience the value of contrast, and out of contrast, to feel your new decisions erupt. There is power in your decision, because once a decision is born within you, that new decision literally summons life force. You might say that contrast is essential to decision, and decision is essential to summoning energy.

Most beings do not have any real sense of how their life unfolds and what vibration and creative control is. Everything is about vibration. And the reason that most rely on taste or touch is that all vibrations you have learned to translate are through your five physical senses. There are other vibrations you cannot decipher that way. You must use another sense, which we call the sixth sense. It is your emotional center… that feeling you get in your solar plexus. Those emotions are your interpreters of vibration. Your Inner Being…that Source which is really you…vibrates at a very high, pure, fast frequency. When you introduce a slower, lower vibration to your higher, faster one, the result of that resistance is a slowing of the vibrations and the way your sensors will tell you that is through the way you feel.

When you feel elation, joy, passion, love, appreciation, that which you call positive emotions, they are your indicator and your "sixth sense" telling you whatever it is that you are focused upon right now, in this very moment, is up to speed with Source. As you embrace that which you are observing that is producing positive emotion within you, it is a vibrational equivalent to your Core Energy. There is no slowing of your vibration and you remain connected to your Core Energy. However, when you feel anger, fear, frustration, guilt or loneliness, what you describe as negative emotions, whatever you are giving [negative] attention to, is not up to speed with who you are. Because you are observing and maintaining interaction with it for longer than 17 seconds (it takes 17 seconds to register in your vibration) then you have included the slower, lower vibration in your mix. That is what causes you to feel separation between your vibrational current and Source Energy.

In the story earlier, Pam was following her sixth sense when she went to California and didn't have a clue why she was doing so. It was only in retrospect that she could appreciate the higher purpose and divine design of connecting with her father.

What is a Personal Vibration?

In *The Wise Child* by Sonia Choquette, PH.D., she shares:

> ...One's personal vibration is the combined energy of the physical body, the emotional state, and the etheric, or intuitive, consciousness. The synthesis of this energy, when in harmony, makes for a grounded, peaceful vibration, like a well-composed piece of music. If, however, any one of the elements of the self is disturbed or out of balance, the personal vibration becomes dissonant, and energetically "off key." To a sensitive person this can be felt usually around the heart, chest, or stomach area.
>
> Our personal vibrations, like fingerprints or the sound of our voice, can be felt by really paying attention to and noticing one another. These personal vibrations relay everything about us, physically, emotionally, and psychically—whether we are strong or weak, happy or sad, sick or healthy, grounded or floating, focused or lost. We attune ourselves to these vibrations through the heart. Do you remember when you fell in love? Do you recall times when the phone rang and you *knew* it was your beloved? What you were tuning in to was a personal vibration. It's like your calling card—as uniquely yours as your personality. The beginning of your ability to perceive personal vibration lies in shifting your attention from your head (thoughts and words) and slipping into your heart and the world of feeling and tone. It is not making an intellectual connection as much as it is a feeling connection.

An example Sonia gives is how children recognize personal vibrations, especially when they are infants. It's how they know you are planning to leave the house before you've made the final decision to do so. It's why they run to the door before you come home. It's what they are responding to when you are angry, sad or fearful and they cower in the corner. It's what they feel when you are happy, drawing them toward you, wanting to share in the good vibes. She notes how important it is to live in the intuitive mode. That means being just as comfortable with the non-physical dimensions of who we are equally as readily as we acknowledge red lights, green lights and stop signs in our physical every day reality. It means acting on your instincts and honoring your feelings without question. I know from personal experience how animals and pets are also very attuned to our personal vibrational signatures.

The Universe Is Ready When You Are Ready

When you believe you are the Creator creating your creations, you take time to listen, feel and be attuned to your vibrations. You take time to make deposits and invest in your well being and your heart's desires. "Doing" is an outer action. Being is an inside job. You take time to connect in with your Inner Being and Stream of Well Being upon awakening or before you start to "do" your day. Visualize having it your way for a few minutes and pre-pave and magnetize your highest outcomes of how you want your day to be. You listen to your dreams, meditate, pray, breathe deeply, and notice the subtle vibrations of how you feel so you have a clear, pure, centered connection.

If you need to use a pay phone, you don't expect to go up and give it a hug. You have to deposit a quarter (or more). If you believe in your creative power, you have to invest in yourself as you follow your bliss, live your vision and are true to yourself and your ideals. It's your personal Law of Attraction in Action and I guarantee you that you will feel more alive, excited, joyous, creative, magnificent, enthusiastic and connected when you allow the energy and clarity of your heart's desires to flow, grow and evolve from your inspired, powerful, pulsating, persistent pre-paving as you eagerly visualize having it YOUR WAY. Be bold and go for the gold.

There is a cute joke that I used in many classes at the university:

> Once upon a time a church gave a banquet. As the celebration took place, three characters watched from across the street— they were a cow, a chicken and a pig.

> The cow said, "Let's go over there and celebrate with them and give them something to share."

> The chicken said, "Okay, I'll provide the eggs."

The cow said, "I'll give some of my milk." The cow and the chicken eagerly crossed the street, but the pig stayed behind. The cow and the chicken looked back and said, "What a selfish pig you are!"

The pig replied, "That's easy for you to say. You are giving a donation. What you are asking from me is a TOTAL COMMITMENT."

Your Total Commitment

That is exactly what it takes to follow your bliss—your total commitment. The most joyous people in our circle of friends, family and colleagues are those who are involved and committed to their personal growth and evolution as Creators. They are fun, loving, exciting, stimulating and delightful people to be around—they aren't sitting on their assets! They celebrate and invest in loving themselves and others, they invest wisely in their time, and they invest energy in being a Deliberate Creator. They make a commitment to floating their corks. It isn't always easy because time and follow-through are the real "biggies" for any Deliberate Creator. However, deliberate creation is a simple formula and enormously rewarding when you create the time to shine and sing and do your thing as you vibrate with attracting your heart's desires and imagine your outcomes fulfilled. This means focusing your energy. It means laying in bed before you start your day for a few minutes to think through the most important parts of your life.

Abraham suggests contemplating those people who are most important to you and see them thriving. Contemplate your own body and imagine positive things about your body and health. Then, consider your work and spend 68 seconds envisioning and creating how you want it to be. Think about your home and family, your relationships, your abundance and then focus, ponder and imagine how you want it to be. You have then done more before you ever get out of bed than you could do by working hard all day long. Feeling and imagination are the keys to your personal vibrational tone and signature of what you will attract the rest of the day. Conversely, when you are in anxiety about your home, your body, your relationships, your career, your finances, you are literally "leaking" energy and miscreating through lack and limitation. The formula is simple: remember you are a Deliberate Creator, embody your heart's desires and consciously attract them by seeing your highest outcomes fulfilled.

Some years ago, Dave Kohr, an advertising executive in one of my classes, loved it when I shared I was a member in Virginia Satir's club called the "I.I.A.F.F.I." which means:

IF IT AIN'T FUN, FORGET IT!

Dave had pens made up with that inscription which he passed out to our whole class. It was so fun and playful to have that reminder in our hands whenever we used that pen. Author, Alan Cohen, says his friend, Lili, has a motto on her business card:

> "Do it only if it's fun—and if you have to do it,
> find a way to make it fun."

As Abraham says:

> "Have Fun With All of This
> All is really well with you.
> Relax and acknowledge that.
> You make too much of all of this—
> what it's really about is FUN and more FUN!
> Pleasure or more pleasure!
> Clarity or more clarity!
> It's about Well Being that you
> are eking out...or Well Being
> that you are allowing to flow
> rambunctiously.
> Well Being Abounds!!
> Sometimes you have to step back
> from the circumstances of your moment
> in order to recognize that."

Crisis Awakens

"You are in physical existence to learn and understand that your energy, translated into feelings, thoughts, and emotions causes all your experiences. There are no exceptions."

…Seth

Since you were magnetized to read this book, you are learning to better understand how energy flows in your life. Most of us haven't known we had a choice about how we would experience "contrast." You now know it is a wake-up call saying "Pay attention…NOW!" If we ignore the gentle and quiet reminders, most of us now realize it will get bigger and develop into a full-blown crisis which then gets our full attention instantly.

CRISIS

Many years ago, I learned the Chinese ideogram for **CRISIS** means **DANGER** on one hand and **OPPORTUNITY** on the other hand. In my university classes, I always shared the principles and meaning of crisis. When we reviewed it the following week, almost everyone would remember danger as one component, and yet were unable to recall OPPORTUNITY. I found that fascinating.

CRISIS is

Danger

and

Opportunity

Crisis is Energy for Change

Crisis is a turning point and always means energy for change. Change comes from a Latin word meaning to exchange. Change does not mean losing—simply **exchanging**—usually for something better, although we may not be aware of it in the moment. Most of us resist change because it often puts us temporarily into the "wobbles" of uncertainty or the unknown. And most of us have a fear of the unknown because the known may feel more secure in the moment.

Some of the Webster Dictionary definitions for change are: to exchange, to transfer, to give and receive reciprocally, to cause to become different, alter, transform, convert, or to pass from one phase to another as in direction or changing directions. The synonym for change denotes making or becoming distinctly different and implies either a radical transmutation or transformation. Actually it sounds quite exciting, yes?

Most of us then undergo a transitional period during crises, which is the process or instance of changing from one form, state, activity, or place to another. A butterfly beautifully illustrates the transition state from caterpillar, then into the interim chrysalis stage and emerges as the transformed higher species of the butterfly. Often we have been strengthened through the "ordeal" of emerging in a similar way to the transformation process of a butterfly, which a caterpillar may view as a crisis while it is occurring! It moves into the unknown on its way to a higher outcome not yet seen. I used to read *Hope For The Flowers* to my grandchildren, and in my classes. It is such a wondrous metaphor for our lives about hope and revolution and caterpillars. A funny joke I love is about two caterpillars who are crawling across the grass when a butterfly flutters by. They looked up and one nudged the other and said, "You couldn't get me up in one of those things for a million dollars!"

The transitional stage of the chrysalis might be analogous to the 40 days Christ spent in the desert. And we are told that Moses wandered in the desert for 40 years. Of course, as the joke goes, it is because they were all men and wouldn't ask for directions! Seriously, the number four has been used in every religion from ancient times to symbolize wholeness and completion.

Most of us feel uncomfortable with change because it is the unknown. Yet here are two caterpillars in our story crawling like worms on the ground barely able to see anything in front of them, when in reality the butterfly had an aerial view and is the true inner essence of the caterpillar.

Crisis Awakens!

Many years ago I read an article on crisis, which was very meaningful and life changing in my understanding of challenges or crisis in my life. Resources tell us the ancients realized that when there were times of great upheaval and the stakes were high and the outcome in doubt, the possibility existed for creating something new and far better. One of my most profound life lessons in learning about crisis and living through it is how **crisis awakens.**

Crisis initially frightens most of us, and we want to turn away from its intensity because of the potential unknown consequences. Usually it occurs when we didn't leave enough room for change or pay attention to the signals around us. When we understand that crisis literally means to sift or separate, we also come to know it is a decisive turning point or crucial stage that can be an ally to compel and propel us energetically into new opportunities and accomplishments. We become what we resist. Thus it is important to listen carefully to our hearts and create an active alliance with our desired outcomes.

Crisis can be an empowering process because it causes us to become more conscious. In his book, *The Seven Spiritual Laws,* Dr. Deepak Chopra clearly speaks about intention and attention. **Intention is your decision and attention is your focus**. What looks like our greatest limitation, in the moment, can become our greatest empowerment. When we reflect on our life experiences, most people realize some of our greatest growth came through crisis and contrast. It is the cosmic nudge which pushes us to new levels of awareness. Just as a seed becomes a plant that breaks new ground to burst forth into its flowering, so are we cata-pulted into our evolution and inner revolution through crisis.

The Healing Magic is Attention

Author Herman Hesse in his diary referred to a dream in which he heard two distinct voices. The first one told him to seek out forces to overcome suffering, to calm himself. The second voice sounded like parents, school, the church fathers, but it also said that suffering hurts only because you fear it, complain about it and flee from it. "You know quite well, deep within you, that there is only a single magic, a single power, a single salvation…and that is called loving." The healing magic is attention.

Crisis often brings intense growth that can be seen as the contrast that jump starts us into huge quantum leaps. We are each potentially the butterfly emerging into our full-blown glory. The Universe provides us with the opportunity to not just go through crisis, but to grow and evolve into new heights and experiences. Thus why I coined the term "Bless The Stress" back in 1980 because of a wondrous infusion of knowing who I am in crisis. I was being awakened into new levels of knowing and unconditional love for myself and others. Remember to focus on the **opportunity** that abounds, rather than detouring into danger and fear in crisis. Crisis is transformation and liberation striving to happen.

Most of us are very aware of the mind-body connection. What is quite recently known as biofeedback in the western world has been practiced for many centuries in the eastern world. Many yogis accomplished seemingly impossible feats like walking barefoot on hot coals. The Menninger Foundation was aware many years ago that a major factor in people recovering from catastrophic illness was their WILL TO LIVE. Dr. Carl Simonton's work with many patients has had "miraculous" recoveries through the use of mental images. Dr. Norman Cousins, when diagnosed with a connective tissue disease formed a partnership with his doctor to do positive emotion therapy and went on to write a book entitled *Laughter The Best Medicine*.

Miracle-Prone Personalities

When I facilitated Dr. Bernie Siegel at Indiana-Purdue University to a sold-out audience of 1500 people through Continuing Education in 1989, he observed, "Spontaneous remission is the accepted medical term for miracles." *A Course In Miracles* states, "Miracles arise from a mind that is ready for them." Most of us are familiar with the expression "accident-prone people" or people who have "disease-prone profiles," as well as others with negative/anxiety-prone characteristics. I believe there are also "miracle-prone personalities" who have a proclivity for attracting and manifesting miracles through their vibration. Like learning to play the piano or training for any sport, when you are thrilled to invest time, imagination and focus in being a "miracle maker" through the Law of Attraction, then MIRACLES ABOUND! While my M.A. is a Master of Arts in Transpersonal Psychology, I also love that it could stand for Miracle Adepts because it is up to us how we focus, attract and magnetize energy.

Miracles Abound, Astound and Surround Us!

We are divine collaborators in miracles as Deliberate Creators. When we have miracles manifesting in our lives, I have noticed that we are loving, laughing, chortling, grinning and having a darn good time. Once we become aware that we deserve miracles, then they are divinely attracted and endowed into our lives.

People who voluntarily walk over red hot burning coals might seem to have little in common with patients and life-threatening diseases and yet both have one common thread—FEAR. Firewalking is an ancient ritual that was well known in Tibet and India which became very popular in the U.S. in the 80's. It first started with Tolly Burkan, a human potential teacher who learned the art from a Tibetan monk. He put together a five-hour workshop called Firewalking which used the firewalk as a magnet to teach how to overcome fear and limiting beliefs.

"The Present Moment is a Powerful Goddess"

...Goethe

On September 20, 1985, I talked two of my Fort Wayne girlfriends, Joanne Snow and Carolyn Jahn, into going with me to a firewalk in Bloomington, Indiana. For me, it was like walking on Cheerios because it felt very crunchy! It was so empowering because when I walked on fire, without getting burned, I had overcome a major FEAR—and I felt so triumphant! I actually walked twice because I truly chose to embrain it into my neurology as it was so exhilarating. I was compelled to repeat it because it was so astonishing and amazing to experience. I got in line again and it was equally empowering the second time. Believe me, walking on red-hot coals keeps you totally focused and absolutely **PRESENT!**

We were blessed with a wonderful Firewalk teacher, Peter Heist, who did several hours of introduction and processing before we actually walked. One of the processes was to go out to the bonfire, which was roaring at that time, and make friends with the fire. I could imagine how many times I had sat around campfires, in the past, which felt very primal and nostalgic.

Expanding Your Belief Systems

The firewalk is one of the most profound and personal graphic demonstrations of how much power our thoughts have in determining the course of our lives. It is a powerful metaphor of how we CREATE our reality and our own BELIEF systems. Again, a thought is only a habit pattern we keep thinking—we can change our thoughts in an instant. A good example is when a parent single-handedly lifts up a heavy car when his or her child is pinned beneath it. The parent doesn't take the time to think about it; the crisis overrides any belief system about weight. The parent knows what has to be done instantly to save a child's life, and the adrenaline and willpower kicks in to accomplish it. Peter was trained in N.L.P. (Neuro-linguistic Programming) which was one of the techniques he used in the firewalk workshop. Firewalking is a dramatic example of an EXPANDED BELIEF SYSTEM, because there is no way you are going to voluntarily walk across hot coals in normal circumstances. People kidded me later and said, "You actually paid to do that?!!"

Two years later, when my husband and I participated together in a firewalk in Taos, New Mexico, several people declined to walk across the red-hot coals. We supported and applauded them for their courage in honoring their current belief system and feelings. Had they walked, there was a strong possibility of being burned because of their fears. Why more people aren't burned is somewhat of a mystery considering the temperature of the red-hot coals. It does reinforce and mirror how we can change and alter our body-mind connection by changing our thoughts and belief system.

The Pounding Hearts Club

A firewalk definitely changes and expands our belief systems. Peter shared that the secret of firewalking…and the secret of success…is that if you are willing to walk through that membrane of fear, your body-mind connection does protect you, although we have to first identify and acknowledge our fears. And believe me, you are certainly very present and focused the moment you are walking over the red hot coals. Everyone is an instant member in the "Pounding Hearts Club."

Before firewalking was popular here in our country, it is reported that 20 men from the U.S. went to India to study with the holy men who could firewalk and also lay on beds of nails. These American men who studied, prayed, fasted and meditated with the masters, were sprinkled with holy water for three weeks. I was told when it came to the actual performances of their firewalk: 13 were burned, 2 actually completed the firewalk successfully and 5 said "forget it" because apparently their belief system was that only masters can walk on fire. I feel we each have to come to the awareness that the true master and teacher are not just "out" there. **Our true teacher is within us as our master ally and creative guiding force.**

Many Polynesian cultures practice firewalks. When we were in Bali in 1997, we also saw "Kechak" dancers perform with fire, as well as walk through the live hot coals as part of their dancing ceremony. In the book, *Miracles, The Extraordinary, Impossible and Divine,* author Carol Neiman shares how Dr. William Brigham, a botanist and curator in Hawaii, told of an incident when he accompanied three *kahunas* (shaman/priests) to an active lava flow near the volcanic mountain of Kilauea. The *kahunas* had told Brigham they could include him in their "fire immunity" so he could also walk across the lava, if he cared to join them. He at first agreed, and when they reached the site **the *kahunas* took off their sandals in preparation for saying their prayers that would enable them to walk across the lava unharme**d. They told Brigham he should remove his boots, because the protection granted by their prayers didn't extend to anyone's shoes. By this time, the sight of the glowing lava encouraged Brigham to change his mind and he refused.

The first *kahuna* strolled across the glowing lava, while Brigham sat a short distance away firmly ensconced in his boots. When the second *kahuna* started across, Brigham stood up to get a better look. He found himself suddenly shoved from behind by the third, and was forced to break into a run across the lava in order to avoid falling down on his face! Much to his relief—and accompanied by peals of laughter from the three *kahunas*—Brigham survived the crossing unharmed. His boots, however, were not so lucky; one had burned off completely, the other was in smoldering tatters, and both his socks were on fire.

Imagine This!

This was indeed Brigham's "trial by fire," as the expression goes! It is noteworthy that the *kahunas* first said their prayers of protection, which is the same vibration and intent of "ask and you shall receive." Their thoughts and feelings were totally aligned in safely walking through the lava unharmed. The root of the word imagination is the Latin word imago, meaning image. Their image, thoughts, feelings and belief was that they were protected and their vibrations were a match for their experience and reality of walking across lava that could burn off shoes and set socks on fire. Imagine!

You Become What You Imagine & Envision Breaking the Barriers

Woody Allen reportedly said, "You know, 80% of success is just showing up!" The fact that my girlfriends and I attended this workshop meant we had, at some level, already made a commitment to move beyond a certain known reality. An example would be Roger Bannister. To run a mile in under four minutes was considered impossible and beyond any human's capability. Then, one day in 1954, Bannister ran a mile in 3 minutes, 59.4 seconds. He didn't have a belief system that said it was impossible (in fact, it turned out to be his "I'm-possible" thoughts which accomplished this feat). He broke through the belief system of the four minute mile—he cut 2.1 seconds from the record which was then embrained into his neurological programming. Once Bannister broke the barrier and record that had stood for 20 years, 30 more people did the same shortly thereafter. When you stretch into new levels of deliberate creation, you can trust and know the Universe is supporting you in fresh, infinite possibilities.

Our belief systems determine our reality and our experiences. I invite you to consider what your most limiting belief is in this moment. If you choose, you can now expand and create a higher outcome in your imagination which becomes part of your vibration through the Law of Attraction.

The evening of our firewalk, everyone eventually had a new mental syntax or emotional-belief equivalent that we could now indeed walk on fire. We became strong and confident in preliminary processing and we successfully did then walk. I used to share an acronym I learned at Unity that FEAR is: False Evidence Appearing Real.

When everyone first goes out to the roaring bonfire and realizes the possibility exists of eventually walking through hot coals, my first thought was a new acronym for FEAR being—Forget Everything And Run! All kidding aside, in the firewalk we learned another acronym for fear which was so powerful. I loved how my fear became:

Forever Experiencing Another Reality

The difference between a master and the "average" person is the master becomes aware of fear and experiences it; and the Master rather than allowing fear to become her "jailer" allows it to become her counselor and teacher. In other words, you learn from it and transform it into **OPPORTUNITY** rather than danger.

Helen Keller said, **"Life is a daring adventure or nothing at all,"** and she overcame more adversity and contrast than most of us could ever contemplate today. She lived a life of victory and was a shining light of overcoming through her expanded belief systems.

Be Inspired Through Your Desires

In Peter's Firewalk, I learned that what it takes to walk over 2,000 degree coals is exactly what it takes to walk effectively and enthusiastically through life—WHO WE ARE AND WHAT WE ARE IS A DIRECT RESULT OF OUR THINKING AND FEELINGS. The implications of that are profound as we become aware of the Law of Attraction in Action. Saturate yourself with inspiring people, books, events, movies and videos, workshops and your desires will soar to new levels of enthusiasm and ebullience. Flow your energy toward your outcomes fulfilled and notice how invigorated and liberated you feel as you unify, focus, attract and relish your vibrational matches. No one can limit your thoughts! Your 17 seconds of pure, high, clear thoughts creates and generates new magnetic experiences.

Once you have expanded your belief system, you feel a greater willingness and commitment to embrace all of your heart's desires. Once you have successfully demonstrated the mind-over-matter phenomenon, the possibilities are awesome. When I awakened the next morning, I still had ashes between my toes. I didn't shower when I returned home at 4 a.m. because I intended to show my husband the evidence of having successfully completed the firewalk. I feel it may have had even more impact then, as it was "soul warming" rather than "sole burning" to realize the power of my body/mind/heart connection.

Someone said, "When fear is given knowledge, it is called enlightenment. Self knowing and self-knowledge is our grandest treasure." This experience personally enhanced and enlightened my understanding that life is simply a platform upon which we can have a rip-roaring good time. When we step into our fears (which are usually illusions) we can gain the greatest pearl of life—the wisdom to Know Thyself. Abraham has said, "Most people tip-toe cautiously through life, hoping to make it safely to death." How sad! Go for the gusto!!

Rejoice In Choice

Most of us in our society have reality by consensus. If we think we can't heal ourselves, we don't. With the firewalk we all knew fire does burn—absolutely! With our expanded belief system, we have now created a new reality by consensus which says we have a CHOICE whether fire is going to burn us. I love the freedom and joy of expanding my belief systems and stretching to new possibilities. I am grateful to have come to understand I am here to deliciously seek, grow, spiral up and evolve to new levels of becoming. It's fascinating that the first four letters of <u>EVOL</u>VE are LOVE spelled backwards. Evolving means we are loving ourselves into grand new adventures.

"A Belief is Only a Habit of Thought You Keep Thinking"

…Abraham

So, reality is what you believe—and what you believe is then REAL for you. Abraham has said, "A belief is simply a thought you keep thinking—it's a habit you keep thinking and repeating." Have you noticed when you are with a group of people excited about personal growth and expansion, how you feel totally supported and a synergy develops. The object of the firewalk workshop was not just to walk over red hot coals. It was to overcome limiting belief systems and fears. It's such a powerful and dramatic example of the power of our mind, hearts, feelings and thinking. Our thoughts are the only things which separate us from all the joy we desire in our lives. We can choose the reality we want to participate in every day with a fresh start. Remember you always have choice! Freedom is contemplating your margin of greatness to become more of who and what you are.

Abraham has noted that about our thoughts…"Your creative mechanism is always functioning. You cannot turn it off. **Therefore, it is of tremendous value to be sensitive to the way you are feeling so that you may be guided to understand in which direction you are focused**. Your creative mechanism does not evaluate rightness or wrongness, the positiveness or negativeness, the goodness or badness of any of it. It goes to work immediately to indiscriminately assist in the creation of that which you have set into motion through your thoughts."

In an anecdote that Dean Morton of the Cathedral of St. John the Divine shares is a story of three people chipping identical blocks of stone. When each was asked what he was doing, the first replied, "Can't you see? I'm chipping a stone block." The second man answered, "I'm earning a living for myself and my family as a mason." And the third one joyously replied, "As you can see, I'm building a great Cathedral." While each person was engaged in the same task, their intents differed significantly. The third stonecutter had a deeper purpose to his craft than just cutting stone. Sometimes our life process is not to become aware of a "wider" vision so much as having clarity and awareness of our true heart's desire.

Every day can be filled with magic and miracles—miracles being defined as simply the right use of energy. Magic is simply a change in consciousness and clarity of focus. You can stop sitting on your assets, invest in yourself and be focused and directed on your highest choices and outcomes fulfilled.

A *Course In Miracles* tells us:

> **"There is nothing miracles cannot do,**
> **but they cannot be performed**
> **in the spirit of doubt or fear.**
> **When you are afraid of anything,**
> **you acknowledge its power to hurt you."**

In the case of the firewalk, we were intensely present and focused on getting safely to the other side. As Peter said that if you think about the obstacles in life, you get obstacles. If you shoot past the obstacles and think about what you are getting on the other side, (as in your outcome) then the obstacle is other than a problem. And if you have any doubts or fears about the firewalk, you burn. Very simple. Or you can transform your FEAR, into Forever Experiencing Another Reality. Like the butterfly, we are all becoming more of what we are. If we exclude our awesome potential from our consciousness, we will always put it outside our reach.

A Course In Miracles also reminds us that:

> **"The mind is very powerful and never loses its creative force. It never sleeps. Every instant it is creating…recognize that your thought and belief combine into a power surge that can literally move mountains."**

Miracles aren't supernatural nor are they new-age "wind chimes and fruit loops." When we accept miracles as natural, then we will be divinely enthusiastic about feeding that energy wave for our inspired delicious creations. Science now knows that particles and waves change when observed. We are the creators who attract our own wave of miracles as we fine-tune our heart's desires.

Bring Your Own Spoon Party

Another wonderful experience I had with my body-mind connection was in the B.Y.O.S. Party, an anagram for Bring Your Own Spoon Party. In 1991, Dr. Brian O'Leary conducted a workshop in spoon bending. It sounded fascinating. Brian is a former astronaut and professor of physics at Princeton. He was formerly very "left-brain" and it was other than fashionable to be "psychic" so denial was his first reaction to anything out of the norm.

He spoke of the margins of reality where moving matter transcends rules of science and interacts with the material world in a way that transforms. Spoon bending is something scientists don't yet understand. He used the example of the Rose Bowl where there is chaotic energy and beer is spilled, etc. Then when a "human wave" is started, the rhythm develops distinct edges and a higher organized force aligns—again like iron filings attracted to a magnet.

Brian drew a square box and showed our society's accepted reality in the center of the box. Outside the box, he wrote outer space, UFO's, crop circles, astrology, the future, such as pre-cognition, prophecy, etc. He talked about a group which had recently been founded called *The New Scientists*. Opening up the borders of the "box" is usually quite gradual. Brian said that Einstein felt the whole purpose of science was to evolve spiritually and is quoted as saying, "Great spirits have always encountered violent opposition from mediocre minds."

Brian said, "The more intellectual you are, the harder it is going to be to bend the spoon." He said on a trip to Australia with a group he was leading, the only one who couldn't bend the spoon was a Congressman from Michigan. That brought lots of chuckle. It was amazingly simple for me once we started. We imagined and moved energy through our arms into our hands and became "one" with the spoon and put Universal Energy in it and did 10 breath cycles. Then we were told to begin to flex the ordinary spoon we had brought from home. It became like putty in my hands. While saying "bend, bend, bend" a window opened up for me as I began to twist it. I got hot while doing this and actually felt like I was sweating both inside and outside from the infusion of energy. One actually allows it to happen. It is like firewalking with the mind-over-matter connection, and the borders and margins of reality begin to dissolve. I experimented and actually did a double knot in my spoon like Brian had demonstrated earlier. As Brian walked by where I was sitting he said, "That's a good one," as I really got into those loops once I knew I could do it. I was on a new frequency band and had fine-tuned my signal as a powerful receiving and transmitting station where I broadcast, focused and flowed energy very deliberately. This B.Y.O.S. experience was seamless and very exhilarating.

Workshops like B.Y.O.S. can be a mirror and a new tool for people stuck in belief systems and limited thinking. Wherever we are feeling challenged in our life, there are always new possibilities of potential if we are open to them. We sure lightened up and had fun with the spoons, as we aligned and tuned in with Source energy—with no resistance. At that time eight years ago, my husband and I were experiencing learning curves setting up a new computer with lots of challenges. After the B.Y.O.S. party that day, we were energized and ready to go home with new expectations and eagerness to program our computer. After all, we had just bent spoons and experienced "magic."

Never Face Reality!

Sometimes people say to Abraham, **"Shouldn't I face reality?"** and he responds, **"No never do that—unless it is perfect in every way."** Contrast will always abound, yet the beauty of it is, we get to choose what reality we participate in. We can survive or thrive. We can be critical and nit-picky, or enjoy and relish our Stream of Well Being. When we speak our heart's desires, the energy begins to flow and in that moment...as my wall plaque says..."All the way to heaven is heaven." The Universe begins orchestrating and manifesting your highest outcome once you line up the energy emotionally and are aligned with your heart's desires. Then you have only to offer your vibration and allow and receive your outcome—with zero resistance. If you have resistance, you will be vibrating in a place where you are not allowing your outcome to be easily magnetized.

According to Your Beliefs, So it is!

According to your beliefs, it is done. If you look at your problems, they will build and stay with you because that's where your point of attraction and attention is focused. Any higher vibration is precluded in bringing a solution, for the most part, because energetically your attention is in some form of resistance through blame, justification or explanation of the "problem." That's what Abraham means in saying, "Don't focus on reality unless it is perfect in every way."

In the past, I had a friend who I thought understood the formula of being a Deliberate Creator, but she kept focusing constantly on what wasn't working. When she returned from vacation, she said how "drained" she was. I asked if she had enjoyed being with her family, and again she said, "I was so drained." I don't usually participate in conversations of that nature very long because it simply doesn't feel good. I kept "re-directing" the conversation and she kept returning to how tired she and her husband were. All she had to do was just summon and ask for energy instead of constantly repeating the litany of how drained she was, which, of course, expanded her reality of being even more depleted and exhausted! This pattern was repeated in her career also, as she continued to regurgitate over and over how intense the pressures were, how many hours she had to work, how little time she had for herself and how tired she was. Apparently she feels it is worth it because she is well compensated financially. However, she pays a big price emotionally. Trust me, this is not following your bliss—this is like a monster getting bigger and bigger. The more she talks about it, the more it expands. Until we are willing to claim what we do want, we will get more of what we don't want—in this case, being drained!

Remember, laughter and joy are great magnetic attractors. I used to tell my classes, if you get too serious on me, I'm going home! Mother Theresa said, "I know God will not give me anything I can't handle. I just wish he didn't trust me so much." Delight in being a joyous Deliberate Creator and know the Universe delivers through your vibrational offering and output. The most important focus is to feel good—keep your valve wide open by choosing thoughts that feel good and you will magnetize your heart's desires. Notice how you are flowing your energy. The Stream of Well Being is always here as pure, positive, passionate, pulsating energy—connect in, ask and bask in knowing the Universe always delivers—it's the Law of Attraction in Action!

Bask in Feeling Good
And Know the Universe Delivers
Now and Continuously!

8
The Risk of Growing

Every blade of grass has its Angel that bends over it and whispers, "Grow, grow."

…the Talmud

Do you know how a lobster is able to grow bigger when its shell is so hard? The only way is for the lobster to shed its shell at regular intervals. When its body begins to feel cramped inside its shell, the lobster instinctively looks for a reasonably safe place to rest while the hard shell comes off and the pink membrane just inside forms the basis of the next shell. No matter where a lobster goes for this shedding process, it is very vulnerable. It can get tossed against a coral reef or eaten by a fish. In other words, a lobster has to risk its very life in order to grow.

The lobster teaches us that the only way to endure the passage of time is to know that we can always grow and change with each year of our lives.

We all know when our shells have become too tight. We feel angry, depressed or frightened because life is no longer exciting. We do the same old things and feel bored. Or we are doing things we dislike or even hate to do and feeling stifled in our shells. Some people continue to smother in old shells that are not useful or productive. They think

116

there may be some measure of safety that way so nothing can happen to them. Some of us are luckier, even though we may be more vulnerable knowing there could be dangers ahead, we know we must take the risks or suffocate. The lobster story was shared with me by someone years ago and the author was unknown. Like the lobster we have the risk and strength of growing through opportunity or suffocating because it feels vulnerable or too scary to grow.

You are the attractor of your experience and nothing is more important than understanding you, which means the risk of growing to Know Thyself more fully. If you don't appreciate your life, then you stay in your safe shell and the status quo; and perhaps you look at your flaws rather than establishing a deep and profound relationship with you. Your Inner Being adores you and is with you to serve and expand you when you remember to ask for and receive inner guidance. Your Inner Being is present when your valve is open and you call upon your Source. Well being abounds! If you are focused on worry, doubts and fears, then that will be included in your vibration and you are stepping on your own hose.

Look for reasons to feel good about yourself and know that nothing is more important than your own personal and spiritual growth. When you seek and allow the vibration of "revving" up your personal evolution by being in the driver's seat, you will find other kindred spirits naturally gravitating to you just as you will be drawn to them.

MIRACLE MAKER

You are the Miracle Maker!
You Will Never Have Any More Power
Than You Do Right Now!

Miracle: The dictionary defines miracle as: mirari—to wonder at, wonderful; mei—to smile, be surprised; an event or action that apparently contradicts known scientific laws; hence thought to be due to supernatural causes; a remarkable event or thing; marvel; a wonderful example.

You are the "miracle-maker" and you will never have more time or power than you do right now. It is your divine right and heritage! You also have to ask, expect, receive and allow. In 1979, I began reading a three-volume set entitled, *A Course In Miracles*, which has now swept the world. The introduction starts with:

"This is a course in miracles. It is a required course. Only the time you take it is voluntary. Free will does not mean that you establish the curriculum. It only means that you can elect what you want to take at any given time. The course does not aim at teaching love…it does aim, however, at removing the blocks to the awareness of love's presence, which is your natural inheritance." The intro also continues with the meaning of miracles as principles: "There is no order of difficulty in miracles. One is not harder or bigger than another. They are all the same. All expressions of love are maximal. Miracles are natural expressions of love. **The real miracle is the love that inspires them**. Miracles are natural and when they do not occur, something has gone wrong."

You can take that to mean that there is no difference between healing cancer or a canker sore, except in your mind and belief system. It has been said that we teach best what we need to learn. So, *A Course In Miracles* provides a means of choosing what you want to teach on the basis of what you want to learn. What you teach, you strengthen in yourself because you are sharing it. It also speaks about contrast in terms of how we choose between pain and joy, hell or heaven and we are each responsible for choosing the feelings we want to experience. For our purposes, you have your own magical magnetic tools to understand how you attract or repel your heart's desires and experiences simply by playing with the magnets and seeing the energy flow.

More Fish and Food for Thought

In 1996, I wrote about a fish story in our newsletter illustrating what they have to do with consciousness. *National Geographic* had a fascinating story about carp and pike. Crucian carp have always thrived in certain ponds in Europe. No pollution, no predators and plenty of food.

However, one day that changed. Pike were introduced into their ponds. Pike often weigh up to 10 lbs. and can weigh up to 30 lbs. Crucian carp weigh about 2 oz. and are no longer than 6 inches. What do you think happened then? Yes, the carp became dessert. Bon Appetit!

Obviously, something had to be done quickly about the pike's feeding frenzy. How did they resolve it? Within five weeks the carp totally changed their mass. They transformed from thin fish to round fish so they could not fit into the mouth of the pike. What is the consciousness of a carp? How big do you think their brain is? The size of a pinhead? Yet these carp intended and willed a permanent new body shape in five weeks! Is that amazing? Now if carp can do that in a very short period of time, what does it mirror back to us about our own personal freedom to evolve and change?!

Goldfish will also grow proportionately to the size of the container they are in. If you remove them from a small fishbowl and put them into a larger body of water like a pond, they will grow much bigger. Initially goldfish often swim in the small circle they were accustomed to in the fishbowl until they realize they are in an unlimited space. It has been said that a mind once stretched by new ideas can never return to its original dimensions or constraints. Metaphorically, what is the size of the consciousness you are playing in? Do you feel comfortable in a shallow pond or do you seek an infinitely larger body of water like a lake or an ocean? How much are you willing to allow your consciousness to expand and express? Would you go to the ocean for water with a thimble or a bucket? Your possibilities are as infinite as your imagination.

Carpe Diem—Seize the Moment

"A miracle is an incandescent, amazing event or moment, big or small."

...Sark

We each certainly have more arenas for transformation through our resonating with creativity, passion and compassion for change and evolving our consciousness than a carp! We have a vast array of extraordinary potential to touch our higher, deeper, true Self at any moment. We are experiencing an acceleration in consciousness in this millennium, which is unlike any opportunity in the history of humankind. This energy is propelling and impelling us to become a richer, riper, plumper, expanded and juicier consciousness as we seize the moment to evolve to the next step in our personal growth We literally are divine magnets for magic and miracles by focusing on what we choose to attract.

"There are only two ways to live your life… One as if everything is a miracle. The other is as though nothing is a miracle."

…Albert Einstein

The ancient symbol of the Tree of Life is found in all wisdom traditions. It is an image of life and growth unfolding in its own natural time. Growing as it does from Earth to the sky, the tree suggests spiritual growth, our evolution toward the One. This image celebrates life in full flowering, the mysterious richness of our Beingness for and with each other.

My physician, Gladys McGarey, M.D., author of *The Physician Within You*, is a colleague. Together we co-create dream workshops for those who choose to move into the tap roots of their soul through dreamwork.

Gladys has shared when it is spring here in the Arizona desert, there is a glory to the kaleidoscope of color as it bursts forth and how we all marvel at the desert trees which withstand the heat and drought of summer, the cold of winter, and then bloom again full of life.

There are, however, some desert trees which do not survive. This has nothing to do with the variety of the plant or apparently even where it is located. When desert trees put their roots down and hit a caliche layer (hard, crusted calcium, clay-like soil), which they frequently do, they have two options. The first option is to put their roots to the side to look for nourishment and water, in the surrounding area—in which case a tree can die. The second option is to put all energy into the tap root. If all of the tree's energy is used to burrow through the caliche layer and hit its SOURCE, nothing can knock it over. Their root system has now made contact with a depth of nourishment that is not affected by the conditions of the surface. They will withstand heavy winds, drought, freezing conditions and even flooding. Because they are secure in their source of energy, they will bloom again in the spring.

**In your own personal Tree of Life...
Are you living on the surface of your life (or)
have you moved more deeply and authentically
into the tap roots of your soul?
Are you surviving...or thriving and
nourishing and flourishing in your life?**

Where are you deepening, strengthening and nourishing your own well beingness—your own tap roots? I choose relationships which are nourishing where we can bloom and flourish together in our willingness to evolve and share deeply. You get out of life what you put into it.

If there are people in your life who are sapping you, then ask yourself how you would like it to be or what your highest choice is with that relationship. Just like the analogy of the desert trees, some friendships won't survive because vibrationally they aren't being nourished by the people involved, especially if they are superficial or one-way streets. If a "roto-rooter" spot arises, and you share your feelings with the other person, often the other person becomes defensive, which only creates a bigger dilemma. The desert trees' tap roots that willingly go deeper have a firm foundation so storms can't knock them around; they are on solid ground. It is the same way with friendships or family issues. Imagine how you would like your friendships to now be. If you are experiencing "contrast" in an existing relationship, then make a new, higher decision and visualize what excites and delights you. Line up the energy for a fresh start. You are the Deliberate Creator and it is important to give your attention to whatever your heart desires. Don't give your attention to what's wrong with the relationship because it will only expand more of what you don't want. Embellish and amplify what you choose to nourish and have flourish with your friends or loved ones.

When Jesus said, "Turn the other cheek." it may sound wimpy to most people; however, it simply means to turn away from the vibration that is displeasing you and focus on what you choose to magnetize. Bless the roto-rooter spots for bringing you the clarity to choose once again. Go into your heart and clarify your friendships and relationships so you can choose to attract uplighting, uplifting, fun, joyful, loving kindred spirits who adore and appreciate you. Law of Attraction is simply focusing on what you desire!

You are the Beacon and the Light House! What and whom do you choose to attract?

When you vibrationally offer a clear signal, you put into motion a fresh start and the Universe conspires to assist you with that new decision. The Universe responds to your upgraded heartfelt focus because now you are flowing pure, positive energy toward magnetizing the kind of yummy friendships, family relationships or associates that you desire. The ones not serving you will vibrate right on out of your life if you don't feed them by becoming embroiled in the issue. I've learned by removing my attention from what's not working, they magically disappear from my life (that's what turning the other cheek really means). If a relationship is draining me, I ask to be invisible to that person or to have them disappear from my vibration. It all comes down to how you are flowing your energy. If you have a "charge" or resentments in a relationship, you attract and expand more of that energy into your life. Nourish and appreciate the friendships that feel good and they will thrive through the Law of Attraction in Action, and you will attract more. It's all in how you are flowing your energy.

The kinds of seeds we plant are the ones which will flourish. You can't plant carrot and radish seeds and expect to have tomatoes grow! I often used to give out mustard seeds in my classes as a metaphor for our inner lives. The will of a seed is a will that is not in opposition to anything. It has no resistance. It simply affirms what it is and strives to become more of the life within. It is amazing how grass and weeds can grow through asphalt cracks in driveways and sidewalks as they seek to express their life force. Author and mystic, Meister Eckhart, expressed it so beautifully, "**The seed of God is within us. Pear seeds grow into pear trees, nut seeds into nut trees and God Seed into God.**" What kind of seeds are you planting in your thoughts and vibrations?

"LISTEN…
Make a way for yourself inside yourself."

…Rumi

There is a wonderful quote that has been widely attributed to Nelson Mandela. This quote was actually originated by author, Marianne Williamson, in her book, *A Return to Love*. It is brilliantly expressed and has touched many hearts:

> "Our deepest fear is not that we are inadequate. Our deepest fear is that we are powerful beyond measure. It is our LIGHT, not our darkness, which most frightens us.
>
> We ask ourselves, who am I to be brilliant, gorgeous, talented, fabulous? Actually, who are you *not* to be? You are a child of God. Your playing small does not serve the world.
>
> There is nothing enlightened about shrinking so other people won't feel insecure around you. We are all meant to shine as children do. We were born to make manifest the glory of God that is within us. It is not just in some of us; it is in everyone.

And as we let our own light shine, we unconsciously give other people permission to do the same. As we're liberated from our own fear, our presence automatically liberates others."

My friend, Joanne Cornog, often says, "SHINE ON" after she heard Pink Floyd's song, *Shine On You Crazy Diamond*. It says volumes about shining on! We are all capable of being shiny and radiant beings like multi-faceted diamonds! My granddaughter, Alexis Rose Warren, was fascinated by all of my crystals when she was young and one day she went home and excitedly announced to our son, "Do you know how many diamonds Grandma has?!" Every since that happened many years ago, I've been called Grandma Diamond by my grandchildren and I love it. We are here to radiate, sparkle and shine!

Dreams: What Shines in Your Night Life?

In my dream classes, one of the most important elements I always share is that **dreams come for a purpose**. There is a life force that has a scope of understanding beyond your conscious mind which is your Inner Being (you can call this aspect the Unconscious or Subconscious also). Dreams help us to become more conscious and expanded. The etymology for dream comes from the English. It means "music, noise and joy," and in the Latin, dream means "gadfly." In other words, dreams pester you until you pay attention and are usually delivered in the form of images, parables, cartoons or non-verbal symbols. Your dream pesters you because it is a wake up call to pay attention to your inner life. Dr. Brugh Joy said, "Dreams are the intentions of our unconscious." In other words, dreams are our window to the soul, and they report back nightly. The royal road to the unconscious and the soul are often paved with spontaneous symbols and potent emotions of our inner transpersonal life that lead us to higher truths.

Dream interpretation books are not often reliable resources because often the material is coming from that author's belief system, which may not be relevant to your dreams at all. Sometimes using a dictionary is useful to prime the pump. One book I do highly recommend is *The Dream Book, Symbols for Self Understanding* by Betty Bethards. My husband heard Betty on Talk Radio in 1987 and raved about her interpretations. After ordering her book, we invited her to Fort Wayne in 1987 as a featured speaker at the university. She is a gifted intuitive. Dr. Brugh Joy and Dr. Carolyn Conger, are experts in facilitating dream work in their transformational workshops, who can take you to deep and life changing levels.

Dreams are concerned with the phenomenon of your life, which is from the Greek, meaning *"to show"* from phantasy and phantasia. It means to make visible and reveal the contents of your unconscious for the purpose of becoming more conscious. Your conscious participation is what bridges the dream from fantasy by integrating and actualizing the dream "message" into your daily life. Phenomenon also has a root form in Phosphorous, which means "bringer of light," and in its base form means, "to shine." The word psyche comes from the Greek root *psuke* which means "butterfly, soul or breath." Any dream that breathes upon you, changes and expands you when you listen and reflect upon it. Your soul intends to give you an account of what shines in your psyche and in your dream life. Once you've heard the "music" of the night, it is up to you to follow through and learn from the insights gleaned from the tap roots of your soul. Dreams are the feeder roots from your Inner Being where your intuition and instincts reside. You have interior maps every night, and it is what you do with the dream material which brings light and shining radiance to your outer life. Carl Jung said:

"A dream that is not understood [not interpreted] remains a mere occurrence; UNDERSTOOD, it becomes an experience."

I had a dream of Heliopolis on August 31, 1980, which was our son, Troy's 21st birthday. That age is a special time that is often recognized as a mark of maturity in many cultures, so it was significant to the dream context. I was going through a tunnel called Unity, and when I came out there was a brilliant light, and I was told by dear friends that I was in Heliopolis. Because of the bright, numinous way in which this dream was presented, and what it evoked in me emotionally, I knew this was a **dream of destiny**. In my commitment to understand it, I wrote it down immediately. It was the first time I had ever heard of Heliopolis so I asked my husband, "Do you know where Heliopolis is?" He kiddingly replied, "Probably south of Indianapolis."

In my exploration, I learned that Heliopolis was biblically known as **ON** and meant city of the Sun, embodiment of light, luminous, radiating brilliance, wealth. I learned it was a city in Egypt and one of the oldest in the world devoted to the worship of God, and refers to Spirit and true spiritual understanding and substance. Since it occurred on a <u>Sun</u>day on my <u>son</u>'s 21st birthday, and Helio means <u>SUN</u>, it was filled with powerful associations. I then explored in greater detail all of the other individual symbols such as a tunnel which often symbolizes new birth.

A short time later, I received a brochure in the mail. When I opened it, I had "god bumps" over my whole body. There was a photo and caption which read, "Obelisk of the sun at HELIOPOLIS." Obelisk means light-house and is a tall slender four-sided pillar that tapers upward and ends in a pyramid (very much like our Washington monument). I immediately called the man who was hosting this tour and asked how I was included in their mailing list. After we explored my dream and this journey to Egypt, he invited me to attend as a presenter with all expenses paid, along with some business details. The whole flow in this dream was pointing to and signaling LIGHT, SUN, RADIANCE, BRILLIANCE, NEW BIRTH.

If I hadn't journaled or paid attention to my Heliopolis dream, I would not have understood the implications of receiving the subsequent bro-chure. I wouldn't have gone to Egypt as a presenter and to Israel on the same trip. The synchronicities were being served up for me to pay atten-tion through the transpersonal realm of dreams. Our dreams are guided and orchestrated as a catalyst for connecting to our Inner Being, but we must take time to understand them. You are exchanging information and accessing layers of consciousness that provide valuable feedback in your daily life. Following your dream guidance brings new depths of understanding and treasures beyond measure.

"What lies before us, and what lies behind us, are tiny matters compared to what is within us."

...Ralph Waldo Emerson

I am an advocate of dreamwork and feel they are letters from our Higher Self or Inner Being. Dreams are one of the pathways to our soul with a focus in assisting our spiritual growth, which is our purpose in being here. You are a co-creator with your soul and you have unlimited access when you ask and expect that doors will be opened. Don't ask and think "maybe" or "try." Have an eagerness and expectation to have a deep connection with Source. You can also ask for counsel and guidance before you go to sleep at night on anything you specifically would like assistance with. The purpose of this short segment on dreams is simply to inspire you to connect with your Inner Dream Team. Many fine books and classes are available to enhance the dream process if you choose to explore and deepen the material further.

Shine On!

One day I was looking for a birthday card for my dear friend, Germaine, and came across a card which made my very heart leap that said "Shine On" on the outside and I was ecstatic. Upon taking a closer look, it was actually in Hallmark's "Mahogany Division" and had a faint image in the background of a black woman's face. I bought it and saved it for another friend, who is African-American and absolutely adores it whenever I say "SHINE ON." It was synchronicity with magic afoot to find this vibrational match! I adapted this card and acknowledge the original resource as Hallmark. While this is written for women, it is equally appropriate for the "feminine" within each man, woman and child.

**"Shine on Daughter of a thousand generations,
send forth your light into this precious world...
Shine on Sister of a thousand dreams,
tend to those dreams with strength and courage...
Shine on Woman of a thousand hopes,
radiating to everyone the beauty within you...
the beauty that comes from knowing who you truly are!"**

...Adapted from Hallmark Mahogany card

You Can Never Love Anything You Fear

As you move through your day, pay close attention to your feelings. Notice where and when you are feeling shiny, happy and uplifted. Be sensitive to your feelings. Notice whenever you are feeling fear, which is defined as anything other than love or whenever you feel disconnected. You will usually observe these feelings when you are pushing against or in resistance. It may be anger, jealousy, anxiety, hurt, discomfort, loneliness or illness. *You can never love anything you fear.* It fact, you usually despise what you fear because you feel controlled or blocked. Being connected always empowers and expands the beauty of your life experiences and your soul. You always have your emotions as a barometer of knowing how you feel.

You now realize there are only two kinds of thoughts (one feels good and the other feels bad), and you can change a "negative" vibration by moving toward the feelings you desire. Most of us initially can recognize these concepts intellectually, but the real power is in getting our "shift" together and integrating them every time we hit a "pothole" or a roto-rooter spot. Your emotions are "e-motion" = (equaling) your energy in motion. These energies are your vibrational signal and indicator of the stance and tone you are transmitting. Continually ask, "What do I desire to experience in this fresh now?" and then focus, create and magnetize the vibration you choose to attract. At any given moment, you can build a bridge from where you are to where you choose to be. The more positive your thoughts and feelings, the higher your vibrational signal transmits. It's your choice.

Sacred or Scared

If you ever think of great Beings, have you ever wondered whether they could have "muffed" it or "screwed" up? Jesus not only fulfilled the spirit of the law of his time, he birthed the new consciousness and vibration of LOVE. He held to his highest vision and bridged the gap by saying, "What I can do, you can do also," even in the most extraordinary difficulties. He didn't have a cushy job or an easy life. I think it's interesting that the word sacred transposes to scared with all the same letters, but represents very different energies and choices. It is just like the polarity of creator/reactor—same letters but a different response energetically. Undoubtedly, Jesus experienced the contrast of love and well-being, as well as fear and resistance, just as we all do. It has been said that the greatest sword that was ever created was never forged of metal. It was forged of superstition and fear. If we were to separate all of the theological dogma that encases this master teacher, there must have been times when he was scared and yet the basic sacred truths of his life emerged and prevailed through the power of love. A wise person said, "Love yourself completely for then you love God...and one day everyone will know this and a new kingdom is born."

I adore the following poem sent to me by my long-time friend, Joanne Snow.

Imagine a Woman

IMAGINE a woman who believes it is right and good she is a woman!
A woman who honors her experience and tells her stories.
Who refuses to carry the stress of others within her body and life.

IMAGINE a woman who believes she is good.
A woman who trusts and respects herself.
Who listens to her needs and desires and
meets them with tenderness and grace.

IMAGINE a woman who has acknowledged the past's
influence on the present.
A woman who has walked through her past.
Who has healed into the present.

IMAGINE a woman who authors her own life.
A woman who *exerts, initiates and moves on her own behalf.
Who refuses to surrender except to her highest self
and to her wisest voice.
A woman who imagines the Divine in her image and likeness.
Who designs her own spirituality and allows it to inform her
daily life.

IMAGINE a woman in love with her own body.
A woman who believes her body is enough, just as it is.
Who celebrates her body and its rhythms and cycles as an
exquisite resource.

IMAGINE a woman who honors the face of the Goddess in her
changing face.
A woman who celebrates the accumulation of her years and
her wisdom.
Who refuses to use precious energy disguising
the changes in her body and life.

IMAGINE a woman who values the women in her life.
A woman who sits in circles of women.
Who is reminded of the truth about herself when she forgets.

IMAGINE YOURSELF AS THIS WOMAN!

...Patricia Lynn Reil

* *I would personally change the word "exerts" to "intuits" in this poem.*

In *The Wellness Workbook* by Dr. John Travis and Regina Ryan, I used to share their "Color My World" process in classes. This involves filling a large circle with names of people and events which are sources of joy for you. You then color "your world circle" with the colors which most signified JOY to you. Each time you inhale, you imagine filling your body and mind with these colors. The process also defines the four basic emotions as *glad, mad, sad, scared*, which are like primary colors that blend into the whole spectrum of human feelings.

Heaven Happens

When you feel "sad, mad or scared," you can magnetize nourishment by making strong statements that will lead you from any current negativity to your desired outcome with positive energy and setting a new tone. On a vibrational meter, this may be anything from happy, satisfied, contented or peaceful to the higher vibrational scale of being excited, ecstatic, fun and funny, inspired or delighted. You might experience *"heaven happies,"* a term which I define as my "JOY DOUBLED, heaped up and running over." There is a bumper sticker that says "S_ _ _ happens." And another bumper sticker which amplifies it even more is "Same s_ _ _, Different Day." You can imagine what the car owners of those bumper stickers are attracting! "Heaven Happens" is also a choice we attract and we get lots of opportunities to practice which vibration we are experiencing.

Building Bridges

Travis and Ryan also share, "Wellness is like a bridge. It is supported by two piers. Each pier is crucial to the bridge's integrity just as the two principles of self-responsibility and love are to the process of wellness. In both cases, the two piers (or two principles) create the pathway between the two distant and contrasting points, allowing movement back and forth. It is the balanced flow between "contrasting" positions, attitudes, or emotions, which defines our well-being." Remember, no one can take responsibility for you, which is from the root word "respond," meaning you have the ability to respond in any moment to the circumstances in your environment.

Intentions Are The Bridges That Span Our Dreams

You are building a bridge from where you are in one (possible) negative moment to where you really choose to be on the higher harmonic positive scale. Regarding bridges, Abraham has said, "Do not try to build a very long span or bridge for your conscious thinking mind will resist that. It has had enough life experience so it is other than 'gullible' as to make a very wide jump. **If you will take small spans, making one positive statement after another in the direction you desire, then you will begin feeling positive emotions.**" Once you have made the transition from negative thoughts and emotions to positive thoughts and positive emotions, you will then be creating in the direction of that which you desire.

What Do I Desire?

Abraham shares a bridging example in your desiring a new red car and visualizing yourself as the owner so you are filled with strong, positive, exciting emotion. Your car is already on its way to you, for you have set it into motion. When you see a car like you desire and you feel happy and excited, that is an indication emotionally you and the new red car are in vibrational harmony. If, on the other hand, you feel depressed or dissatisfied because you do not have your car yet, then know your negative emotions are an indication you are creating **against** your desire and are pushing it away rather than attracting it. The etymology of desire is, "from the stars." You live in a benevolent Universe that responds and perks up its ears when you speak from your heart. Decree means to speak with feeling! You have to ASK (and yet not keep score of "reality" in this moment). Just know that it is already here whenever you decree your heart's desire by naming and claiming it.

Negative Emotions Attract
Negative Reactions

Abraham would share that you can stop your negative reactions immediately if you build the following bridge by affirming, "I desire a new red car like that one. I have set the creation in motion. Now I have only to allow it to be and it will be. For a moment, I realized I was pushing it away. Now I have stopped that and I am again attracting it by my strong desire. I am excited when I think about having and driving my new beautiful red car. Only my thoughts can push it away. My thoughts are again attracting my new car. I know that, because I FEEL excited and positive."

There is great value in recognizing, in the early stages, when you are upon a negative thought path so you can divert it and instead create in the direction of that which you choose. Negative emotion can be of great value for it alerts you to negative creation. If the negative emotion goes unnoticed and the Law of Attraction expands it, then it becomes larger and what you desire is pushed away. Remember, what you think about always expands!

As you apply the Belief Bridging process, you will find yourself responding to negative "warning bell" emotions in the early stages before other negative thoughts are attracted. The negative emotions start out subtly and then, by the Law of Attraction, build into something much bigger and more painful. Remember, as soon as you identify what thought, word or action has brought forth the negative feelings, ask "What is it I desire?" immediately.

The Best Way to Predict the Future is to Create It!

Tune into your own emotional patterns and recognize those warning signals, which start out gently and then build into a full fledged warning bell. Make new choices and be a conscious creator rather than reactor. Cultivate speaking your heart's desires in meaningful directions and notice when you detour by justifying, blaming or defending when experiencing "contrast." Notice how crucial your bridge's integrity is for the two principles of love and self-responsibility to strengthen and balance energetically. You must have both self-love and self-responsibility, which is your "ability to respond" as a Deliberate Creator with infinite possibilities.

♥ Free Falling Into Your Heart ♥

I had a delightful couple in my university class years ago and the man was what I call a "skeptic." He was an attorney who was very analytical and he didn't believe in some of the topics being shared. For instance, he had never heard of synchronicity before and it seemed too far out for him to even see it as a possibility...until he began to pay attention and noticed all kinds of synchronicities emerging in his daily life. One evening we were discussing the implications of out-of-body experiences and near-death experiences, which were even more controversial 15 years ago. Later, at the conclusion of a special one-day workshop, a powerful piece of music and meditation was played and this dear man had an out-of-body experience! Talk about a quantum leap in the circle of all possibilities. If you had polled the group, the consensus would be that this person would have been the least likely candidate to have this kind of experience. He and his wife came to me immediately afterward and asked if we could go somewhere and talk!

Finding Your Own Rhythm & Balance

He said, "You know you have talked about human potential and paradigm shifts, but I just didn't believe a lot of this...and yet, it just happened to me and I can't deny what I just experienced." For him, this was no longer a head trip of intellectualizing these possibilities. This was an authentic and empowering experience. We each assemble our puzzle pieces differently to get the whole picture. Reading a book about riding a bicycle is very different from getting on the bike without training wheels and experiencing the wobbles and uncertainty of falling again and again. This is then followed eventually by an exhilarating feeling of finding our own balance. It's a wonderful metaphor for our own lives of finding our own speed, rhythm and balance. It was so touching to see this dear man lose his mind intellectually and fall into his heart and feel the truth of what he experienced. A deep inner knowing was revealed to him that he will always remember.

The Bridge Across Forever

In the wondrous book, *The Bridge Across Forever*, Richard Bach says,

> "Things around us…houses, jobs, cars, they are all props. They are settings for our love…empty settings…how easy it is to chase after settings and forget the diamonds! The only thing that matters, at the end of our stay on earth…is how well did we love…what was the quality of our love."

Trust Your Gut and Follow Your Heart

Another point Abraham stresses is how it is of great advantage to give much concentrated thought in the direction of those things you desire and to give little or no thought toward those things you do not want. A fleeting negative thought is other than going to harm anyone. Dwelling upon negativity will eventually magnetize and bring the [undesirable] creation into your experience. Unless you invite that which you do not desire by giving undue thought and focus to it, you will preclude attracting undesirable experiences.

When you effectively utilize the marvelous guidance system which comes forth from your Inner Being, *in the form of emotion*, then you will be in a position to always effectively create what you desire, while you deliberately avoid creating what you do not want. As you become sensitive to the emotion you are feeling in any moment, you will know if you are creating toward or away from that which you desire. Always trust your inner guidance for it comes forth from the broader, wiser part of yourself which has the advantage of knowledge of both physical and non-physical.

As I've often said, "Trust your gut and follow your heart" and I would now add with emphasis, "And let the good times roll." Set your own style and tone by practicing and choosing deliberate thoughts and good feelings until they **feel familiar**. It is the difference between being in the driver's seat at the wheel of your car directing your destination vs. sitting in the passenger's seat where you are simply the observer.

My Karma Ran Over My Dogma

As mentioned earlier, karma means in its root form "come back." In other words, through the Law of Attraction in Action, we create our own reality negatively or positively. Every action has its "reaction" or comes back—not as "booga booga" or something to fear—it is simply energy in motion. You know now there are only two emotions—one feels good and the other feels bad with a wide range on either end of the vibrational scale. This is why you always have a choice to set deliberate intentions. Allow them to be magnetized by keeping your valve open…with low resistance and high desires and a fresh new start.

Above All, Don't Wobble!

In the book, *The Way of the Peaceful Warrior*, by Dan Millman, his mentor, Socrates, was discussing how every action has its price and its pleasures. Recognizing both sides, you become realistic and responsible for your actions. And then you can make the "warrior's choice"—to do or not to do. There is a saying, "When you sit, sit; when you stand, stand; whatever you do, don't wobble. Once you make a choice, do it with all your spirit."

Dan had a wonderful story he shared about how one night he was complaining that people at school didn't seem to act very friendly toward him. Socrates told him, "It is better for you to take responsibility for your life as it is, instead of blaming others, or circumstances for your predicament. As your eyes open, you'll see that your state of health, happiness and every circumstance has been arranged by you—consciously or unconsciously."

Dan didn't agree with Socrates and said, "I don't know what you mean." Socrates responded, "Well, here's a story about a guy like you, Dan."

On a construction site in the Midwest, when the lunch whistle would blow, all the workers would sit down together to eat. And with singular regularity, Sam would open his lunch pail and start to complain.

"Son of a gun!" he'd cry, "not peanut butter and jelly sandwiches again. I hate peanut butter and jelly!"

Sam moaned about his peanut butter and jelly sandwiches day after day after day. Weeks passed, and the other workers were getting irritated by his behavior.

Finally, another man in the work crew said, "Fer cripesakes, Sam, if you hate peanut butter and jelly so much, why don't you just tell yer ol' lady to make you something different?"

"What do you mean, my ol' lady?" Sam replied. "I'm not married. I make my own sandwiches!"

"Let the beauty you love, be what you do."

...Rumi

You can easily see now why our consciousness bridge span has two piers of self-responsibility and love—let what you love, be what you do. We all make our own sandwiches in life!! Once we are aware we have the ability to respond, our life becomes more creative, exciting, flexible, clear and energetic. Do what you love and love what you do and the Law of Attraction will bring more of whatever you think about.

The following poem succulently describes this process:

The Book of Mirdad by Mikhail Naimy

"So think as if your every thought were to be etched in fire upon the sky for all and everything to see. For so, in truth, it is.

So speak as if the entire world were but a single ear intent on hearing what you say. And so, in truth, it is.

So do as if your every deed were to recoil upon your heads. And so, in truth, it does.

So wish as if you were the wish. And so, in truth, you are.

So live your life as if God Himself had need of you, His life to live. And so, in truth, He does."

Mikhail Naimy was a friend and contemporary of Kahlil Gibran with whom he founded a dynamic movement for the rejuvenation of Arabic literature.

My good friend and colleague, Dr. David Viscott, whom I adored, was such an intuitive psychiatrist with his own syndicated talk radio show. He also wrote a book entitled, *Risking*, where he said:

"If you cannot risk, you cannot grow.
If you cannot grow, you cannot become your best.
If you cannot become your best, you cannot be happy.
If you cannot be happy, what else matters?

All you can be is what you are.
All you own is what you experience.
All you are is what you are aware of now.
To live in ignorance of yourself is to be incomplete.
You cannot take strength from the good parts of yourself you
do not know.
If you want to see the world most clearly, turn your eye inward before
you look about…"

And then the day came when the risk
to remain tight in a bud was more painful
than the risk it took to blossom.

When Was the Last Time You Did Something for the First Time?!

9
Is Your Life Chance or Choice?

When you choose to live your life on purpose through creative choices, you are focused on goals and outcomes. I invite you to start a journal. Date and write down specific intentions of what you choose to create and receive. Notice the word receive indicates you other than have to "work" for this. As you write, play or draw, let it be joyful, enthusiastic and fun. This is your magical moment to rekindle the thrill of your heart's desires and to magnetize your creations. Get out your magnets again and feel their power of attraction in your hands.

When our grandson, Skye, was 11 years old, he was playing with my set of magnets and he attached a whole line of large paperclips one to another. About ten large paperclips kept generating their own magnetic energy to dangle down one through another until they were all in a long line through the power of magnetic attraction from the original source. And then Skye did something really amazing. He took one of those paperclips, and it magically stayed on his finger without being attached to the magnet he had set on the table. In other words, that paperclip apparently had enough magnetism left in it to attach to his skin's inherent electrical body energy. He was so delighted. And I was thrilled to see this electro-magnetic body energy demonstrated so easily, all through the instincts and play of a child.

The Vibration of Enthusiasm

Next, write **why** you choose to receive your heart's desire. I choose it because "_____," I receive it because " _____," or, I desire it (or deserve it) because " _____." When you feel the excitement and thrill generated through your enthusiasm, you will know your wish is in alignment. Enthusiasm in its root form means "*enthos = in god*," and it is your enthusiasm vibration that radiates and pulsates the power for drawing your "coming attractions" to you. Your inspired feelings, emotional tones and energy literally become the magnet. Enthusiasm and appreciation generate high magnetism and attraction. If you had a vibrational meter in your hands, where are you today on a scale of 1 to 10? Only you can "up" your vibration by choosing energies that feel good.

Once you have begun your Deliberate Creations and intentions in the back of this book (or a separate journal), review them before you fall asleep at night. Imagine and see yourself succulently, sweetly and successfully receiving your outcome(s) fulfilled now. Vividly experience the juiciness of your wishes granted and *feel* the excitement radiating from you, which energetically accelerates your process. Consider the following: **Who are you with, what are they saying to you, and what are you feeling and doing**? Then give thanks and appreciate yourself and your highest choices for today. This focusing can become an exciting part of your lifelong process as a delicious, divine Deliberate Creator.

As you write and review your goals, imagine they are every hue and color of the rainbow. What colors are they? I suggest you use colored markers and pens and make a spectrum of yourself and your goals. As you weave your highest outcomes, imagine they are a tapestry mirroring your life. Create a collage of your wondrous self. Design the outcomes you magnetically choose to attract now. Let your heart and mind soar. This is your opportunity to grandly imagine and be your magic genie (imagine = i am a genie = your divine plan). Notice what you say to yourself and know what you consent to be true is woven into the threads of your life force and vibration consciously in this moment.

You are the Genius and the Genie,
The Deliberate Creator,
The Flow-er of Your Heart's Desires
As You Intensely Feel and Consent
To Your Outcomes Fulfilled Now!

Feeeeeeeel good and think only about what you desire. As Abraham says, "You are the focuser of energy, you are the perceiver, the decider, the flow-er, the seer, the creator, the anticipator, the executor, the intender, the desirer." The Universe always responds to your vibration. Your clarity is what creates divine order and divine timing in your outcomes being fulfilled. The Universe is ready when you are! Remember to hold yourself in vibrational harmony with your desires at all times. All you have to do is decide and intend what you desire and why. That is the deliciousness of hands-on creating for the sheer pleasure and the anticipation of it. Then you have a buffer of time to be very clear and you can change it, re-arrange it, augment or fine-tune it more specifically before it manifests as your heart's desire. The Law of Attraction in Action *always* responds to your vibration.

"Appreciation is the fastest tool for personal growth."

…Abraham

I initiate and align my outcomes prefaced with these three magical words: **"I give thanks!"** Then I state whatever I am choosing to create. This acknowledges it is already here. It literally sets up the Law of Attraction in Action. When you give thanks and appreciate all of your creations and conscious goals fulfilled, you'll attract more of your heart's desires easily and effortlessly. APPRECIATION IS ONE OF THE STRONGEST EMOTIONS YOU HAVE FOR WHATEVER YOU CHOOSE TO CREATE NOW! Stay focused! Follow your heart! Imagine being the highest and purest vibration you can be and let your words and feelings match your highest choices. Remember, having an attitude of gratitude accelerates the process! Walt Whitman said, "I do not seek good fortune—I am good fortune!"

Go for the Gusto!

A legend tells us that one night in ancient times, three horsemen were riding across the desert. As they crossed the dry river bed, out of the darkness a voice called, "Halt!" They obeyed. The voice then told them to dismount, pick up a handful of pebbles, put the pebbles in their pockets and remount. The voice then said, "You have done as I commanded. Tomorrow at sun-up you may be both glad and sorry." Mystified, the horsemen rode on. When the sun rose, they reached into their pockets and found that a miracle had happened. The pebbles had been transformed into diamonds, rubies, gold and other precious stones. They remembered the warning. They were both glad and sorry—glad they had taken some, and sorry they had not taken more.

When you invest time in your life as a Deliberate Creator and focus on your creations, you are fulfilling a divine work of art. You are the master and centerpiece of your life. No one can do it for you, although we can be midwives and assist by helping one another in birthing our creations. You are the sculptor and you are the clay. You are the weaver, weaving your sacred tapestry. You are the knower, the knowing and the known in oneness and vibration. You are the prayer and the one who grants and answers the prayer.

Invest in Yourself—Be Bold—
Go for the Gold!

Neville asks, "What prayers of yours have been answered? What would it mean to you to know whenever you pray or intend your heart's desire and outcome fulfilled that something definite would happen now? A prayer granted implies that something was done in response to prayer. Therefore, the one who prays must be the one who grants the prayer. To pray is to elevate the mind to what you seek, so lift your mind and heart by assuming the feeling of the outcomes fulfilled. Experience in your imagination what you would experience in reality when your prayer is answered. Hold your attention upon the idea of the wish fulfilled until it is focused and crowds out any other ideas that are other than in your best interests."

The Good News

Dr. Christiane Northrup, who wrote the visionary book, *Women's Bodies, Women's Wisdom*, recommends avoiding TV or listening to news on the radio for 30 days. In our beautiful warm winters here in Arizona, I often go for a walk around sunset and immerse myself in the beauty of nature rather than watching the evening (often "bad/sad") news. Don't be on negative information overload. Christiane says that human beings were never designed to act as "receiver sets" for the bad news of the planet.

"Icky" Garbage Thoughts

Abraham has an excellent analogy of a buffet dinner. If you try a certain food, and it doesn't taste good, you don't eat it. You spit it out or push it aside on your plate. Unfortunately, many people consistently hold "icky" thoughts, instead of focusing on what they want. None of us would think of eating garbage yet many people constantly hold "garbage" thoughts. You can't hold positive thoughts and energies and then keep observing your reality of what doesn't feel or taste good in your life. Change your thoughts so you are summoning and flowing energy toward what you desire. You attract new levels of well-being and what tastes good in the smorgasbord of life because you always have freewill and choice.

Stay Out of Reverse

As a teenager, I'll always remember the first time I had to put a car in reverse to back out of a long driveway. It was both embarrassing and hilarious as it looked easier than what it actually was. My husband really enjoyed Dr. Richard Carlson's book, *Don't Worry, Make Money*. We appreciated his insightful story entitled "Staying Out Of Reverse" that points out how it is impossible to move forward in reverse gear. Carlson comments that reverse sounds like the following, in day-to-day living: "Can you believe what happened yesterday? Those guys were jerks. Every time I work with them, it gets messed up. I'm still mad at what she said to me." He clearly states that anytime you are fixated about something from yesterday or 10 years ago, you are in reverse gear. As he notes, it's boring, unforgiving and counterproductive. The reason people stay there is that they can easily justify being there. As you know from using your magnets, "reverse" is pushing against rather than moving forward and flowing your heart's desires.

Finding your own balance is very rewarding and liberating because it creates boundaries from distractions. Be discerning about what serves you and is life enhancing. Stay out of reverse gear! Often we do things out of habit, like turn on the TV or radio when we could nurture our creativity or appreciate the beauty that surrounds us. Invest in rituals for your inner self and find the resources which nourish your mind, heart and soul.

Dreams—Free Movies Every Night The Star of the Show Is You— This is Your Life!

Even though dreams were covered earlier, I have a sidebar here to emphasize the importance of how you awaken in the morning. You get "free movies" every night about your life, where you are the producer, creative director, the writer and the STAR of the show. In my experience, your best and most important dreams occur around 4 a.m. Set the intention to program yourself mentally for what time you choose to awake. If you have a particular timeline to meet, then program music, rather than an alarm clock. Notice the language I'm using is not deadline; it is timeline. Watch your words, as your subconscious hears every word you say and takes you literally. I've heard people jokingly say, "I can't think of what's-his-faces name—I'll probably remember it at 3 a.m. this morning." Guess what? Your subconscious happily follows your directions and has no sense of humor about whether you meant it or not. Be prepared to be awakened at 3 a.m.! Instead say, "I choose to remember his name. It will come to me any minute." That direct command brings it forth from your unconscious much more quickly. You can also "program" yourself to awaken at any appointed time you desire.

"The life we want is not merely the one we have chosen and made. It is the one we must be choosing and making."

...Wendall Berry

143

One day, after an appointment with Abraham-Satarcia, Patricia Mulreany and I were having lunch and she pointed out to me that the word ritual is in spirituality.

Ritual is the Heart of Spirituality

When I drew it out on paper at that very moment, I was amazed I had not ever noticed ritual contained in "Spiritual" or as a centerpiece in "Spirituality." Ritual is embodied in both the above words and I love to play with anagrams and rootforms. My enthusiasm for ritual, which for me is personal excitement imbued with divine energy, sparkles and shines as soon as I awaken! It is an important and essential part of making each day magical and sacred. *Ritual helps me to remember my spirit*.

"I thank God, every time I remember you."

…Philippians 1:3

Ritual is summoning and flowing energy in a heartfelt vibration in your sacred space. You can easily create daily ceremony or ritual for your highest outcomes and heart's desires if only for the few moments it takes to light candles. I have a series of seven-day glass candles in beautiful stained glass holders I light every morning for my personal prayers in connecting and remembering Spirit, as well as specific candles for loved ones. They last for months, as they are only lit for an hour or two daily. I have two sculpture pieces entitled "Circle of Friends" with a candle in the center which I specifically light for my "tribe's" intentions, which we discuss for our individual or collective heart's desires. Having co-creators stimulates, enriches, enlivens, accelerates and feeds our dreams. By focusing on specific prayers as I light each candle, it amplifies my heart connection to each person as I feel them in my heart. I keep some beloved photos of my friends and family with sweet memories in this sacred space. I send prayers on their behalf and imagine their radiant well being, as well as how precious they are in my life. I also give thanks and appreciation to Source and Master Teachers, angels and my Inner Being who divinely guides me. Philippians expresses it beautifully as, "I thank God every time I remember you." And in that moment, you are remembering Spirit. Your one-pointedness is essential in lighting your candle(s), as it sets the vibration for specificity and focus in your prayers.

On Oprah's TV program in 1998, author Sara Ban Breathnach said to a woman in the audience who appeared to be on the pity pot: "**Blessed am I to live in such a beautiful temple**" referring to her body. You can appropriate that for your body as a temple, or the temple you live in. Spirit's presence permeates every cell in your body and every room in your home. As Psalm 144 states: "I will sing praises." We named our home *Desert Song* because it gives voice to the music of our Spirit and because it is truly a song in our hearts. Bless your home and your life, as you light candles. When you connect with your Stream of Well Being, your life is filled with the sweetness and presence of Spirit as you give thanks and acknowledge "God is and all is well."

I am aware that some people who have been raised in a tradition where they often light candles, find rituals become "rote" or routine rather than a celebration of our connection to Source. Always follow your heart and do what feels good!

Uplighting Your Connection

In the few minutes it takes to light my candles, I'm remembering and illuminating my connection to All That Is…the Spirit of God within me and within my loved ones. We are born with a connection to God and the invisible realms. Our prayers are uplighted as luminous fibers streaming out as we flow and focus our energy from our ever-present Stream of Well Being. You will read more about the vibration of *uplighting* in Chapter 12. As you remember your connection by lighting a candle(s), send thoughts and prayers that shine and radiate love, blessings or healing.

Spiritual Relationship

Authentic rituals feel good to the very core of your being because deep inside you know you are inherently divine. As you become more aware of Spirit, you cherish the "uplighting" times of your life. I love creating space for connecting and remembering Spirit for it opens the passage-way to transmitting and receiving with Source. It may be as brief or as long as time permits. Perhaps your schedule only allows five minutes, but your intent and focused vibration prepaves your day and way in amazing grace. For me, this sets the whole tone for my day. Rituals are about relationship. They are a conduit to the Universe and All That Is. Rituals are my daily soul journey encoded with my personal I AM imprint as I pray, invoke, intend, create, attract and meditate.

If you are going to be using candles in your daily ritual, consider using scented or perfumed ones. Fragrance can be a powerful vibration of connection. It is as potent as remembering the fragrance of baking bread, perking coffee, popcorn popping or a crackling campfire and all the nostalgic memories these scents evoke within you. I sometimes make my own candles as a ritual and summon sacred intents and prayers while playing special music.

Remembering to Remember

Author Jean Houston, a well known authority on Egypt, quotes Kabir via Edmund Helminski by reminding us: "We are forever in parts and yet wish to be whole. We are distracted and yet wish to concentrate; we are scattered and yet wish to be gathered…we are fragmented when we wander from our own center. When our attention is merely reacting to outer events, or when it is being dominated by something, it loses contact with its own source."

Rituals help us to "re-member" our source and the divine spark within us. It brings all "members" and aspects of our being back into the wholeness and fullness of who we are. Spirit renews and resurrects those holy pieces being found and "re-membered" and gathers you 'round in pure love and power as you induct prayers in your sacred space.

"To thine own self be true."
…William Shakespeare

When you "intend" your highest choices through ritual, it clarifies your specific heart's desires, which are then magnetically set into motion. You become aware of what has heart and meaning for you and what your true passion is. Appreciate yourself for your willingness to write your intentions down. Invoking and reading them out loud is also very effective. You will be amazed if you haven't done so before. It makes a much deeper connection. Ceremony expands your commitment to grow, change and upgrade your deliberate creations because you are summoning and flowing energy. You can also sing, laugh, skip and play. Give thanks for your "ah-hahs" and appreciate your inspirations and aspirations. Music can restore and elevate your soul, as does aromatherapy through the exquisiteness of fragrance. Your authentic commitment engages your will and your power to direct your thoughts to manifest your heart's desires. Your inspired feelings and pure, positive emotional energy literally begins to magnetically draw and pulsate a higher level of well being. The Universe always supports you when you commit to your vision and believe in yourself and follow your bliss.

Goethe beautifully expressed it this way:

> **"Until one is committed, there is hesitancy, the chance to draw back. Concerning all acts of initiatives [and creations], there is one elementary truth, the ignorance of which kills countless ideas and splendid plans.**
>
> **The moment one definitely commits oneself, then Providence moves too.**
>
> **All sorts of things occur to help one that would never otherwise have occurred. A whole stream of events issue from [your] decision, raising in one's favor all manner of unforeseen incidents, meetings and material assistance which no man [or woman] could have dreamed would come his/her way.**
>
> **Whatever you can do, or dream you can do, begin it. Boldness has genius, power and magic in it. BEGIN IT NOW!"**

The legend of the three horsemen powerfully illustrated being unlimited in imagining and fusing your heart's desires as you come from your wishes granted. Allow and align with the thrill of already having your precious creations fulfilled as gems of joy—"heaven happies" mirrored in your daily life. Passionately follow your bliss. By thinking from the outcome fulfilled, it magically results in magnetizing miracles. You are divine partners and co-creators with Source.

BEGIN
"The true name of eternity is today."

...Philo

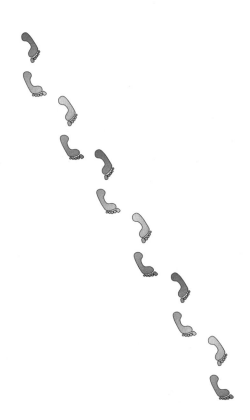

10
Learning Gives Way to Being

Nasrudin, The Persian Rascal

The story is told of Nasrudin, the Persian rascal-sage who found himself on the bow of a tiny ferry boat with a pompous intellectual. Bloated with his own self-importance, the scholar begins to quiz and criticize Nasrudin's education.

"Have you ever studied astronomy?" asked the professor.

"Can't say that I have," answered the mystic.

"Then you have wasted much of your life. By knowing the constellations, a skilled captain can navigate a boat around the globe."

A few minutes later, the learned one asked, "Have you ever studied meteorology?" "No, I haven't," said Nasrudin. "Well, you have wasted most of your life," the professor chided. "Capturing the wind can propel a sailing ship at astounding speeds."

After awhile he inquired, "Have you ever studied oceanography?"

"Not at all," said Nasrudin.

"Ah, what a waste—awareness of the currents helped many ancient people find food and shelter," the professor said.

A few minutes later, Nasrudin began to make his way toward the stern of the ship. On his way forward, he nonchalantly asked the professor, "Have you ever studied swimming?"

"Haven't had the time," responded the professor. Nasrudin replied, "Then you have wasted all of your life. The boat is sinking!"

I have a whole book on Nasrudin jokes and truisms which I love. This particular story came from Alan Cohen, author of, *I Had It All the Time*, who said that sooner or later we reach the point where living the truth becomes more important than seeking it. Knowledge pales in the face of the riches of the heart—learning gives way to BEING.

I've been aware of the importance of our words and languaging for many years. It was upgraded when Robert and Helena Stevens of *Mastery Systems* became colleagues and friends. Their primary work is to teach and share the importance of clearly "speaking the word" for only those things you choose to have manifest. This is done in workshops they present on using creative language to empower, transform, and align your words with successful outcomes. Some of the words which sabotage our language are: "I can't, I'm not, I won't, I must, and I should." I've told classes for years, "Don't should all over yourself." I became more aware in *Mastery Systems* how often I was using the word **not**. Yet how do you speak without the "nots" and still language it appropriately? For example, "I'm not going to the party" would become "I am **other than** able to attend."

Someone once said, "Every thought is a prayer." If that is true, can you imagine what we create with expressions like, "it will blow your mind" or "doesn't that just blow you away" or "drop-dead gorgeous" or "I crashed and burned" or "I'm sick and tired" or "it's killing me" or "I just love you to death." If we had instant manifestations from those phrases, we would have large holes where our brains were blown away, or drop dead from being gorgeous, be in a morgue from crashing and burning and totally lethargic from being sick and tired. Since our unconscious takes us literally, the importance of what we speak becomes a self-fulfilling prophecy. Someone said to me, "I desperately want a relationship," and I invited her to reconsider that she would attract a "desperate man" using that languaging. I've had many people say to me over the years, "I just love you to death," and I say, "I'd rather have you love me to life!" They look at me momentarily startled and then a lightbulb comes on in their awareness and they realize what they said.

Several years ago, my dear friend, Joyous Lesperance, sent me the following BE ATTITUDES and I adapted the languaging.

Be Attitudes

Be **A** ware… of the infinite possibilities in each moment.
Be **T** rusting…of the life you are creating.
Be **T** rue…to yourself and to the highest potentials within you
Be **I** ngenious…with your creativity and passion for possibilities.
Be **T** hankful …for the generosity of life and friends. Appreciate!
Be **U** nderstanding of others for we are all on the same path,
                    …in different places along the way.
Be **D** elighted…with the wondrousness and gift of Life.
Be **E** nergetic and expectant of love, joy, and highest outcomes.
(author unknown)

Swami FedEx

In his book, Alan Cohen shared a story about the secret of life in a chapter, *Always Had It, Always Will:* "What would you do if someone swore that you knew the secret of life and put you up on a stage to tell it?"

A totally hidden video television show set up a prank on precisely this theme. For the gag, a Federal Express driver was asked to deliver a package to a religious temple (fabricated by the TV show). Unknown to the driver, the pranksters had taken a photo of the Fed Ex driver himself, and replicated it as a painted portrait depicting the young man dressed in the royal regalia of this fictitious sect.

When the Fed Ex delivery driver arrived, the disciples (actors hired by the TV program) took one long look at him and began buzzing excitedly. They ushered him into the front of the sanctuary and invited him to sit on a plush cushion of honor. Then they revealed to him to be the "Chosen One," the long-awaited prophet foretold in their scriptures. To dispel any doubts, a servant parted the altar curtain where, lo and behold, hung the majestic portrait of this Fed Ex driver which appeared to be painted centuries ago. "Please give us some words of wisdom," begged the disciple.

The driver surveyed the portrait and looked over the throng of expectant devotees and a hush fell over the assembly gathered therein. He sat down on the pillow, took a deep breath and spoke, "Life is like a river." the sage explained. The disciples "oohed" and "aahed" on the heels of his utterance, hanging fervently onto every word. "Sometimes life flows easily, and sometimes you encounter rocks and rapids," the guru continued, "but if you hang in there and have faith, you will arrive at the ocean of your dreams." Again the students swooned with ecstasy. More "ooohs and aahs." This was indeed the day they had waited for. "Well, that's about it," Swami FedEx curtly concluded. "I have to go now and make more deliveries." Reluctantly the devotees rose and bowed reverently and cleared the way for the anointed one. Amid profuse veneration, he made his way to the door.

Federal Express

Now, the amazing P.S. to this true story, according to Cohen, is the TV show played the same trick on several Fed Ex drivers, each of whom had profound wisdom to impart the moment they sat on the cushion. The invitation to wax poetic brought forth inner wisdom in these unassuming people. As Cohen states, "Deep within our hearts, each of us knows the truth. The answers we seek, the power we strive for, the acknowledgment we attempt to gain, abides in us. Given the opportunity—[in this case being placed on a cushion], or the challenge [being pushed against the wall], we know what we need to know, to do what we need to do."

Goethe said it this way:

**"If you treat a man as he appears to be,
you make him worse than he is.
If you treat a man as if he already were
what he potentially could be,
you make him what he should be."**

152

Your true self is on a path of self-discovery…becoming more of who and what you authentically are. Dr. Brugh Joy, author of *Joy's Way, the Map for the Transformational Journey*, has noted, "The key word is 'appears,' for how often do we ever see the totality, including the potential, not yet manifest in ourselves or any other human beings?" In Brugh's workshops, he asks participants to spend an afternoon re-phrasing Goethe's quotation into a contemplation of the following:

**"If I treat myself as I think I appear to be,
I make myself less than I am.
If I treat myself as if I already were
what I potentially could be,
I make myself what I can be."**

In his book entitled, *Breaking the Rules*, author Kurt Wright asks us to contemplate in a way similar to Brugh Joy's adaptation of Goethe with questions posed such as:

**What are we like at our best?
When does it happen?
What is your level of awareness of this?**

Wright suggests pondering when things go especially well for you—when you are on a roll, have you taken time to explore how and why you got there? Most people wait until they fall off "being on a roll" and then wonder what's wrong. Wright's book is accurate in exploring how often we are accustomed to focusing on what is not working to build upon what is working. When we remove our attention from trying to fix what appears to be broken, we open to new inspirations by focusing and attracting solutions.

His approach has been to study those who are doing super-well to find out **WHAT'S RIGHT**? Wright asks people to re-focus upon "**what's going right**" rather than what's wrong even in the midst of corporate crises where he was a well-paid consultant. Again, it's a matter of contrast in diversity.

Stinkin' Thinking vs.
The Fragrance Frequency

What if we had a monitoring device to "catch" ourselves instantly when we judge, blame or have thoughts of "exclusion." This device would immediately give us feedback through an unpleasant odor. It would be an instant "alert" that we are in resistance, pushing against, mismatching or miscreating. Imagine how quickly we would "stink" up our vibration. We could immediately choose to re-align, re-focus, and upgrade our language and feelings by getting back "on course." When we revel and appreciate our ability to be a Deliberate Creator, the pleasure fragrance would be self-evident—can you imagine how that would feel?! We would then consistently know and be the point of attraction to vibrate with our outcomes.

I'm sure we would consciously choose to re-align our thoughts quickly and know how to get back "on track" with an experiment like this. Our radar signals would be beaming out either "Stinkin' Thinkin" (i.e: noticing the resistance) or telegraphing and beaming out deliberate, creative thoughts that are what we are excited to attract magnetically. This instant feedback would provide an upgrade immediately. Right now in the Valley where we live, it is spring and the orange blossoms are flowering on the trees. It is one of the sweetest fragrances on the planet and if we really understood that as we think we vibrate, and as we vibrate, we attract, we would consciously choose to be the fragrance we adore. It's all according to how we are flowing and outputting our energy. If we had a built-in "odor meter" we would consistently know what we were outputting. Fragrances and odors have a distinct signature vibration. We would always know our tone and frequency by our words and feelings. I invite you to flow and know the fragrance you appreciate.

Blame, Guilt or Appreciation

I had a situation arise by e-mail from an acquaintance that was a temporary bump in the road, which occurred as I was writing this chapter. I realized he was simply disconnected from Source. He was into blame regarding something he had heard from a third party. I reminded him you can never, in reality, control or change another person. I didn't match energy with his tone. His information was skewed and inaccurate.

However, he was into a mode of justification (pushing against) so I suggested he create a higher outcome rather than stay focused on his explanations and defensiveness.

On an Abraham tape, I appreciated an analogy he described as a pie chart, which was entitled **"Blame, Guilt or Appreciation."** It is a very meaningful, quick tool to use in contrast, because you know instantly which energy section you are on the pie chart. In this situation above, I summoned higher choices vibrationally, lined up the energy, listened to the responses and we all learned something. It is helpful to remember that when people have a charge and are into the "blame game" while claiming integrity, you can bring this chart into awareness of blame, guilt or appreciation. From contrast, new clarity and decisions are born. It was interesting this occurred as I was just about to write the next topic on manure and fertilizer. The Universe does have a sense of humor with cosmic alarm clocks going off. I did have to giggle at the divine timing for this segment. We teach best what we need to learn.

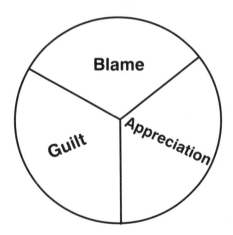

The Magic of Manure

There's a joke about a mother who took her twins to a psychiatrist because they were so different from one another. One boy was a pessimist and the other boy was an optimist. The psychiatrist put them each in an observation room that had a two-way mirror where he could see them. In the center of each room was a big pile of manure and a shovel.

The one boy he watched was crying and having a hissy fit shouting, "I hate manure!" The other twin took a shovel in his hand and was excitedly tossing the manure in the air with great relish in order to get to the center of his manure pile saying, "There's gotta be a pony in here somewhere!"

Reality is for People with No Imagination

It's all a matter of focus and you can use contrast to make new decisions and line up new energy for your heart's desires or stay in the "manure" of blame, guilt, explanation and justification. Which would you rather have? The pessimist saw "what was" and observed "reality." The optimist twin goosed up his imagination and created his own reality. You can bet he found a "pony" wherever he was. Like the bumper sticker my friend, Germaine saw: "Reality is for people with no imagination!"

In her presentations many years ago, psychologist, Patricia Sun, used to share an analogy by asking how many people liked the fragrance of baking bread and naturally everyone raised their hand. Next, she would ask how many people like the smell of feces and of course no one raised their hand. She then explained how feces used to be thrown out of the window from chamber pots, and later dumped into rivers and polluted them. However, when it finally was put in the soil, a miracle happened! It became sweet and made the soil fertile and rich, which fertilized the wheat for the flour we use to bake the bread into the fragrance we do appreciate.

Fertilizer For Your Spiritual Evolution

The magic of manure helps us understand there are no accidents in contrast. It is the compost or fertilizer for our personal growth and enrichment. We have a choice about which energy we choose to participate in. I earlier quoted Richard Bach saying, "We seek problems because we need their gifts." There have been times in my life when I felt like I was drowning in my "opportunities" known as "challenges." However, when I stayed conscious enough to realize it was a "set up" I created for my personal growth as a "wake up call" to pay attention (rather than an "upset" as an "outside" event), it **always** turned out to be a big shift or transformational point. Any problems that crisis precipitates cause us to become more conscious! Know that the Universe is lovingly and magnetically responding to your prayers and heartfelt requests.

The poet, Rumi, beautifully expressed it this way:

"The breeze at dawn has secrets to tell you.
Don't go back to sleep.
You must ask for what you really want.
Don't go back to sleep.
People are going back and forth across the doorsill
where two worlds touch. The door is open and round.
Don't go back to sleep."

If you are out of sync with any family, co-workers or friends, look at what resistance issues are up. Don't go back to sleep! I'm sure you will remember this Brer Rabbit tale from your childhood.

Tar Baby Creates Resistance

Do you remember Brer Rabbit and how Old Mr. Fox had enough of his tricks so he mixed a big jar of turpentine and sticky tar and made what he called a Tar Baby? Then Fox hid in the bushes til Brer Rabbit came hopping down the road and as he approached Tar Baby, he said, "Good Morning" and Tar Baby didn't reply. So, Brer Rabbit raised his voice and Tar Baby just sat where he was. Now that made Brer Rabbit mad and he said, "Are you deaf?" and called Tar Baby "stuck up" and said he was just the one who would cure him of a "big head." And if he didn't answer like Brer Rabbit thought he should, he was going to draw back and give him a good wallop, which of course he eventually did.

Now Old Mr. Brer Fox just chuckled from his hiding place in the bushes. So, next Brer Rabbit smacked Tar Baby on the lips and then he became stuck too, as Tar Baby was sticky as glue. So Brer Rabbit then says, "If you don't let me go, I'll wallop you again," and then struck him square on the chin. Naturally by then Brer Rabbit was really stuck again and shouting demands and trying to kick out all of Tar Baby's stuffings which only made things worse as both his feet stuck just like his hands. So, he squealed and he struggled and he cussed and even butted his head and got totally more stuck instead.

"Brer Rabbit & His Tricks," Ennis Rees Hyperion Paperbacks for children

Remember...What You Resist Persists

By now, you get the bigger picture of "what you resist persists." We all have had Tar Babies in our life where the more we cussed and resisted, the more it expanded. Rather than "react" to Tar Baby situations when you've been "set up" by someone like Brer Fox, you can pivot and give your attention to re-directing your energies by knowing and trusting you have the resources to get back "on course." We can attract solutions of what's working and choose to re-focus on pure, positive attention to pulsing with our Stream of Well Being.

You will notice what happened to Brer Rabbit when he's blaming and shouting at Tar Baby. It's just as "mucky" in your vibration when you have negative emotions or "control" or "power issues" or sweep things under the carpet. It just gets lumpier and bigger. As you recognize negative emotions or resistance, you will quickly realize you are actually flowing energy in opposition to what you'd like to magnetize. You will always know when you are moving in the direction of your heart's desires as you feel exhilarated, clear and uplifted.

When you find yourself metaphorically "banging your head against a wall" with a "sticky" issue, ask yourself, "What do I choose to create, what is my highest outcome, and why?" Once you begin to re-direct the energy, you feel the power of transformation moving from manure to fertilizer, which bakes the bread and attracts the fragrance you choose to appreciate. It's so liberating and freeing...and life feels so delicious and fun with your Windex Sky clarity. So, go where the juice is and connect in with your Inner Being, your core desires and your divine counterparts. Be a Deliberate Masterful Creator and Co-creator. You get to dream it and attract it now and continuously!

"You Can Lead A Horse To Water But You Can't Make'm Drink"

A recent story I have permission to share is from a dear friend who called and asked me what "water leaks" meant as a life metaphor. She had been experiencing significant water "challenges" in her life. First, she had a major pipe break during a heavy rainfall and it leaked into the home she was selling (and no longer residing there). It caused a lot of damage to the home's interior. Later, the water meter at this home also broke and flooded the street.

Meanwhile, the roof in her beautiful new home started leaking, and she had buckets placed all around. Then, as she was rinsing dishes in her kitchen sink in her new home, she felt water gushing at her feet, and a perfectly good pipe had somehow become disconnected. It was implausible that it even happened the way it did. She said "What does all this mean?!" I told her water is usually emotional issues, and I suggested she take a look at what was going on in her life that she was consciously (or unconsciously) avoiding. She acknowledged there were definitely issues she needed to deal with. I told her, "The issues will continue to expand unless you really get the point of what this is telling you symbolically now. You have the power for a fresh start that feels good. Offer a new dominant intention and signal to reconnect by taking time for yourself." At this rate, with water surfacing constantly, it was so obvious the Universe was asking her to pay attention now.

As Abraham says if you are ignoring something, "Don't worry, it will get bigger!" Many of us laugh out loud at that, as we have noticed how true it is in our own personal lives. In this case, the pipe becoming disconnected was a major clue of inner work which needed to be addressed. You can't continue to put whipping cream on top of garbage. The avoidance tactic just kept muddying up the whole vibration.

Water, Water Everywhere and Not a Drop to Drink!

Five days later my friend called and said, "Well, you were right, Sharon, it just got bigger!" She was at the same kitchen sink in her new home, and the pull-out sprayer completely disconnected from the faucet! The force from the maverick hose shot water across to the other side of the kitchen, onto the walls, the ceiling and pictures. She called me even before she cleaned the water up while it was still dripping all over. She really knew this time that the hose disconnecting and going out of control was the final wake up call. The only way out for her was going within by taking time to re-focus, acknowledge and own her authentic feelings on these emotional issues.

Water metaphorically often represents our emotional energy. It is our feeling nature. In this case, leaks popped out in the most unusual and bizarre ways. The leaks kept getting bigger so she couldn't possibly miss the emotional issues at hand. They kept re-surfacing over and over. Many times we feel we are too busy with current life happenings and ignore what is really important. This became a major wake-up call for this sweet soul to pay attention to connecting back into her Stream of Well Being as the beautiful and capable creator she is. I've seen miracles occur in her life and I knew she had the inner resources to magnetize her heart's desires simply by acknowledging that she deserves to take time for herself. It meant listening to her Inner Being who is always here whenever she chooses to reconnect. She needed to take time to flow positive energy and attract deliberate creations and vibrational matches of what she desired. The Universe is responding to our signal. Many times we are unconscious of our vibrational output until incidents like this are mirrored back. We have to summon and flow pure, positive energy—in and out—in and out—in and out and notice what is being reflected back in our daily lives.

Insanity is Doing the Same Thing Over and Over Again and Expecting a Different Result!

My topic for this segment was, "You can lead a horse to water, but you can't make him drink." However, my philosophy is…you can make him thirsty! Your Inner Being will quench your thirst the moment you begin to pay attention to your wake-up calls and remember your Spirit.

"No more words Hear only the voice within."

Rumi

Imagine!

"Imagination is More Important Than Knowledge."

…Albert Einstein

You can empower your dreams in your imagination by consenting and believing they are already true and already here. Appreciate and give thanks they are already done effortlessly—a self-fulfilling prophecy! Be emotional and passionate and hold the vision of your decision(s)! Claim them now! Feed the energy wave of what you desire, what feels inspired and stay connected vibrationally to your Stream of Well Being by noticing how you feel! Light a candle to focus and set the tone for your intent! Go around singing, "I DID IT MY WAY." Act as if it is already here and imagine how it feeeeeeels so you are revved up to experience it fully! Take lots of deep breaths and be infused with the energy of freedom (sometimes it feels like relief also) knowing you create your reality! Then, consider it done!! Play with your magnets often so you feel the sense of wonder and JOY of moving powerfully and magnetically with your dreams fulfilled through the Law of Attraction in Action! There is such an intoxicating and enchanting sense of power and anticipation when you flow energy as a Deliberate Creator!

"A desire fulfilled is sweet to the soul."

…Proverbs 13:19

My dear friend Germaine had found the home of her dreams and she and her husband, Steve, purchased it contingent upon the sale of their current home. So, we flowed energy as divine partners and Deliberate Creators for 52 days and on July 22, I had an experience where I absolutely **knew** her home would be sold that day. I called her and said, "Today's the day!" and told her what had transpired. That evening at

6 p.m., I was surprised to learn it hadn't sold because I had such a strong and total sense of knowing it was already fulfilled. When I awoke the next day at 5 a.m., there was an exhilarating fax from Germaine on the sale of their home at 8:30 p.m. the night before, which was magically completed!

I later went shopping for housewarming presents for their new home named *"Silver Oasis."* I prepaved and serendipitously found a *START FRESH* mug, a *silver* angel candle holder and a *silver* heart-shaped candle holder. The card I gave them said: "A DESIRE FULFILLED IS SWEET TO THE SOUL" from Proverbs 13:19. Indeed how sweet it was, is and will continually be when we flow positive energy as Deliberate Creators! As Ralph Waldo Emerson said, "A friend is someone before whom I can think aloud." You can have such fun co-creating vibrational matches.

The Windex Sky Approach

When you have clarity in magnetizing your heart's desires, it benefits all your relationships. It's really a clearer vision—a Windex Sky approach—with the sky being the limit when you practice more thoughts of what you desire with 17 seconds of pure vibration on your relationships. The Universe will respond, deliver and match your desires in divine order and timing. This is the Law Of Attraction in Action from the Stream of your Well Being. Many years ago, William James said, "**The discovery of the power of our thoughts will prove to be the most important discovery of our time.**" The clarity and beauty or the ugliness of our thoughts is up to us. What we praise grows and what we condemn withers and dies.

I've been involved in "mastermind" groups where it is so fun, fruitful, and delicious to come together with focused intentions to line up the energy for our heart's desires. You can also co-create and partner with just one other person who is like-minded. It isn't the number of people, it is the vibrational intent. It is powerful to share and align our mutual dreams knowing the Universe will respond to our vibration and commitment.

"You can't depend on your judgment, if your imagination is out of focus."

…John Kennedy

Years ago in the *Science of Mind* magazine, I read where an airplane was diverted from several large airports because of an unusually severe storm in the northwest. The plane was low on fuel and had to land at the only available place, a small-town airport. Just as the plane was nearing the airport, there was a power failure in the electrical system on the ground, and all the lights marking the landing strip went out.

A quick-thinking airport manager made some hurried phone calls to the local radio station, which in turn announced the need for cars to go the airport to help light the concrete runway. In a short time, each side and the ends of the landing strip were clearly marked with car lights and the plane landed safely. Today safety regulations would probably prohibit a plane landing in such circumstances. What a brilliant and inspired idea from the manager who followed his impulse and intuition! As John Kennedy expressed so well in his quote, it shows how this manager's imagination was the well-spring for creativity and quick answers.

Margaret Mead said:

"Never doubt that small groups of committed concerned citizens can change the world. Indeed, it is the only thing that ever has."

This plane story is a brilliant reminder that several people with a focused intention make a huge difference when the energy is lined up. In this case, what a great analogy of how people responding with their bright lights made a big difference. One car in the dark would have had little impact. Our love and aligned vibrations are a light shining in the dark and the Universe resonates and responds to our highest choices and outcomes.

Some years ago, I read a touching piece, which reminds us of the power of a group being together in a common direction. It was written by Milton Olson entitled, *Lessons of the Geese*. I later heard the lesson applications for this on an audio tape by Angeles Arrien, a cultural anthropologist.

Lessons of the Geese

1. As each bird flaps his wings, it creates an uplift to the birds who are following. By flying in a "V" formation, the whole flock adds 71% more flying range than if the birds flew alone.

    Lesson: People who share a common direction and sense of community and networking can get where they are going quicker, easier and faster because they are traveling on the thrust of another.

2. Whenever a goose falls out of formation, it suddenly feels the drag and resistance of trying to do it alone and gets back quickly into formation to take advantage of the lifting power of the birds immediately in front.

    Lesson: If we have as much sense as a goose, [that always makes me giggle] we will stay in formation with those who are headed where we want to go and be willing to accept their help, as well as extend help to others.

3. When the lead goose gets tired, it rotates back into the formation and another goose flies up to the point position.

    Lesson: It pays to take turns in doing the harder tasks in sharing leadership. With people, as with geese, we are interdependent on each other.

4. The geese in formation honk from behind to encourage those up front to keep up their speed! [This always makes me laugh out loud—it's so true.]

    Lesson: We need to make sure our honking from behind is encouraging and not something else [like criticizing, complaining or competition].

5. When a goose gets sick or wounded or shot down, two geese drop out of formation to help it and protect it. They stay with the goose until it is able to fly again or it dies. [Imagine that—they stay with it until it is able to fly again or it dies— what a wonderful metaphor of being one in heart and spirit]

Then they link up on their own, or with another formation or catch up with their flock.

Lesson: If we have as much sense as the geese, we, too, will stand by each other in difficult and stressful times, as well as when we are strong.

I always feel such a sense of camaraderie in sharing *Lessons of the Geese* in classes because it seems to be a universal touchstone for everyone. It is about being vibrationally together in heart and soul through the resonance of attraction. As Jane Howard said in her book, *Families*, "Call it a clan, call it a network, call it a tribe, call it family. Whatever you call it, whoever you are, you need one."

One day I received a "marshmallow" story from our dear friend, Joyous Lesperance, that beautifully illustrates how very important your tribe is, even those behind the scene.

Who's Packing Your Parachute?

Charles Plumb, a U.S. Navel Academy graduate, was a jet fighter pilot in Vietnam. After 75 combat missions, his plane was destroyed by a surface-to-air missile. Plumb ejected and parachuted into enemy lines. He was captured and spent six years in a Communist prison. He survived that ordeal and now lectures about lessons learned from that experience. Here is his story:

> One day when Plumb and his wife were sitting in a restaurant, a man at another table came up and said, "You're Plumb! You flew jet fighters in Vietnam from the aircraft carrier Kitty Hawk. You were shot down."
>
> "How in the world did you know that?" asked Plumb.
>
> "I packed your parachute," the man replied.
>
> Plumb gasped in surprise and gratitude. The man pumped his hand and said, "I guess it worked." Plumb assured him, "It sure did—if my chute hadn't worked, I wouldn't be here today."
>
> Plumb couldn't sleep that night, thinking about that man. Plumb says, "I kept wondering what he might have looked like

in a Navy uniform—a Dixie cup hat, a bib in the back, and bell-bottom trousers. I wondered how many times I might have passed him on the Kitty Hawk. I wondered how many times I might have seen him and not even said, 'Good Morning or how are you,' or anything because, you see, I was a fighter pilot and he was just a sailor."

Plumb thought of the many hours the sailor had spent on a long wooden table in the bowels of the ship carefully weaving the shrouds and folding the silks of each chute, each time holding in his hands the fate of someone he didn't personally know. Plumb also points out that he needed many kinds of parachutes; his physical parachute, his emotional parachute, his mental parachute and his spiritual parachute. He called on all these supports before reaching safety when he had to jump from his jet.

Now, Plumb asks his audiences, "Who's packing your parachute? Everyone has someone, and many times more than one person who provided what you needed to make it through the day. Recognize and be gracious to people who pack your parachute!"

Shared by Gary on the Kryon web site—Marshmallow Stories

Consider who's packing your parachute and have an attitude of gratitude for your clan, both seen and unseen! It's a wonderful story to acknowledge how connected we really are.

Sometimes in our busy world, we forget what is really important. Saying how are you and really meaning it; saying "I appreciate you;" radiating a smile that lights up a person's day; sharing loving words from your heart; performing a random act of kindness or "paying it forward" (based on the book title) makes such a difference to the vibration of well being in our world.

Birds of a Feather

The saying "birds of a feather flock together" is again a matter of magnetizing. As we have discussed, magnets have a positive pole and a negative pole, which when properly aligned have a very strong "drawing" together power. These magnets are so strong they can even lift heavy scissors and staplers, which helps you to understand metaphorically how strong the pull is of the Law of Attraction in magnetizing your heart's desires.

The earth has a magnetic center and yet when our astronauts move beyond the earth's magnetic field, they experience "weightlessness" which is described exuberantly as an "uplifting" experience. The power of your vibration also draws your "tribe," your "flock" to you, which is your personal spiritual magnetism pulling kindred spirits to you. *We are then divine magnets for and with each other.* We can choose to grow and evolve with elegance and ease. Seize the moment of doing what you love to do and you will automatically co-create magnificent allies and attract magical alliances.

"The ideal you seek to attain will not manifest itself, nor be realized by you, until you imagine you are already that ideal."

...Neville

12

The Sacred Spiral— Return To Center

I love spirals and have seen them carved on petroglyphs worldwide in sacred sites from Egypt, Greece, England, France, India, Bali, and in Native American glyphs here in our country. The spiral is the mark of time.

Author and teacher, Lynn Andrews, tells a story how the spiral begins in your earth walk. Then you move further and further away from your center, from your original nature, until you are on the outer parameters of the spiral. At some point, most people eventually ask, "What is the purpose of my life...or what is the meaning of life?" That is always a turning point when you begin to ask that question for it is a quest to return to your original nature. You begin to retrace your steps or tear away the veils of conditioning with all its limitations and dogmas. Lynn calls this the process of going back home, for we are here to become more enlightened. And yet, she says it is the one thing we seem to be the most afraid of. We have fears of life, fears of death, fear of power, fear of failure, and some people have fear of success. They are called "energy knots"—these fears are ones of feeling "not good enough." Who we truly are at our soul level vibration is love, joy, goodness, Spirit and God.

Many of us have had a church background where we are conditioned to the story of Adam and Eve and original sin. Unfortunately, we absorbed and believed that message rather than the one of our true original nature being pure love. Sin is archery term, which simply means missing the mark. And when you miss the mark, you don't flagellate yourself, you simply aim again and again. **When you know better, you do better.** Someone said that sin is an acronym for <u>S</u>elf <u>I</u>mposed <u>N</u>onsense. So, loving yourself is the first step back to your original nature. The essence of my teachings, no matter what the course material might consist of, is that we are each divine beings unfolding and remembering and becoming more of who we are.

Remembering God

There is a wonderful anecdote, which I've heard shared by various speakers. I understand that Dr. Gerald Jampolsky and Dan Millman, both well-known authors, have similar versions. The essence of this touching story is that a baby was born into a family, which already had a four- year old child. As soon as the baby arrived home, the daughter asked if she could be alone with her new brother. The parents were somewhat concerned that the older sibling could inadvertently harm the newborn baby and so they were initially reluctant. However, the young girl insisted it was very important and the parents finally agreed. The bedroom had an intercom system and the parents monitored the children's first encounter alone. They heard their daughter approach her brother's crib and say, "Please tell me about God, I'm starting to forget." It's such a special story because it is so true. We are here to remember our Spirit and summon and flow energy with Source.

The True Master

It has been said that "The true master is not one who has produced the most students or disciples, but the one who empowers and produces the most masters." As a teacher, I have always said that I wasn't teaching anything that at some level the participants didn't already know. So often, people want to put others on a pedestal. It is far more important to trust the miracle of your being and the teacher within you.

When you are ready to awaken to the sacred spiral, you will create a teacher for yourself to recognize what is already within you. The etymology of the word *recognize* is to *know again*. We are simply remembering who we really are…divine beings and Creators. Focus on your goodness and magnificence rather than on "sin" or unworthiness. As Richard Bach said in his book, *Illusions-The Adventures of the Reluctant Messiah*:

**"Argue for your limitations and
sure enough they are yours."**

My highest outcome is that we vibrate and celebrate our divine, original innocence and goodness.

Remembering Your True Original Nature and Living an Authentic Life

There is a beautiful story shared by a number of teachers in various forms. It is about a mountain lion who was about to give birth and she came down out of the mountains to find food before she delivers her cub. She came upon a goat herd and in the process of killing a goat for food, she dies herself. However, the cub is born and adopted by the herd of goats as one of their own. The cub, not knowing the difference, thinks it is a goat. The cub lives grazing and making noises and acting like a goat. Then one day, Grandfather Lion comes down the mountain and he sees this young lion and can't believe it is living with the goats. He smells the lion and its scent was that of a goat, but it was really a lion.

Grandfather Lion grabs the small lion by the scruff of the neck and takes him to the river and shows him his reflection and roars, "Now take a good, long look at yourself and your reflection in the water. You are a lion just like me. You are not a goat!" And sure enough, the small lion realizes he is not a goat. It is quite a rude awakening because he has been living a life that is not real. He has not been true to his authentic nature. So, the lion goes off with Grandfather Lion and learns how to regain his original nature. Metaphorically, the lion is our intuitive nature that has been repressed or forgotten…living like sheep or goats rather than seeking and living an authentic life.

You Are the Eternal Dance of the Sacred Spiral

The sacred spiral is the transformation point for metamorphosis and you begin to learn and become teachable when you remember your original nature. You come to know that the "wobbles" and the "scariness" is better than living a life that is not genuine. Every time you come to a new perspective, a new "ah-hah" or expand your awareness, you are "uplighted" and uplifted. Then, you complete another circle in coming home to your original nature on the eternal dance of the sacred spiral—your true essence. Sometimes in life, you may feel like you are going around in circles, but each time you move inward on the spiral you have a clearer understanding of your true nature. The Universe conspires and empowers your journey in becoming more of who you are when you name and claim your divine, original nature as a Deliberate Creator.

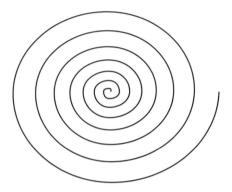

Like Attracts Like Light Attracts Light

Light always attracts more light. Be lighthearted. Lighten up! Always look for more light and upliftment in your life. Be a visionary and give reality a rest by knowing you always have a choice, even when choice looks unavailable in the moment. You are the only one who can adjust your life to a higher octave on the sacred spiral by being a Deliberate Creator.

Uplifting & Uplighting

In April, 1998, at a women's meeting in my home, I shared an intention I had written out and invoked that was very uplifting. It was for my personal journaling and also for my book which had been recently birthed. I was choosing to amplify my heart's desires. They were so excited with my "alignment" statement and wrote it down. I volunteered to type it out later and they each affirmed, "You must include this as a highlight in your book!" This was setting my tone for what I chose to imagine, magnetize and attract:

> "I desire with all my heart to be stimulated and guided to a fuller connection of who I truly am now and eternally. I choose to vibrate who I AM in Spirit, grounded into 3-D reality. I ask for huge access to stimulation of *uplighting* thoughts, inspirations and ideas now. I say YES! YES! YES! to magnetizing and

171

manifesting my magnificence and my heart's desire for health, wealth and divine well being now."

You'll notice an unusual word in this intention which isn't in any dictionary. It is "**UPLIGHTING**." Over and over while writing this book or typing faxes and letters to friends, I would mean to type the word uplift. However, it came out "**UPLIGHT**" or "**UPLIGHTING**." My friends loved it and said, "Keep it!" although I felt most people would wonder about this unusual phraseology. So, now you know my Stream of Well Being has coined a new word and energy to be shared for the first time through this book!

Headed for the Light

There's a humorous e-mail story to illustrate this point shared in an e-mail from my dear friend, Laurie Hostetler. It is about a man new to fatherhood many years ago.

> In the backwoods of Scotland, Ian's wife went into labor in the middle of the night. The doctor was called to assist in the delivery. To keep the nervous father-to-be busy, the doctor handed him a lantern and said, "Here, you hold this high so I can see what I'm doing." Soon a wee baby boy was brought into the world.
>
> "Whoa there, Ian!" said the doctor. "Don't be in a rush to put the lantern down…I think there's another wee one to come yet."
>
> Sure enough, within minutes, he had delivered a bonnie lass.
>
> "No, no, don't be in a great hurry to be putting down that lantern, Lad. It seems there is yet another one besides!" cried the doctor.
>
> Then Ian scratched his head in bewilderment and asked the doctor, "Do ye think it's the light that's attractin' them?!"

172

☀ What Lights You Up? ☀

What lights you up and really turns you on? The etymology that comes closest to uplighting I could think of would be the word illuminate, which literally means "a light" or "to light up." Illuminate also means to brighten up; animate; to make clear; to enlighten. What is your deepest inspiration? Does it light you up? Inspire means "in spirit" or to be breathed upon, infused and animated…to be guided and motivated by divine influence. When you are "in spirit" you are infused with a purpose.

- ♥ **What is your highest passion?**
- ♥ **What divinely inspires you?**
- ♥ **What are you eager and enthusiastic about?**
- ♥ **What fulfills you?**
- ♥ **What feeds and nourishes you?**
- ♥ **What thrills your soul and animates you to new visions and inspired decisions?**
- ♥ **What are your aspirations?**
- ♥ **Are they fun, joyful and exhilarating?**
- ♥ **Do they make your heart soar?**
- ♥ **Are you a vibrational match to your heart's desires?**
- ♥ **What shines in your soul that is seeking to express and bless?**

A Dhammapada passage translated by Thomas Byron says, "However young, the seeker who sets upon the way shines brightly over the world. Day and night the one who is awake SHINES in the radiance of Spirit. Meditate. Live purely. Do your work with mastery [and joy]. Like the moon, come out from behind the clouds. Shine!"

"Uplifters Unite and Uplight!"

…Sharon Says

I truly believe *UPLIGHTED* is a fresh divine vibration for you and me to clearly feel and know in our heart of hearts what lights up our lives. It is not something we acquire, it is divine energy already within us waiting to be released. Every enlightened prophet or text has told us, "You are the light." *UPLIGHTED* means you are plugged in, turned on and connected to Source energy. Ecstasy is a new "frequency" as you feel the

173

surge and thrill of flowing energy. It is when the highest in me meets the grandest in you! To be uplighted is the divine circuitry of pure, positive, passionate, pulsating, powerful energy that guides and "enlightens" you. I believe this special word, *uplighted*, was "downloaded" in me because a bright shiny light is abirthin' in us. I salute you as an uplighter and invite you to play by bringing this energy into your vibration. Ask to be uplighted! We had so much fun when this first came through that our "motto" became "UPLIFTERS UNITE AND UPLIGHT!"

Deliberate Creators
Attract More
Light
Light
Light
Light
Light
Uplifters Uplight

"We have no future except that which we envision…and what we envision will draw itself to us."

Philip Rubinov-Jacobson

13
Delicious Rituals
Let's do the Deal!

Treasure Mapping—Door #1

Years ago in at least one class, I would devote a segment on what is called "Treasure Mapping." Participants were asked to bring in a large poster board, along with magazines and pictures of their heart's desires.

Unity Church teachings have described this as a "pictured prayer" demonstration. Mary Katherine MacDougall wrote a book, *What Treasure Mapping Can Do For You,* which states, "A road map indicates the way to a planned destination; a treasure map helps us get what we desire—healing, supply, job, possessions, happiness. Physically, it is a piece of paper on which we have placed pictures of what we want with statements of faith that God wants us to have in our life now. It may be a large wall map or a small one tucked into a book."

"Any idea seriously entertained tends to bring about the realization of itself."
...Joseph Chilton Pearce

I always suggested to my students to collect pictures of the trip or cruise they would love to experience, or the new car they would love to purchase. I even proposed going to an actual car dealership and obtaining a full-color brochure of their heart's desire in order to attract a precise vibrational match. It is even more wondrous to test drive the car to get the "feel" of it emotionally and to take a whiff of the scent of new interior. Be enchanted with your creations by bringing all of your senses into play.

In dreamwork, a car often represents your physical body, so ideally, selecting the color, model and price range would make it vivid and real emotionally. If they were seeking a special relationship, then I would ask them to describe in detail what qualities they would seek in their beloved. Often they were seeking "the perfect partner." I would suggest they reconsider languaging it as "my ideal partner" with the desired characteristics pictured and outlined. The Universe takes your intentions very literally so specificity is essential.

We would have a fun and exuberant time in creating our special treasure maps by all sitting on the floor, cutting out pictures and sharing magazines, scissors, glue pots, and colorful markers. A wonderful camaraderie and synergy developed as we talked and inspired one another. Music is an important component in any of my classes so it would be playing energetically in the background or we'd be singing and humming along.

Devoting a three-hour class segment was playful and creative. At the end of the class, we would share our treasure maps (show and tell) and I would play a clip from Reverend Ike's tape on "**Feelings,**" which had everyone all charged up and laughing. It was such a wondrous, uplifting mirror of energy for a vibrational match to our Treasure Maps. We were jazzed! We were telling the Universe we were ready to receive our highest good. When you have a visual outpicturing of your highest outcomes, it is a powerful tool to magnetize your heart's desires. It was our joyous vision and creation at its best with everyone vibrating to the max. This energy was flowing with delicious, fresh, new vibrational signals and intents.

Stand and Deliver

"For God's sake, choose a self and stand by it!"

...Psychologist William James

First, you decide what your focus is and that will be your central inspiration. Collect materials for a week or two and put them in a special folder as you gather them. Let your imagination soar in selecting the colors, sizes and materials. You will also want to date your Treasure Map. When you get ready to mount your materials on poster board, consider placing your personal photograph in the center of the map. Then arrange what you have collected as a magnetic outpicturing of what lights you up. Be colorful and vivid with your markers and pens. Be bold!! You can also add your written affirmations and prayers. Appreciation is always a key component so you could start with: "I give thanks for ____(be specific)____ easily, effortlessly (and quickly or affordably if that is a consideration). Or you can use spiritual quotes which are personally meaningful to you.

**"'Que Sera Sera' is a lovely song,
but a lousy philosophy.
Nothing worthwhile was ever
accomplished by anybody
who met life with a shrug.
Instead, your motto should be:
'Que quiero sera'—whatever I will, will be!"**

...Edwin C. Bliss

There is POWER in the written and spoken word. Specificity is important in conscious languaging and imagining your highest choices. These are your dreams and outcomes being fulfilled. It can be anything from personal possessions like a new computer with all the bells and whistles, a magnificent home on dream property, beautiful furnishings, wondrous cars, more money in your bank accounts for abundance, stock portfolios, educational goals. You can include positive, stimulating relationships with your parents, children or family, as well as great co-workers and loving, yummy friends.

Name It and Claim It!

You can envision exciting promotions, a career doing what you love to do, or owning prosperous businesses. You can picture attracting your beloved and the qualities your heart desires, or your current divine partner as one who adores and appreciates you. Your map can mirror your heart's desires for radiant health (or healing if you have a concern), unexpected lavish income (like inheritances, lotto, contests, benefactors), freedom, wealth or visualizing specific personal successes (name and claim them.)

Your map may involve your spiritual growth or workshops of that nature that includes books, tapes, CD's, etc. to enhance your unfoldment. If you choose to attune more clearly and easily with your Inner Being, holy pictures may be appropriate, or photos of celestial beings like angels. You may choose to attract more passion, love, joy, freedom, peace, harmony, inspiration or plenty of time with your family and friends who are kindred spirits that adore you. Your map could include body concerns like dropping weight or being your ideal size, which may involve new forms of exercising or fun sports activities being pictured. You can plan your heart's desires for vacations, cruises or travel adventures.

You can create your treasure map on separate poster boards by subject. You can also create sections on one large poster board so your outpicturing has specific designated segments. These might include home, career, relationships, and personal growth with joyous expansion. Name and claim your heart's desires. You are learning how to flow energy in any arena you desire which is the whole purpose of this process—to be a conscious Deliberate Creator. For instance, if you are choosing prosperity, put a $100 bill in the center of your abundance area (or take a photo of any denomination which makes you feel wealthy). Carrying a crisp $100 in your wallet (without spending it) is indeed a vibrational attraction, as you automatically feel delight in "green energy" and financial freedom every time you see it. An earlier chapter emphasized the importance of having an attitude of gratitude. For example, in your relationship to money and wealth, you want to be vibrating with the Law of Increase. Play with it and enjoy what money represents as an energy flow to acquire your heart's desires.

"How was Einstein able to conceive the Theory of Relativity? He said the one crucial thing that helped him was his ABILITY TO VISUALIZE... what would it be like to be riding on the end of a light beam?"

...Anthony Robbins

Read books that expand and inspire you and coincide and align with your Treasure Mapping. *Think and Grow Rich* by Napoleon Hill is a classic and a legend in its own right. Our son attended a seminar entitled, *The Science of Getting Rich*, which is also a book that is materially and spiritually based. There are many wonderful personal growth resources available now. I find the Abraham-Hicks materials to be very clear resources of inspiration. Abraham tapes, books, videos and events are uplifting, as well as practical, joyous and easy to integrate. These delicious Abraham teachings are available through Esther and Jerry Hicks, who beautifully facilitate and co-create the *Science of Deliberate Creation.*

Treasure Mapping for Others

If there are areas of concern with family or friends, remember they have free will. You can always say "I give thanks for _____ (whatever your prayer or affirmation is for them or in your mutual relationship). Your treasure map creates the loving space for them to be receptive. Focus on your highest choices and ignore current reality! Trying to change or control anyone is other than productive. This treasure map is your loving "pictured prayers" for the highest good for everyone involved.

Intentions—Door #2
Reality is a Result of Your Design!

After moving to Arizona in 1989, I became aware of Barbara Marciniak workshops. The message on one tape from *Bold Connections* is: "Have a good time and change the paradigm and INTEND WHAT YOU DESIRE, while going beyond any current limitations. State your desires with clarity and then watch your manifestations magically appear. Have fun with a big purpose, get excited and find the miracles. As you call to yourself what you want, you will get it. The best kept secret in this Universe is you create your reality! Trust! It is not going to happen unless you call for it. Each of you must get more feisty with reality. REALITY IS A RESULT OF YOUR DESIGN. Effortlessly intend that it come about. You are a result of your thoughts. 'Trying' is not doing! State: 'I am intending, I am doing, I am creating, I am manifesting'—not I am trying! I INTEND IS THE TOOL FROM WHICH YOU CREATE YOUR REALITY! Get clear on what you want. You create whatever it is you focus upon. You are creating what you desire and what you fear quicker and quicker."

Intentions are a wonderful and powerful tool in your consciousness tool kit. It accelerates your abilities to create your reality faster and more joyfully. When we were doing a large workshop in Rio Verde, Arizona sometime ago, we shared our experiences and then focused on how to create specific intentions. One woman, who is a good friend, called excitedly the next day after the class. She had a piece of land which had been on the market for several years without any success. Within two days, she had two offers from two separate buyers after we assisted in fine-tuning her intention with specificity and clarity. Fine-tuning with specificity results in greater effectiveness.

"I may not be perfect, but parts of me are excellent."

…Ashley Brilliant

Another man's intention was to attract the "perfect relationship." He called after the workshop to tell us how excited he was regarding his intent and I invited him to re-consider by creating and attracting the "ideal partner." He laughed and understood the reasoning right away when I asked him if he was perfect. Within 24 hours, he had someone new come into his life based on his intention and attracted his reality easily and effortlessly. Again, the Universe is ready when you are! Spirit will bring it in a variety of unexpected ways with infinite possibilities so allow and receive and give thanks it is already here. Don't tell the Universe **how** to do it—all you have to do is identify why you want it and be specific what your heart's desire is and how it feels. Then bypass your current "beliefs" or "reality" and CONSIDER IT DONE! The world is awash in angels, both visible and invisible, who deliver wishes granted. When you call Pizza Hut for a pizza delivery, you don't expect a fish dinner to show up. So, "stand and deliver" your heart's desires and flow your energy creatively and positively! Visualize! Let your inspired thoughts and feelings vibrate and pulsate, as you confidently relax into knowing your dreams are fulfilled.

My husband and I were considering moving from the adult community we had lived in for five years to relocate here in Fountain Hills. We set our intentions for the ideal piece of property with all of our heart's desires for beautiful mountain views, being able to see sunrises and sunsets, affordable land cost, ideal location, and then gave thanks it was already here. We also say "Thy will be done" for often there is a higher Law Of Attraction operating that may be even more divine than we envisioned in our heart's desires. Several times we had something close and yet not fully 100% in alignment.

One day we looked at another land parcel and declined it. Later in the day, as I was leaving Scottsdale, I asked for guidance from my angels and said, "I know the ideal parcel is available for us in Fountain Hills. Please take my steering wheel and guide me to the land now. Thank you for my answered prayer!" When I arrived in Fountain Hills, I was impulsed to turn on a street I had not taken before because of the high land costs around the golf course. I saw a sign that said "auction" and I was so elated as I intuitively felt this would be our divine appointment.

The views were gorgeous and surpassed anything we had previously seen. I had "God bumps" from head to toe, even though it was on a steep hillside which is considerably more expensive for excavation costs. The beauty of the mountains, the lush golf course several hundred feet below, and the 600' tall fountain in the distance were so inspiring that I felt I was in heaven. It also encompassed unlimited views for both sunrises and sunsets. Ideally, "all the way to heaven is heaven." We are creating our reality moment to moment through our thoughts and vibrational offerings!

I called the agent listed who said the auction had already been held recently, but the land had not sold due to the seller's "reserve" bid. My husband was concerned with the degree of the steep hillside slope so we hired a local engineer, who was knowledgeable about any potential difficulty with hillsides and their inherently higher construction costs. Based on his expertise, we made an offer on the land. The realtor asked us to deal directly with the buyer and he cut his commission substantially. We purchased our dream land with a magical outcome! Three years later, the vacant parcel next to us sold for two and one-half times more than what we paid. The home next to that land just sold for $1.1 million. Naturally, we were ecstatic! This is divine order and co-creation at its best and we are thrilled with our outcome! It was even better than we had imagined!

Your Magical Creation Box—Door #3

Your Desires Must be Given to You!

In a taped forum in 1995, which is now online on the newly-created Abraham-Hicks web site [www.abraham-hicks.com], the Magical Creation

Box is discussed at length. For us, this is an easy and delicious process. The following italicized parts are extrapolated and shared from the Abraham dialogue regarding the Creation Box:

If you are wondering what you are vibrating, observe your life. It's a perfect match. What you are living is what you are vibrating, without exception. So, if you have something you don't like, you must identify what it is within your vibration that is giving it to you. And the thing we most want you to hear is what that is, every time or nearly so, is that your power of observation is simply stronger than your power of visualization. The Law of Attraction is powerful, friends, and whatever you are vibrating, the Universe will match.

Some of you have been listening to us for awhile, and you listen to our never-ending stream of processes. We always have another great idea for you to apply, and the reason we are offering these processes is because we desire to assist you in finding ways that cause you to vibrate more in harmony with your own desire. That's all.

**All you have to do is get into vibrational harmony
with your desire, and your desire must be given to you...
and the Universe will find endless ways of bringing it to you.**

Imagine you are sitting in a chair, and next to your chair is a good-sized box and you accept that this box is your creative arena. It's your point of attraction. Now, you are like a giant sitting here in this chair and you have the ability to reach out anywhere in the Universe and anything you see that you like, you can just pluck it and bring it back to your Box. And as you do so, it will vibrate here and then the Universe will match it with a physical equivalent.

In the beginning, Esther played this game mentally only by just imagining. And, it then became so much fun, she actually got a box and started tearing things out of magazines and dropping them in. Doodlings. Esther does not draw very well although she is an effective doodler. She would doodle on little note cards and drop them in the Box or put snapshots in. And, what she began to notice, right from the first day, is that whatever was in the Box, the Universe began to respond to.

*We are going to give you a new game—we call it the **Creation Box Process**. It will serve you in two very powerful ways. One, it causes you to be a better visualizer. It causes you to use your power of observation more constructively and*

182

be a better visualizer. And the other thing it does is help you be aware of how many things you're bringing to your box that you really don't mean to bring here.

A few weeks ago [this was recorded as live audio tape in 1995], as Jerry and Esther were leaving New York, Esther was mentally playing with her Box as she was packing the night before their flight. Esther was imagining a bright beautiful sky so that when they lifted from LaGuardia Airport, she could see the Empire State Building and the Statue of Liberty and all the landmarks she loves to see from the air. She imagined her playful, happy mate sitting next to her and a delicious meal served to them in the first-class cabin. She imagined happy flight attendants and a smooth comfortable flight. And then Esther thought, "I hope that the United Nations meeting that is coming to an end today does not have the security so increased at the airport that it makes it hard for us to get around and make us late for our flight or makes our flight late for us." And then Esther laughed and said, "Now, that's a silly thing for me to bring to my Box"...because she is beginning to recognize that whatever she focuses upon, she vibrates.

Now, we want you to hear about this Box and about your point of attraction. We would like for you to think of them as one and the same thing. What this Creation Box process will do for you is cause you to purify your vibration. Now, what do we mean by that "purify your vibration?" Well, think about it. Law Of Attraction is responding to your vibration. So, if you are thinking "I would like to have lots of dollars," you are vibrating in that desire and the Universe is responding to that desire. But, when you say, "I don't have any dollars," that's in the Creation Box too. So, your vibration in the Box is not pure. You are offering a contradictory vibration. And, the Law of Attraction, which always responds to everything, is responding to both of those vibrations. It is responding to 'more' money and to 'no' money, and that leaves you standing pretty much where you were.

Start purifying your vibration
so that you are consistently visualizing.

*Now, friends, the thing that you have to do, even though it's hard and you don't want to, you have to **STOP FACING REALITY** (you always hear laughter in the background on the tape when Abraham tells the audience this). In other words, you have to begin to say, "It doesn't matter 'what is,' I'm working on my Creation Box."*

Have you ever awakened from a dream that is so magnificent that when you woke up you were disappointed to be awake and you would like to go back to sleep and dream that dream some more? That's the way we want you to feel about the Creation Box. A place where you go for fun, a place that soothes you, a place that you go often, a place that you go with the singular intent of purifying your vibration. As you begin to play in your Creation Box, you will be excited by the speed and efficiency with which the Universe responds to your purer vibration in the Box.

One of the first things Esther actually put in her Creation Box was when she was looking through a magazine and she found a picture of a beautiful oriental rug, which was a magnificent color and design. So, Esther tore it out of the magazine and dropped it into her [Creation] Box. About three days later, a postcard came in the mail from a furniture store in San Antonio announcing the opening of a rug gallery in their store, and they had a picture of an oriental rug on the postcard. It was the identical rug Esther had torn out of the magazine a few days earlier. She was just about as excited as if she had come home and found the rug on her floor, because it was evidence to her that the Universe was responding to her vibration.

One day she was sitting at her desk, opening some mail, and there was a solicitation from the Spurs Foundation—Spurs is the basketball team in San Antonio. Jerry and Esther do not attend sporting events and probably will never go to a Spurs game, but as Esther was holding this advertisement for tickets, she was fantasizing for about fifteen seconds, "Wouldn't it be fun to get some tickets for Tracy (Esther's daughter) and her boyfriend." They often go to Spurs games. And Esther imagined their delight at receiving the tickets, and then Esther thought, "Well, I'm really not ready to order these tickets because I don't know when David works," but she did drop the brochure in her Creation Box just the same. Two hours later, Jerry and Esther were in the grocery store in San Antonio, and as they were in the check-out line, a woman who Esther had not ever seen before, turned to her and said: "You know, I have two extra tickets for tonight's Spurs game. If you know of anyone who would like them, I would be happy to give them to you." Esther nearly fell over with the speed with which this manifestation occurred. She took them joyously.

**Your vibration doesn't have to be strong,
it just has to be pure.
You don't have to think about
something over and over again.
You just have to think about it PURELY.
You have to other than contradict it
with your own vibration.**

Now, the reason that the Universe delivered a nearly instant manifestation on those Spurs tickets is because Esther's vibration is pure about Spurs tickets. She has never before thought about Spurs tickets so she didn't wake up thinking, "Where will I get Spurs tickets?" She didn't go to bed at night thinking "Not enough Spurs tickets." When she was a little girl her Mother didn't say, "There will never be enough Spurs tickets...you have to accept that lot in life as being Spur ticketless." None of that. Her vibration was pure, since this was the first time she ever thought about it. And since she thought about it in the context of the vibration, CREATION BOX, which had already been working for her, her vibration was pure.

And, on and on it goes. One night Esther was sitting tearing pictures out of magazines and dropping them in her Creation Box. One of those pages was a picture of a wall, with many pictures upon the wall and what that represented to Esther was the desire to gather some nice pieces for the walls of their new home. They don't have many walls, mostly windows. And she couldn't really see what the pictures were. It just represented the desire to attract more of that. Another thing in that same sitting was she tore a cover off of a jewelry magazine which represented her desire to attract some nice neck pieces. And she dropped them in the Creation Box. About three days later, they went to Albuquerque, and two people came with gifts. One brought a magnificent print of a tempura painting that she had done. When Esther saw it, she squealed with delight. She said, "If I had seen this in a gallery, I certainly would have purchased it." Another brought a necklace from Santa Fe with a piece of turquoise in it. Esther said "This Box is dangerous!" [Meaning how quickly you actually create your reality.] A few days later came another magnificent metal sculpture for the wall.

**When you are in vibrational
harmony with your own desire,
the Universe will find endless ways
of cooperative, joyous beings
to co-create with you
in your creating.**

Whatever you are focused upon, be it real or imagined, whatever you are focused upon causes you to vibrate—and your vibration is what the Universe accepts as your point of attraction. So, if you are predominantly observing "what is" and therefore having a vibrational response, that is your personal point of attraction and the Universe cannot deliver to you anything other than that.

**The Universe does not know or care
why you are vibrating as you are vibrating.
It only responds to your vibration!**

Work on achieving vibrational harmony with your desires, because when you are in harmony with your desires, the Universe will deliver to you that which you are choosing.

We want so much for you to come to recognize that you are Deliberate Creators, and as Deliberate Creators, your work is to use the power of observation and visualization, and to use the magnificent contrast to catapult you into stronger, clearer, purer vision. And when you are envisioning purely, the Universe magnificently manifests to you. No more justification. No more proving worthiness. Just simple, pure vibration with the Universe answering your every desire as you live happily ever after. We are complete. [End of article on web site.]

After reading this stimulating material, my husband and I discussed what to use as our Creation Box. In fact, Duaine even referred to it as Treasure Chest. That keyed me into remembering I had bought several of the currently-popular decorated boxes with handles on them. I exclaimed, "I have one with ANGELS decorated on it that would be perfect for our Creation Box!" It is approximately 6" high x 12" across and was ideal for our purposes. I also had a smaller matching box that was 7" x 7" where I put all of my creation supplies (which are discussed later in this chapter).

The following is our formula for our Creation Box, which we played with and personalized from Abraham's "recipe." You can make up your own to put on the outside top of your box or inside the lid so that it is personalized for magnetizing your heart's desires. We also place our photographs and other inspirations, special stones, flowers, colorful and pretty papers with specific intentions, etc.

> ## OUR CREATION BOX EQUALS =
> ## OUR POINT OF ATTRACTION!
> ### What we are placing into this Creation Box
> ## VIBRATES AND RESONATES
> ### all through the Universe and the Universe matches it with yummy physical equivalents now and continuously.
> ### Thank you! Thank you! Thank you!

We dated and signed the above "alignment" statement as Deliberate Creators. Periodically, we go through and clean out our Creation Box. We then do a new alliance by dating and signing it for a FRESH START in magnetizing our divine, deliberate creations.

We have shared the Creation Box formula with our family and friends. It is wondrous fun to co-create and celebrate together. My dad, Don Curtis, who lives in Kalamazoo, Michigan, is now 85 years of age. He became very ill and was hospitalized in 1998. It was a discouraging and scary prognosis after having had good health for many years. I sent him a Sony Walkman and began sharing the tools of deliberate creation, as well as my book material. It has made a huge difference in his well being and even his doctor told him recently, that whatever he is doing to keep it up. This is the first time my dad has participated in anything like this. It is amazing grace to see his improvement, physically, emotionally and spiritually. The expression, "You can't teach old dogs new tricks" is not necessarily true. My dad's not an "old dog," but he sure has learned new "tricks" in becoming more of a Deliberate Creator. We are now "birds of a feather flocking together!"

Powerful, Portable, Pulsating Tools
Delegating Your Desires Daily

Abraham said, "If you want to change what you are living, you have only to change the balance of your thought." I have an Abraham daily calendar, which has enriching "quotes" on one side. The reverse page is appointment times on one-half of the page; the other half is where you assign your desires to the Universe to work on in your behalf. The inspirations are nourishing and are a daily connection to consciously remember your Stream of Well Being. Oprah expresses this vibration so well in the "Remembering Your Spirit" segment of her show.

Often when we make lists, we feel in "whelm" because we realize we don't have enough time to accomplish everything on the list. So, our desires carry one creative, pure, positive vibration, while our belief (current reality) carries another vibration of not enough time or money so it doesn't get done. By delegating to the Universe, you develop vibrational harmony between your desires and beliefs. It then becomes a positive habit to change the balance of your thoughts.

Abraham says, "When you delegate to the Universe some of the things you want, you leave out your habit of thought that opposes. When you assign to the Universe something like, 'Universe, please orchestrate a happy outcome to such and such a situation,' you do not include your feelings of not knowing how to orchestrate it. This helps you offer a vibration that is purer and more in vibrational harmony with your own desires. It is exciting and stimulating to find tools which are literally like lightning rods in launching your rocket of desires. My Dad is so cute as he tells people about me by saying, "My daughter either has been in it, is in it or will be in it." I totally acknowledge that I am on an accelerated, adventuresome, joyous, tapped in, tuned in, turned on glorious path of evolution! It is delightful to have instant, simple, quick upgrades in following your bliss more easily and effortlessly.

"The Universe loves symbolic gestures."
…Louise Hay

I keep one set of magnets in my Creation Box so they are easily available. They also symbolically magnetize and vibrate with our creations constantly by letting the Universe orchestrate the details.

In anything you choose to create, whether you decide to develop a Treasure Map, write out your intentions, or produce your own Creation Box, know that these energies are catalysts for connection. You are seeding and magnetizing your heart's desires. Passionately summon and call forth your creations with inspiration and specificity. Your decision to breathe life into your project brings forth new visions of clarity. Remember, when you ask, it is given! When you allow, you receive! Your dominant intention must be to FEEL GOOD.

Your Creation Book
New Doorways and Horizons

After integrating and using the above-mentioned tools, I designed my own original, individualized approach through a ledger which I call MY CREATION BOOK. It is such an easy, fun and joyous expression for me to create in! You can purchase a "ledger" or an affordable large scrapbook at a multi-purpose store. If your Creation Book is a solid color, decorate it with inviting images that inspire you. You can also laminate an image for the cover to personalize and energize it. You can also mount an enlarged photo of you on the cover to personalize your creation vibration.

Your Creation Toy Box

I suggest you purchase a decorative, small box (creatively decorated, of course) to keep your supplies in so it's all at your fingertips. You will need the following:

♥ Scissors (Deckle scissors are also fun to have, which are available in various designs)*

*2003 Note: The scrapbook industry has become a multi-billion dollar industry since writing this book in 1999. The market place now has thousands of fun tools and fabulous items for creating your heart's desires visually

- ♥ Colored pens and markers and highlighters—assorted sizes and colors

- ♥ Glue stick

- ♥ Paper clips (clipped to your magnets)

- ♥ Scotch tape

- ♥ White-out pen or correction fluid

- ♥ Pretty papers

- ♥ Stickers of your choice to decorate with—like hearts, flowers, angels, money, musical notes, shooting stars, and now they even have stickers with your personal name in glitzy letters.

- ♥ Photos of you "radiating" joy and feeling "shiny" and "heaven happy."

- ♥ Miniatures of anything you'd love: car, baby, graduation, computer, etc.

- ♥ Jewels (found in small packages at craft stores—great decorations)

By purchasing special papers to write your creation statements upon, I find it adds energy and impact. You can find affordable packages of 100 sheets at most office supply stores and more expensive individual sheets at some arts and craft stores. Cut them into any size and shape you'd like or do your scripting on them.

Visual Creations Attract Good "Vibrations"

I collect and save special or pretty greeting cards, Christmas cards, personal photos, and magazine pictures, and fun glow and glitter stickers. I keep them in a pocket folder so I can easily pick out whatever inspires my creativity for doing mini-collages effortlessly and quickly. These can be used for any single aspiration or for multiple heart's desires that strike your fancy anytime. In other words, they are for passions you are excited to magnetize. Create whatever has heart and meaning for you. If I have had an especially potent dream, I depict the essence of it in a collage and title it as if it were my movie for that night. This truly enhances and energizes it in a memorable way.

For instance, if you would like to swim with the dolphins, get photos, brochures or images of them and make a collage of where, with whom, when and how excited you feel in being with dolphins. Imagine it being your outcome fulfilled and describe it as if it has already happened. Your collage then becomes your intent and vibrational match for your heart's desire. If there is a particular piece of land or a beautiful home you adore, then explore it, take photographs, visualize joyful possibilities and develop them. Have a friend take photos of you in front of the land or home you desire so you are literally "in the picture" on all levels! Office supply stores carry large poster boards in a variety of beautiful superimposed photo images of clouds, flowers, ocean life with dolphins, parchment scrolls, etc. They are energetic, magnetic attractions.

Our grandchildren love to draw on these colorful image posters and embellish them with their heart's desires. My granddaughter, Chelsea, who was eight years old in 1999, wanted to swim with the dolphins. She used dolphin stationary and wrote her heart's desires and then put a real shell from the ocean on that page of her Creation Book. She also cut up a photo calendar with these images for her Creation Book. The wished was granted for both my grandchildren in 2002 when we went to Sea World. They both participated in the Dolphin Interaction Program and had the best time! My grandson, Skye, who was 11 at the time, wanted his own treehouse. He drew it out on a poster and then also entered a contest on why he wanted a treehouse where he said, "I am a Tree Musketeer," (he named it and claimed it). He then kept one color copy of his heart's desire in his Creation Book and put one in his Creation Box. In 1996, Robin Mullin showed me how to create an "intuitive" collage on poster board on my birthday, which was very meaningful.

My Creation Book is an energetic pictorial record of my life and my dreams from day to day and week to week. It could also be from month to month—whatever is easy and fun timewise. My Creation Book is the bigger picture that encircles my life with my family and friends. It is an infinite mirror of following my bliss on the wheel of time through the Law of Attraction in Action. I focus my deliberate creations on my body and health, my relationships with my self (including dreams), my friends and family, my home, my career, my work and play, my abundance, and my spiritual growth and evolution. Include your wildest dreams of anything you choose to magnetize.

Being Your Colorful Self
In Your Creation Book

One day I cut out a wondrous magazine picture of an avant garde woman. Around that image I defined all the qualities of my WONDER WOMAN aspirations. I claimed them vibrationally as I journaled. It is such a an energetic and delightful experience to create, envision and magnetize your heart's desire.

All of the things you consider for a Treasure Map can come into play in the Creation Book. The only difference is you are doing it in page-by-page segments whenever you choose to. I like this format immensely because it is an organized pictorial collection I can leaf through at any time. This is your life! It provides a colorful, magnetic timeframe for your life attractions and creations. Date the pages and also go back and insert post-it notes of gratitude to update when your outcomes manifest and evidence abounds. Journal how you feel and go on a rampage of appreciation! These are your living, breathing, vibrating creations being outpictured through the Law of Attraction in Action. Congratulate yourself for your commitment and willingness to be a Deliberate Creator and go for the gusto. Your Creation Book will provide such warm, special memories of your dreams and heart's desires being fulfilled.

I Choose the Colors!

LaUna Huffines in her book, *Connecting*, said that what amazed her most after years of helping clients was how little most people ask for. I have found that to be true also, as most people don't take the time to ask and receive.

There is a wondrous story about a handicapped man with a club foot who had a difficult time getting around. Yet this man had an amazingly successful life and had done extremely well. While being interviewed for a newspaper article, the reporter commented that being handicapped must have been very difficult for him, and how it must have colored his whole life. He replied, **"Yes, but I choose the colors!"** In other words, you can choose the circumstances and the quality of your life in any given moment through the power of choice and attitude.

You are the Imagineer

Again, I invite you to be specific and imaginative in your Creation Book. Ask the Universe for your heart's desires. In my thoughts and prayers, I always ask for this creation or something "better," which is another way of allowing the Universe to bring something even "higher" and more delicious than you could have imagined. Specificity is so important because if you simply say "I want to be rich" or "I want to find a mate" or "I want to be happy" it is too vague.

Get out your magnets and imagine and have clear, precise feelings about what being rich means to you—how rich and what does it include? A new home (define your new home in great detail, where is it, what did it cost, what does it look like both inside and out, who lives in it with you, what kind of furnishings, style, landscaping, colors, etc), or, if you desire a new car (what model, color, cost, year, etc.), a new relationship (with whom and what qualities do you choose your beloved to have—list all of them very clearly that are important and dear to you). These days many people have children from a previous marriage so be specific about whether you could embrace having a "ready-made" family which would include current children. Also, if you desire to have children, you would seek a beloved who adores children and wanted to have them.

Many times people will say, "I want to make more money." First of all, the only people who "make" money work at the U.S. Mint. Second, how much more income do you realistically desire to have now (remember the bridge span discussed in an earlier chapter). It is easier to attract more money and wealth if you know what you will do with it. What will you spend it on? Who will you spend it on? How does it make you feel? If you concentrated on only one single important element of your life right now, what would you choose? Be specific and fine tune your focus!

"What you love is a sign from your higher self of what you are to do."

...Sanaya Roman

Place your images and visualization in your Creation Book or Creation Box. The more specificity, the easier to magnetize. If you are too vague you will get vague results and little outcome or evidence. If you focus on too many things initially, your energy can be scattered like buckshot. Instead, pick one or two things that excite, delight, ignite you into inspired visualizations and creations. You carry a personal signature vibration, which is your signal for attraction and connection in the same way. You recall the story earlier of Carolyn and Cork at a company party when someone asked another colleague if they were wealthy. Your friends and colleagues carry an image of you, just as you have an image of yourself. Are you feeling wealthy and abundant or are you carrying an image that comes from lack, can't afford, not enough or struggle. Have you noticed how most people love to be around and are attracted to those who are genuine, joyous, fun and loving? Those are magnetic qualities that attract just like bees to honey. Become the person and life vibration you want to attract and you will be living on purpose easily as you follow your heart. Dr. David Viscott told the story years ago of a famous producer who was asked the secret of his success and he responded, "Stay away from losers!"

Shine and sing and do your thing as you deliciously explore and expand your Stream of Well Being. Follow your bliss and your heart's sweet, succulent, pulsating passions.

Rituals are the Law of Attraction in Action That Create and Magnetize Your Dreams Fulfilled Now!

Any of these rituals can be your personal Law of Attraction in Action that creates and magnetizes your wishes granted now! You become what you imagine! You are the wings beneath your delicious, divine dreams! You're gonna soar and have a "roarin" good time with new glorious visions and delicious decisions!

194

"We connect to something larger than ourselves when we perform a ritual. Think of it as a Spirit Fax.

…Carolyn Casey

Do It Now!

14

Mind Mapping/Focus Wheels

"...For where your treasure is, there will your heart be also."

…Matthew 6:21

Many years ago I was intrigued in reading, *SUPER LEARNING, Have A Supermemory*, by Sheila Ostrander and Lynn Schroeder. It introduced a revolutionary new system that let you master facts, figures and skills two to ten times faster than you ever thought possible. As they stated, "We've cracked the cocoon—we can start shaking out our wings; it's time to claim our birthright. We can be so much more than we are."

All of us recall inspiring teachers who made a difference in our lives. Unfortunately, they were few and far between. I recall Ms. Meyers in first grade who was kind and gentle. Mr. Andrews at Milwood Jr. High was fun and inspiring to the point where we felt comfortable occasionally visiting his home because he was "always there" for us. His wife was an educator also and warmly welcomed us. They were wonderful mirrors of doing what you love to do. Then there were Mr. Wallace and Ms. Sternberg, my favorite teachers in high school because they genuinely cared and went the extra mile. They were shining, caring professionals who loved what they were doing and were authentically interested in their students.

I was once given a plaque that read, "To teach is to touch a life forever." It has meant so much to me through the years. When I taught in mental health, the students gave me a gift of an exquisite Butterfly Crystal by Swarovski, which is so special and represents our potential. I believe we are here to evolve and go higher in becoming more of what we are. I love this old French poem by Appollinaire.

"Come to the edge," the teacher said.
The students said, "We can't. We are afraid."
"Come to the edge,"
"We can't! We will fall!"
"Come to the edge."
They came. He pushed them and they flew!

So often there are grand potentials waiting to be explored…just beyond our reach, if only we had eyes to see and the courage to "fly." Mind Mapping, Treasure Mapping, Focus Wheels, Creation Boxes and Creation Books are all wonderful tools to support you in your process of magnetizing your heart's desires. They are the wind beneath your wings. You can also magnetize kindred spirits and teachers as you stretch to new possibilities who assist you in soaring to new heights.

In 1985, I attended a *New Dimensions In Learning* conference (a.k.a. superlearning) being held in Chicago with Charles Schmid. He said, "We're not really teaching anyone anything…we're unlocking what's already there, helping people get in touch with the enormous potential they already have, enabling them to regain that whole-brain balance they all had as imaginative children."

It was here I was first introduced to the power of hands-on mind-mapping skills and inherent artistic abilities from a holistic viewpoint. Most people are aware that the left brain is our verbal, rational, logical, mathematical, scientific and analytical hemisphere. Our right brain is just the opposite of the left because it is "non-logical" and "non-rational" whereby we know through the qualities of our intuition and creativity. It's where our artistic abilities, the sensual, non-verbal, and psychic impressions reside, as well as music, metaphors, and symbols, such as in our dreams. It's also where love and feelings originate and our imagination is evoked.

Using the right hemisphere is when you feel like trusting your gut and following your heart in spite of what current reality seems to be in that moment. The right brain has often been neglected because we have starved this faculty in most educational and business approaches. Some corporations are now realizing the value of meditation, exercise, relaxation, power naps, and brainstorming sessions, such as mind-mapping. What happens when you engage the whole brain is, as Ostrander and

Schroeder point out, "the difference between learning and super-learning." They also report learning foreign languages in often less than half the time previously necessary.

There was a quantum leap for me that weekend in my artistic abilities, which usually made me break out in a cold sweat whenever the subject of art was approached. I felt I had little talent with drawing (and I had "evidence" to support that conclusion). I was very pleasantly amazed at what came forth. The example provided is like thinking of an orchestra with brass, percussion and strings. When the horns are featured, the drums and violins don't try to pound against them; they play in concert. Usually in our efforts to learn, we've separated ourselves into pieces. Superlearning works to put Humpty Dumpty back together again, so he can see what he can become. There are many books and tapes available on mind-mapping which go into much greater detail if you choose to explore it further.

An important component of superlearning is music being played in the background. Baroque music has been found to be the most effective in superlearning. We play Tom Kenyon's *Acoustic Brain Research* audiotapes, which are excellent and lifechanging. Tom is a psycho-therapist, musician and researcher who spent many years studying the effects of sound, music and language. He is also the author of the acclaimed book, *Brain States*, which discusses how the mind works and notes the distinction between brain and mind. Our Bali trip together was lifechanging in 1997.

Focus Wheels

Setting The Tone— Upgrading Your Vibrations

Abraham shares what he calls a Focus Wheel, which is a similar concept to Mind Mapping. For instance, right now you might have a health issue which is something you other than desire to have. It might be an injured knee. Your knee injury is a challenge and so you would desire to change and upgrade your vibration because obviously somewhere there is a certain limiting belief and contrast is being shown to you through your knee. You will remember Abraham's definition of a belief is: "only a thought you keep thinking." So how do you keep focused on thoughts which are a match to your outcome, in this case getting your knee healed and healthy? Most people have a habitual pattern which becomes a rut in thinking and turns into a self-fulfilling prophecy because they have evidence through their pain rather than focusing on health and well being.

The way the Focus Wheel process works, as described by Abraham on an audio tape in 1997, is by drawing a circle in the middle of a page. Instead, I draw a large HEART, as it energetically mirrors my heart's desires. The reason you do a focus wheel is to have the Law of Attraction in Action. With magnetic attraction, you know how powerfully the magnets instantly attract or repel either positively or negatively. Your thoughts are equally as powerful in doing your Focus Wheel. So, you begin to write brief, general statements to set the tone of offering a pure vibration which is specific to your intent.

Abraham says if you start with, "I know I will heal my knee," you can tell the energy isn't lined up because you have the contrast in this moment that your knee isn't yet healed. Instead, start by writing something like, "I know that my physical body responds to my thoughts." We know that is true. Then, feel around for something even softer like, "For the most part, my body is doing alright" and will probably feel pretty good to you. Then, the next line radiating out from the [heart] center of your focus wheel might be, "I believe the Universe matches my vibration." That one will stick since you already know how your magnets attract or repel. The next statement could be, "My physical body has been very good to me." If you believe that, you are beginning to feel a sense of relief and your vibration is now more of a match and lifting.

When Shift Happens, Relief Happens!

Abraham says, "You will know whenever you've found a vibrational match because you feel **RELIEF**." In other words, the statement soothes you and feels better. Let it be general, comforting statements:

"I like the idea of being a Deliberate Creator."
"I like having desires and the Universe responding to them."
"I appreciate my physical body."
"I love how well my body has served me and continues to serve me."

"I'm excited at being able to deliberately focus and feel my body respond."

"I am coming to understand anything can be altered or changed, it simply requires my focus."

"I appreciate the clarity I have in desiring my vibrant health."

"Even this experience with my knee has clarified my desire for well-being."

"Even while my 'knee issue' has been 'inconvenient', it is clarifying."

"This is a good experience to set me on a strong path in my physical experience."

"I can now appreciate this experience of contrast."

As Abraham points out, in the beginning, some of these statements would have seemed absurd and even untrue initially.

Claiming Your Stance, Creates a New Vibrational Tone and Dance

As you continue to be uplifted, you would write, "My knee is well" and "My knee is healed" because you are now vibrating in a pure place relative to this subject because you have achieved a whole new vibrational stance. Your point of attraction is now substantially different than when you began the Focus Wheel. Once you have claimed your new stance in the Universe, you've set your own tone. You have staked a new claim of THIS IS WHO I AM and you will feel a vibrational difference. You arrive at a whole new space and relationship with your body and specifically with your knee.

"If you do not rest yourself, the Universe will rest you...The STOP NOW PLAN..."
…Alan Cohen

When we were really considering whether we would stay in the Midwest, it was because our families lived there—both sets of our parents lived in Kalamazoo, and our children and grandchildren lived in Fort Wayne. In December of 1988, I was a pedestrian in a marked crosswalk in Fort Wayne and was hit by a professor driving his car after an ice storm. I went to an emergency clinic where they took X-rays, bandaged me up, gave me crutches and medication and predicted I would have to stay off my feet for six weeks. My leg was painfully swollen and I was hopping around on crutches during the Christmas season. Naturally, I was wondering how I had attracted and created this situation. I knew there had to be a pony in there somewhere. Obviously, I now had a window of time to reflect on this seeming "misadventure" and contrast. It was clearly an opportunity to seriously consider living in a moderate and warmer climate. I questioned why we remained in a city with only 165 days of annual sunshine punctuated with many gray, rainy, icy and snowy days, plus high humidity in the summer. We could live anywhere we desired and it was time to consider new possibilities.

In the book, *I Had It All the Time*, Alan Cohen said, "If you do not rest yourself, the Universe will rest you…the forced rest plan is not pleasant or gentle, and you may end up wishing you had chosen peace before life chose it for you. If you are overworked or overscheduled, you may be decked by an accident or illness that requires you to stop and find yourself. While this is a painful route to take, the long range results are invaluable. Those on the Stop Now Plan are given time to redevelop time with themselves, their loved ones and their spiritual source…what began as an inconvenience or tragedy reveals itself to be a blessing and a gift." This was personally so true for me because it provided the means to really slow down, evaluate our options and listen to my inner voice.

My mentor, Dr. Carolyn Conger, a profound and powerful teacher I was sponsoring for a four-day intensive in early 1989, arrived from California in January. We discussed my situation and both arrived at similar conclusions. The Universe had gotten my attention with a "cosmic shove," as a "wake-up call" to consider sunny, dry climates. Even though this accident happened when I was clearly in a crosswalk in broad daylight where I should have been safe, it took this dramatic situation and having six weeks off my feet to consider our options. Once we chose Arizona, magnetizing our home in Rio Verde was created easily and effortlessly through treasure mapping and intentions. I always feel my "accident" in the crosswalk was a crossroads in my life to get us to Arizona.

Rituals for Children and Teen-Agers

We've covered many rituals and personal examples in this chapter of how to make you feel good. I was touched by a recent story in the *Parade Magazine* in *Lynn Minton Reports Fresh Voices*. One boy wrote in about his family ritual: "At the table each Sunday, my mom makes us say 'I love you' to each person and give a compliment. I wish we did this every day." Another teen-age group was asked about rituals that made them feel good and Micah responded: "I was a counselor-in-training at a camp and for 'cabin time' we had each camper in our group go around and say something nice about every other person. I had 11-year-olds, and they're really insecure—there's always a kid who doesn't quite fit in. And especially for those kids, it made them feel accepted by the hip campers who don't usually pay attention to them or hang out with them. This ritual created respect for everybody."

Erika responded to what Micah had shared: "I'd like to have an experience like that. Or what if it was just me and someone else, and I didn't like that person? It would be nice to think: 'What's a good quality about this person?' And then say to the person, 'I just thought I should tell you, you're a very good listener.'" And Antenique chimed in too by saying: "That could be a good beginning—you make the person feel, 'Maybe she does like me.' It creates an openness, a 'yeah, we can talk.'"

I loved this article and was so touched at the sensitivity of sharing from these teenagers. They already have a strong sense of being uplifters and how to achieve vibrational matches through rituals that make everyone feel good! The Columbine High School tragedy would never have happened with this kind of sensitivity.

> ## "Every time you say, 'I appreciate that. I really like that. I applaud that! I acknowledge value in that!' Every time you do this, you invest your energy. It is this energy that creates a vacuum, so to speak, or an attraction that draws more."
>
> …Abraham

202

Lining Up Your Energy

Tapped In, Tuned In and Turned On!

…Abraham

Once you understand how the magnets with this book are your hands-on tools and mirror to understanding energy as it repels or attracts, you simply re-direct your energy or focus. You can feel the power of being a masterful, Deliberate Creator, rather than a reactor, by reconnecting with your Stream of Well Being which is always inclusion. You will always know if you are connected because the better you feeeeeel, the more attuned you are. Abraham calls it being "tapped in, tuned in and turned on," and when you are feeling enthusiasm, joy and love that is always a match to your core energy. When you are feeling discomfort and "exclusion thoughts," then you're not a match to your core energy. That's why when Jesus healed, he never saw a person's sickness because he was other than a vibrational match to any illness. Whenever anyone is in the mode of exclusion, it is a vibrational match to "separation." Jesus saw people as whole and healthy and so he was a vibrational match to their healing by being "solution oriented." He said, "Pick up your bed and walk, Dude." It was not a wimpy "Do you think you can do this?" or "Let's try and see if this will work." He healed with a clear vision of their wellness and then said, "Go forth and tell no others" because doubters and disbelievers would be skeptical and cause you to doubt also. He knew and acknowledged that his energy was lined up and connected to Source.

Stressed Is Desserts Spelled Backwards!

I love that "stressed" is desserts spelled backwards! How sweet it is when we realize our "opportunity" in crisis or stress is to discover that greater potentials are being born. If you were an acorn, you would be snug and protected in your "shell." It would be very comfortable for awhile. Then one day, your shell develops a "hairline" crack and you get drenched with rain. You could say, "Oh no! My world is wet, rotting and cracking all around me! Why me? Why is the Universe allowing bad things to happen to me?!" In your complaining and staying on the "pity pot," you fail to notice what is happening. You are germinating and ripening and beginning to grow! In your anguish, you wonder what you did to deserve this, rather than celebrating that your shell has cracked wide open and you are exposed to a bright new world. You have "graduated" to a new level of beingness with moist dirt, soft moss, bright light and shiny stones all around you. You can forge ahead now as you continue to grow and flourish and notice the pressure is diminishing. Instead of being fixated on thoughts of "lack" such as, "It sure is hell to break out of this shell!" or "I'm so stressed!" you can focus on appreciating your freedom and flowing energy. An acorn essence inherently knows, on some level, that it is going to become and grow into a beautiful, majestic and strong leafy oak tree which will be admired in all its magnificence! How wondrously liberating to see how contrast serves our greater growth.

Two ways to get to the top of an oak tree...

I used to tell my classes, "There are two ways to get to the top of an oak tree. You can sit on an acorn and wait for it to grow or you can climb the oak tree to see new vistas and horizons." And I followed it by saying, "And, too many of us have been sitting on our acorns!" which would produce lots of laughter. Unfortunately, too many people are sitting on their acorns blaming and projecting rather than seeing how we are strengthened through life circumstances by blossoming more fully into who we are. Because we are constantly changing and growing, ideally our lives are getting richer, better, truer to our self. We are then feeding the higher energy wave through the thrill of flowing energy toward our heart's desires. We leave behind old outworn shells (jobs, relationships, etc.) that no longer serve us as we evolve and graduate through diversity and contrast. By using imagination, we can create new visions and decisions to spiral up in our relentless commitment to our becoming "more" of what we are. The happiest people I know are those who are joyfully invested in personal growth, and who willingly share and inspire others as Deliberate Creators magnetizing their outcomes fulfilled!

Inspire Through Desire

It was an enormous gift for me when Abraham said never pay attention to reality and to instead flood your environment with Source energy. Rather than being frustrated with people or situations, be unwilling to see them as they are now. See them as you know they want to be and hold that vision. Hopefully, they will rise to higher expectations. You hold the frequency and broadcast a higher outcome. Occasionally, a person or situation may vibrate right on out of your life because you are no longer a match. Enhance your imagination and have fun being in vibrational harmony with your heart's desires and being with those who are mutually enthusiastic about being Deliberate Creators.

"Your Experience is Always the Sum Total of the Content of Your Vibration!"

Abraham has said the Law of Creation is:

"As you intend it and allow it to be, it is."

He added that as you set forth positive thoughts of your desires, you are at the same time experiencing positive emotion. You are, in that moment, in the perfect position for receiving or deliberately creating that which you are giving your thoughts and feelings to. The higher the intensity of emotion, the faster creation is occurring. If you give thought to that which you are not desiring, and experiencing fear, doubt or negative emotion, you are then in the position of having negative thoughts and emotion to create the very thing you are not desiring. It is the Law. In short:

You get what you think about whether you want it or not!

According to Abraham, in order to create anything you are desiring or intending, you have only to set forth a clear deliberate thought of intent and then *allow* it to be. If you suppress desires because you have wanted and not received them, and you have given up on your desires, then being ineffective at the wanting part of the equation is not usually what is keeping you from deliberate creation. It is that you do not allow anything that is extremely important because you allow only within the boundaries of your beliefs. And so, in many cases, your beliefs must be altered to harmonize with your intentions. Also, when you understand that your beliefs are creations set into motion because of previous experiences, then you realize your beliefs are not unchangeable; they are pliable and moldable. You alter your beliefs by applying new or additional thoughts to those beliefs until you have molded them into what you now prefer. It is of great advantage to give concentrated thought in the direction of the things you desire and little or no thought toward those things that you do not desire. As you become sensitive to the emotions you feel, you will know if you are creating toward or away from that which you desire. The following chart will assist you in always knowing what your vibrational signal is.

Vibrational Meter Illustration*

PASSION	PEACE	FRUSTRATED	ANGRY
Lots of enthusiasm High, fast, pure vibration DESIRE IS STRONG Summoning lots of energy NO RESISTANCE A Deliberate Creator	Contented Mellow Not much desire, but no resistance. Notice and feel the difference between peace and passion	Mild, negative emotions— Some resistance and some desire	Strong frustration & displeasure Lower, slower vibrations Strong Desire Strong RESISTANCE Strong Reactor Lots of Contrast

The Universe is responding to your vibrational output magnetically through the Law of Attraction. You can easily notice the important role that your emotions play in attracting your heart's desires because you are always transmitting a vibrational signal. When you observe how you FEEL, then you will know whether you are moving toward your heart's desire (attracting as a Deliberate Creator), or repelling because you will have resistance and know you are pushing against (Reactor). There are infinite notches or stops for a vibrational meter—these four are depicted so you will understand your life force.

CONTRAST gives birth to desire—in the midst of contrast, you will have the option to make a new decision. Allow contrast to produce new desires for fresh choices and to focus on higher outcomes. Ask and it is given! As Deliberate Creators, you are modulators of energy and you summon life force through your new focused desires. Don't push against what you don't want— because you are including that in your vibration (use your magnets to demonstrate resistance). You want to FEEL GOOD, which means a high, fast, pure vibration with no resistance. You magnetically attract your heart's desires by focusing on what you do want to create for fast, powerful vibrational "matches" (use your magnets to demonstrate how good and fast that feels)!

* Excerpts from Abraham-Hicks adapted as a chart illustration with supporting material to understand vibrational output that Sharon created for a workshop using the magnets which accompany this book.

Magnetic Mirrors

This is why using the magnets with this book is such a powerful tool. You will always know whether you are attracting or repelling your desires by seeing and feeling what transpires with the magnets. And you know through your reacting (resistance and pushing against) or creating (attracting by harmonizing) that you will attract more of whatever you are thinking about you.

While writing this book, I had shared these magnets with some friends and family for them to use them as demonstration tools in attraction and resistance in their own thoughts and beliefs. They all were impressed with having a hands-on tool. I realized I would need more magnets for future classes and for the book prototypes to be sent to agents and publishers. I sent a fax off to the wonderful woman who had handled my previous magnets order so promptly. When I didn't receive any response to my fax after two weeks, I called her. I learned that only 30 minutes earlier she had called me and didn't receive an answer. I was on the phone with an important business call and ignored the call-waiting beep. We laughed as it was pure telepathy on my part to call her only shortly after she called me. She literally had my address label and fax in her hands at that moment to tell me why the order had been delayed. This was another instant and fun mirror of the Law of Attraction in Action. I was inspired through my desire, which in this case was attracting more magnets!! We were literally on the same "magnetic" wavelength.

Worry Is Miscreating

In contrast, we received a phone call from someone who exclaimed, "I was so worried about you," because she hadn't received a letter for two weeks. What happened is she became even more concerned by her thoughts and her beliefs that something must be wrong. This resulted in more anxiety because she was dwelling on it. Again, the Law of Attraction is neutral and works either way, depending on what you focus upon. Someone wisely said: "Worry is prayer turned inside out."

The Creative Power of Words

Iyanla Vanzant, in her beautiful book, *One Day My Soul Just Opened Up*, quotes author Maya Angelou about the power of words:

> "Poet Maya Angelou once talked about the power of words. She said that words are like little energy pellets that shoot forth into the invisible realm of life. Although we cannot see the words, she said, words become the energy that fills a room, home, environment, and our minds. Ms. Angelou described how words stick to the walls, the furniture, the curtains, and our clothing. She believes the words in our environment seep into our being and become part of who we are. When I reflect on the negative words I have heard about myself and the years I have spent in battle with them, this makes perfectly good sense to me. Words are so very important in our life. The written and spoken word determines what we do in life and how we do it. And, since words ultimately guide our actions, it is important for us to speak words of truth, love and every good thing we desire to experience into existence. Self-affirming words and actions are necessary to counteract the unpleasant things we have heard about ourselves."

Focus Only on What You Choose to Attract

Thoughts which don't have heartfelt emotion accompanying them are not usually powerful enough to manifest. Therefore, it is important to focus upon only those things which you choose to magnetically attract. When you are sensitive to your thoughts and emotions, you will constantly know whether you are attracting or repelling that which you desire.

Delicious desires means focusing your energy. When you begin to consciously notice the direction of your thoughts—positive or negative—you then have an awareness of what you set into motion. For example, in my Creation Book, whenever I see my new Cadillac SLS, I am really excited! I've already picked out the interior and exterior colors. I see myself owning and driving it. I actually test drove it and loved it. I also put my personal snapshot in the driver's window of the car brochure and glued it in my Creation Book. I delegated my heart's desire to the Universe and considered it done.

Later this spring, I called the Cadillac salesman and told him what I was specifically desiring in accessories and color. He excitedly called me one day recently and said this SLS is precisely what you asked for and the color is champagne. He offered to bring this car to our home; I drove it, he gave us exactly what we had in mind for our trade-in, he called the dealership and it was authorized all within one hour. Done deal! After I had initially put the SLS photo in my Creation Book, two months later I had glued in a picture of the On Star system as an accessory and dated it as being my heart's desire also. This car came equipped with the On Star Satellite feature. Evidence abounds! The Universe delivered on all levels—and literally right to my front door! It happened easily and effortlessly and in amazing grace! I named her PRINCESS.

Your Vibrational Statements to the Universe

Our bodies and the clothes we wear, the friends we attract and celebrate life with, the homes we live in, the cars we drive, and the goals/outcomes fulfilled that we experience are all vibrational "statements" to and from the Universe. Each expresses an energy. Be clear in knowing, feeling and visualizing the highest choices of your heart's desires from the deepest places within your Being. Then be willing to allow, receive and accept what you have asked for. Create it the way you choose it to be (and ignore current reality unless it is perfect in every way)!

"I celebrate myself."
...Walt Whitman

It takes courage to be who we are. When the writer, Carlye's complete manuscript about the French revolution was accidentally destroyed in a fire, he was desolate. Yet, he summoned and flowed energy to rewrite the entire book. Can you imagine? Author Jack London received over

600 rejection slips before he was published. That is a massive amount of rejection, and yet he believed in himself and kept re-submitting his manuscript. No one ever said life was easy; however, the formula for deliberate creation is simple.

When poet Walt Whitman said, "I celebrate myself," the thought is so exuberant and delicious. Imagine the joy that comes with celebrating Self—our achievements, our experiences, our very existence. Imagine what it would be like to look in the mirror and say, like God did, 'That is good, very, very good."

Someone told me that Kenny Rogers wrote a song entitled:

"Don't be afraid to give up the good, to go for the great."

Celebrate Yourself!
Appreciate Yourself!
Do It Now!

Summary

In her wonderful book, *One Day My Soul Just Opened Up*, Iyanla Vanzant shares the following:

"When your life is working there will be an absence of drama."

"In the absence of drama, conflict and chaos, lasting change is given the opportunity to take place. I encourage you to be patient with yourself. Be gentle with yourself. Know that all things are working in your favor. If you take one step toward the light of Spirit, Spirit will take five steps in your behalf."

Drama is time consuming, exhausting and attracts more of the same "crazymaker" energy. I believe it is our divine destiny and heritage to be Deliberate Creators through the Law of Attraction when we consciously and creatively live our life on purpose. Once we understand that the Law of Attraction is no different than the law of gravity—the law simply IS—we become more sensitive and aware how and what we are vibrating. We then have the opportunity to make new choices (while ignoring reality as much as possible). One cannot vibrate in pain or conflict and attract the vibration of JOY. As you are now aware through experiencing the magnets, you can see how you attract or repel through your thoughts. Just as any metal (like nails) are caught up in a magnetic field, so is your vibrational tone and what you attract. By setting your tone, you attract your heart's desires and create your grandest outcomes.

Being a conscious, delicious Deliberate Creator means summoning and flowing energy by magnetizing your heart's desires through the steps of Deliberate Creation. These energies are literally in your hands as you connect and stand in your Stream of Well Being.

Hands On!

Your left hand (right side of the brain) represents receiving, love, heart, symbols, dreams, intuition, and your sacred connection. It is holistic in nature. As you will see by the hand imprint illustration on the following page, your life purpose revolves around five primary areas which match each finger of your left hand.

- ♥ Your body and mind
- ♥ Your relationships
- ♥ Your career and work
- ♥ Your home
- ♥ Your imagination, dreams, inspirations and aspirations in the life arenas outlined above.

The right hand (left brain) is your practical, verbal, daily "hands-on" life creations that are action oriented and grounded into the world through your clarity, vibration and passion.

The Steps of Deliberate Creation

- ♥ Know what you do NOT want.
- ♥ Know what you do desire and feed that energy.
- ♥ Create a vibrational match to your heart's desires through strong emotion and feelings.
- ♥ The Universe provides! Look for evidence abounding.

Magnetizing Your Heart's Desires

Creative Intentions—It's In Your Hands!

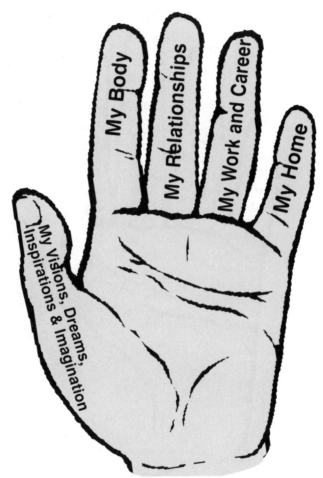

- ♥ You are a Deliberate Creator through your expectations and eagerness to flow energy.
- ♥ As you vibrate on purpose by aligning with your heart's desires, your highest outcomes are being fulfilled.
- ♥ Allow your words to be creative and unified.
- ♥ Notice how your thoughts vibrate and attract.
- ♥ Know that the Law of Attraction is always in action, negatively or positively.
- ♥ Imagination is the key.

Magnetizing Your Heart's Desires

Steps for Deliberate Creation
It's In Your Hands!

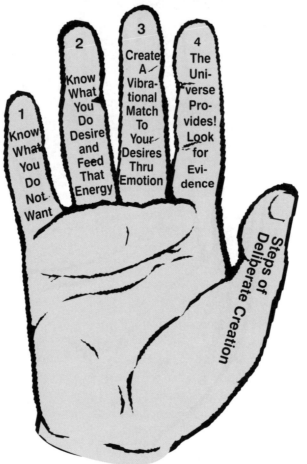

❤ Eagerly launch fresh new rockets of your inspired heart's desires.

❤ The more you are in conscious connection pulsating and radiating pure, positive energy, the more vibrational matches you attract.

❤ Passionately hold the vision for your decision.

❤ Name it and claim it now and continuously.

❤ When you are connected, you will always feel uplifted, elated and excited.

Your Life is in Your Hands

There is a beautiful Indian story about a Master who lived in the Himalayas and the children of the village wanted to out-smart him. So they decided to fool the Master by having one of the children hold a bird behind his back in his hands. They would then ask, "Master is the bird dead or alive?"

If the Master said "The bird is alive," they would then wring the bird's neck to make the Master wrong. If the Master said, "The bird is dead," then they would let the bird live and the Master would be wrong. Either way, the children figured he would look foolish and the children would be pleased to have outwitted him.

So, they went to this wise old Master and said, "Master, what do we have in these hands?"

He replied, "A bird."

They asked, "Is it dead or alive?"

And he replied, "**It's in your hands.**"

Your life is in your hands. It always has been and always will be. Ultimately, who you are really matters only to you. And who you are is a direct result of your thoughts, feelings and vibration as a Deliberate Creator. You have only you to depend upon. Love what you are, invest in yourself and let your LIGHT SHINE!!

Years ago when my husband and I taught a class entitled, **LOVE**, at the Aldersgate Methodist Church in Fort Wayne, we received a sweet thank you card from the class with this verse:

"A candle is just a simple thing
It starts with just a bit of string,
Then dipped and dipped with patient hand
It gathers wax upon every strand
Until complete and ivory white
It gives at last a lovely light.

Life seems so like that bit of string
Each deed we do a simple thing
Yet day by day when on life's strand
We work with patient heart and hand
It gathers JOY and makes dark days BRIGHT
and gives at last a lovely LIGHT."

…Susan Squellati Florence

I invite you in this moment to light a candle to your glorious self and radiant Spirit. This is a reflection of your inner light. You are adding your bright light to the millennium energy every time you remember who you are. Burning candles is a sweet ritual that invites and ignites renewal and honors your personal illumination and vibration. **Ritual** is the heart of spi<u>rituality</u>—sacredness is our natural state.

To light our way into the 21st century, each of us can summon and flow our energy as divine Deliberate Creators for our highest dreams and grandest outcomes. By having clarity in our commitments as we "light our fire," we are inspired to imagine and know what nourishes our souls and spirits. It fosters a deeper connection to our ever-present Stream of Well Being in magnetizing our heart's desires through the Law of Attraction.

Shine on in Your Luminous Light
And Shiny, Sparkly Spirit!
I Wish You the Brightest of Blessings
In a Radiance of Love and Joyous Expansion
Always!
Shine On!
Shine On!
SHINE ON
SHINE ON
in love, light and laughter
in magnetizing your heart's desires
through the Law of Attraction in Action.
You are the vibration of Divine Creation and
the light of the world shines in your face!

> "The end of all exploring will be to arrive at our starting point and know it for the first time.
>
> …T.S. Eliot

"We live at the edge of the miraculous."

…Henry Miller

Appendix 1

Who are the Invisibles?

"It is with the heart that one sees rightly; what is essential is invisible to the eye."

Antoine De Saint-Exupery, The Little Prince

On November 12, 1994, I went into a meditation, which turned out to be an experience of profound amazing grace. I had an angel appear who was all shimmering golden sparkly bright light. I was so deeply touched and the experience to this day is still beyond words to describe. The Angel said her name was **Souleiah**. At the time, I didn't know how to spell it although I knew the sound phonetically (Soul-lee-ah). She said she came as a master teacher and she was a very radiant feminine essence with beautiful features. According to my mom, I was named after the Rose of Sharon. I experienced a heartfelt fusion wherein Souleiah and I were flowering and blending together as one essence and presence—she even had a rose-like appearance. Afterward, as I pondered the significance of this experience, I sketched a large drawing with a gold-ink pen in my journal. It was a day I would always remember...a golden moment in time, which was a turning point of truly knowing the presence of a glorious light being.

Shortly thereafter, I talked on the phone to my artist friend, Linda Ashburn, within a half hour of this meditation. That morning at the same time I was receiving Souleiah, Linda was painting a new card with an angel, which she entitled, *Incoming Angel*. We became very excited at the synchronicity of the angelic timing for both of us, as well as being impulsed to call each other.

A Convocation of Angels

In early December, less than 30 days later, I was awakened at 12:30 a.m. hearing indescribable sounds that were unlike anything I had ever heard. The fluttering or rustling of wings? It was also a vibrational sound, although I wouldn't have described it that way then. I went out to the kitchen and lit some candles, which made crackling and popping "noises" and the wick itself was doing unusual "funky" things. The "sounds" continued as I sat down and began to write. It was as if I was taking dictation from a convocation of angels. I was given guidance, both personally and for my family, for hours.

"We don't need a new religion, just a new experience of ourselves as the vibrations of a single and eternal flow of energy."

…Alan Watts

At some segment in this transmission, it seemed almost unbelievable and I really questioned it with thoughts like, "You've got to be kidding!" I was told we would "go global" and I didn't have a clue what that meant. When I later shared this with our son, Troy, he immediately and intuitively "knew" it was the World-Wide Web. In 1994, very few people had knowledge of the "super information highway" and no one we knew was online. It turned out to be absolutely clear guidance and our son went online and became a Web Master and consultant. He built a web site for us within four months, which featured lots of angels. We were later given an award honoring us in the top 5% category for being one of the best Web sites. While reading, *The Celestine Prophecy* by James Redfield, which we had given Troy as a Christmas present, he had an experience on New Year's Eve weekend with an angel in a hotel room. He called us immediately and said, "Can this be true—is this for real

219

what I saw?" My angelic guidance turned out to be "right on" in the course his life took, which seemed out of the realm of reason at that time when it was "channeled" in December. For us, the guidance was impeccable. What we chose to do with it was up to each of us.

> ## "The very presence of an angel is a communication. When an angel crosses our path, God has said to us, 'I am here. I am present in your life.'"
> Tobias Palmer, An Angel in My House

As the guidance continued, I thought to myself, "Duaine will never believe this—it's too incredible!"—and even I was amazed at the extent of it. When Duaine awakened around 4:30 a.m. and came into the living room, I started to cry when I told him what had transpired and said, "You will never believe what has transpired for the last couple hours." As I began to share, he took my hand tenderly and said, "I do believe it and I have confirmation of this through my dream." While I was being guided by angels, his dream was very biblical in nature and he was taken to many different spiritual plateaus. Eventually, his dream culminated beneath a huge Redwood tree with words from the radiance of the Virgin Mary. We both knew this was a golden moment in our lives and we trusted what had been imparted to each of us. We both felt such an inner peace and intense soul expansion in being elevated to new sacred awareness and profound knowing. It was the presence of shining angels and Mary which had infused us in different ways, and yet, vanquished any doubts. We were both filled with serenity and gratitude. Shortly thereafter, we named our business, Angel Express, and our lives changed dramatically.

To those who believe in angels, there is no need for further explanation of what unfolded in my personal encounters. And to those who question and doubt the reality of angels and the "invisibles," then no explanation is possible. I believe that the presence of the "unseen" beings from non-physical will accelerate in the millennia and culminate in more people's heightened ability to see, hear and feel them in their midst. Truly, these shining, light beings bring tidings of great joy and reveal our connection with All That Is in the non-physical realms.

So, Who in the World is Abraham?!!

In 1998, after my Dad had been hospitalized, I sent him some draft chapters from my book, as well as Abraham material and tapes. Later, when we were speaking on the phone, he asked me to explain what channeling was, as I had used that term as a reference regarding Abraham's teachings and audio tapes. I went into quite a lengthy explanation for a few minutes and then he said, "Oh, you mean the Invisibles?" I about dropped the phone because it was an instant "ah hah" and I excitedly responded, "That's it, Dad—what a brilliant way of expressing it!" We are all very aware of our physical world, but the Invisibles, who are Non-Physical beings, are always with us. We have only to tune into them. My Dad's health has improved significantly, which we attribute to these teachings, as well as our dear friend, Dr. Charles Ruckel, a chiropractor in Fort Wayne, who has made a huge difference with his holistic approach to regaining wellness. My Dad's heart specialist was simply stunned at his renewed health and said, "Whatever you are doing, keep it up!"

Abraham says they are a group of highly-evolved teachers, sharing their broader Non-physical perspective through the physical consciousness of Esther. Esther and Jerry Hicks disclosed their experiences with Abraham to a few close associates in 1986. Esther was definitely a "reluctant" channel and had a lot of "booga booga" issues around anything of this nature. I'm sure they thought she would only be a "closet" channel for their guidance. Originally, when Jerry studied some of the Seth material, Esther didn't even want it in the house. I love it when the Universe sets things up and waits for us to tune in and turn on. Esther would never have dreamed back then that Abraham would one day become so universal, with world-wide attention and an ever-widening circle of seekers and participants interacting with Abraham in many key cities.

Abraham speaks to our level of comprehension, from their present moment to our now, through a series of loving, allowing, yet brilliantly clear and simple recordings in print via books and audio recordings, as well as interactive workshops. Abraham guides us to a clear connection with our Inner Being and upliftment—from our total self.

I am eternally grateful for having been introduced to the Abraham materials by Mimi Greek. I am divinely enthusiastic about their clarity, practicality and humor which touches my soul. Abraham is so much fun and brings forth the JOY vibration with high, pure, positive energy. As you can see from this book with many Abraham quotes, they have enriched our lives enormously. Our tribe is in deep appreciation for Abraham's valuable teachings and "uplighting" guidance.

See page 228, "Resources," for contact information.

"The delights of self-discovery are always available."

…Gail Sheehy

Appendix II

Magnets

In a booklet entitled, *Investigating Magnetism,* from the Magic Penney Magnet Kit (which I bought for my grandchildren), it states:

"Magnetism is a force generated whenever an electrical charge is moved. All substances are made of atoms which are continually moving. All atoms have a positively charged center (nucleus) around which one or more negatively charged electrons continually orbit. In magnetic materials, the atoms cooperate with each other to some extent. Each atom can act as a small magnet (a magnetic dipole) with a tendency for groups (domains) of adjacent atoms to line up in the same direction. If enough domains are aligned, the material as a whole can exert a magnetic force on other magnetic materials.

The zone of influence of a magnet is known as its magnetic field. It is conventional to describe magnetic fields by drawing lines of force emerging from the north-seeking region (north pole) of the magnet re-entering the south pole."

The History of Magnets

The booklet also stated it is felt that Chinese armies probably were the first to use magnets as magnetic stones over 4000 years ago to guide them in bad weather. Magnetic stones made of the ore magnetite were mined near the ancient Greek town of Magnesia. The ore contained iron oxide. The stones were called leading stones or lodestones because when suspended freely, they consistently pointed in the same direction and were useful in guiding the way. Before magnets were discovered, travelers found their way by following the stars.

William Gilbert (1544-1603) was a physician to Queen Elizabeth and the pioneer of magnetism. His first book gave an account of his investigations and described the earth as having the properties of a bar magnet.

About the Author

Sharon Warren, M.A. is a catalyst for transformation and empowers people through her life changing classes and teachings. Her Master's degree is in Transpersonal Psychology. Sharon was an associate faculty member and taught at Indiana-Purdue University for 17 years. She also facilitated and coordinated major events and sold-out audiences with well-known notables, such as Dr. Bernie Siegel, Dr. Brugh Joy, Stuart Wilde, and Dr. Carolyn Conger, Dan Millman, Dr. David Viscott, Betty Bethards, Mataji Indra Devi, Drs. Jordan and Margaret Paul, while teaching at Indiana-Purdue University. In Arizona, recent events also include authors, Neale Donald Walsch, Gregg Braden, and Tom Kenyon. Sharon and her husband, Duaine, moved to Arizona in 1989 and love living in the sacred southwest. They have traveled the world over together, as well as facilitating group travels to sacred sites. Sharon has a zest and enthusiasm for life that is contagious.

In 2003, well-known personality, Michele Blood, interviewed Sharon in California and featured *Magnetizing Your Heart's on MpowerTV.* You can view this 20-minute video online at www.mpowertv.com by typing in Sharon A. Warren on the "search for author" link. Sharon also presents at The Learning Annex in San Diego. You can contact her directly for future seminars. Personal coaching sessions are also available by contacting Sharon through her personal web site at: www.amazinggracenow.com, e-mailing: iam@amazinggracenow.com, or telephoning for further information.

Sharon's *Flowing Your Energy* columns appear in *Arizona Together Newspaper,* as well as online at her website: www.magnetizingyourheartsdesire.com. These columns may become the basis for a future book.

For workshops, classes and product orders contact:
> Sharon Warren
> Amazing Grace Unlimited
> Phone: (480) 816-9930
> Fax: (480) 816-9960
> E-mail: iam@amazinggracenow.com
> www.amazinggracenow.com
> www.magnetizingyourheartsdesire.com
> www.lawofattractioninaction.com

♥ Notes ♥

♥ Notes ♥

♥ Notes ♥

♥ **Resources** ♥

For information on Abraham-Hicks contact:

Jerry and Esther Hicks
P. O. Box 690070
San Antonio, TX 78269
Phone: (830) 755-2299 or FAX (830) 755-4179
Online: www.abraham-hicks.com

Sharon's business website: www.amazinggracenow.com for book orders and testimonials

Available also at: www.sharonwarren.com

Sharon's <u>Arizona Together Newspaper</u> articles and her *Flowing Your Energy* online columns
are at: www.magnetizingyourheartsdesire.com

E-mail Sharon at: iam@amazinggracenow.com

Sharon's articles are often featured at www.kryon.com (In the Spirit E-magazine link), as well as www.aquarius-atlanta.com

www.lawofattractioninaction.com (link)

Amazing Grace Unlimited Press
Phone: (480) 816-9930 (Monday to Friday, 9am to 4pm MST)
Fax orders: (480) 816-9960
www.amazinggracenow.com
e-mail: iam@amazinggracenow.com

Magnetizing Your Heart's Desires©
by Sharon A. Warren, M.A.
(ISBN 0-9674990-1-1)

Please send me _____ copies of *Magnetizing Your Heart's Desires* at $22 each, which includes a set of magnets.

Ship to:
Name _____

Address: _____

City: _____ State _____ , Zip _____

Phone: (AC)_____ _____ Fax:_____

E-mail address_____

Our data base is confidential and your information is respected and private.*

Shipping and handling U.S. mail only: $6 includes **Priority Air Mail** for the first copy, $2 additional for the second copy and $1 more for the third copy. **Media Mail:** $3 (takes up to 7-12 days for delivery).

Payment (U.S. funds only)
Check or money order _____
Credit card:
Circle one: VISA.   MasterCard

Card number: _____

Name on card: _____Exp. Date: _____

Signature: _____

Price: $22.00 each $_____
Shipping: (see above) $_____
Total: $_____   **Thank you for your order!**

Conversely, please do not use our mail, fax or web site for personal solicitation purposes.

Additional joyous products available from Amazing Grace Unlimited:

Quantity	Product Description	Price	Total
MAGNETS			
	* Magnets–1/4" dia.x 1" high, nickel plated, rare earth	$7 set	
OTHER BOOKS:			
	Interactive Guidebook for children and adults: Master-Mind/DreamMakers, In Power, In Joy, In Love, Mimi Greek	$24.95 ($6 shipping)	
	TOTALS THIS PAGE		

Magnets may chip if not handled properly. Not recommended for children under 10 years old.

Quantity discounts on large orders for *Magnetizing Your Heart's Desire* are available. Inquiries are welcomed and appreciated.

Please see reverse side of order form for postage and applicable tax for Arizona residents.

MasterMind DreamMakers, In-Power! In-Love! In-Joy!

Benjamin Franklin Best Book Award, May 2002

This glorious book is wonderful for children and parents (plus grandparents and teachers) to romp through and enjoy together. The colorful art visuals are stunning combined with heartfelt tools and games for DreamMaking/Masterminding that will long be remembered. *MasterMind DreamMakers* is sure to win top acclaim for its brilliant, original and unique interactive approach. Mimi Greek's message is inspiring and joyful with fun empowering "hands-on" processes. This book is a magical catalyst for positive well being and self-esteem. Children and adults will find it captivating from beginning to end. My grandchildren adore *IN-POWER! IN-LOVE! IN-JOY!* We have enthusiastically explored and enjoyed many hours together of self-discovery and laughter in this wise, witty and wonderful book.

Sharon A. Warren, M.A.
Author, *Magnetizing Your Heart's Desire*

Thank you from South Africa!

Sharon Warren, I want to THANK YOU for your book, *Magnetizing Your Heart's Desire*. It's magnificent! I am so thrilled in working with the book's material and it has really lifted my spirits. You have a wonderful way of writing-it is so infectious! I am recommending this book to everyone I know.
Cynthia Taylor, South Africa

Most exciting and refreshing book I've read...

WOW! *Magnetizing Your Heart's Desire* is the most exciting and refreshing book I have read in a very long time! It is so unique! It is so inspiring! It is also the first book that incorporates FUN into philosophy. There are so many neat ideas in your book that jumped out at me and helped me think "outside the box." I've learned to 'lighten up' and my mission is to change my lifestyle so I can actually live my life with style. I intend to use your book and tools to keep me on track!
Deb Boyd, Auburn, In.

Absolutely thrilled.

I am absolutely thrilled with *Magnetizing Your Heart's Desire*. I have read many, many "how to" books over the years. No other book has ever taken me step-by-step to the pinnacle of achieving my desires so fully, quickly and dramatically. It is so complete and powerful! This great book is a "must read immediately." I have already magnetized miracles!
Jean Ann Burger, Retired Teacher, Torrance, Ca.

All the good you can imagine!

A delightful, inspirational, easy to read guide to understanding the universal concepts that underlie the life we all live. Follow Sharon's guidance and tools and create a consciousness that will attract all the good that you can imagine.
Bruce I. Doyle, III, Author, *Before You Think Another Thought*

A Beacon Of Light!

Sharon's words directly reflect the heart of life. They are like beacons of light showing us the way to who we truly are. Inspirational, encouraging and a vital guide to illumination. I refer to this book often in my workshops.
Serge Mantel Runningwolf

You're Worth It!

Magnetizing Your Heart's Desire gives practical methods of aligning yourself with the flow of Universal energy. Placing yourself in this flow, easily creates your highest potential. Go for it...you're worth it.
Steve Rother, Author, *Beacons of Light—Reminders From Home*

A sampling of comments from readers at Amazon.com—2002

From Costa Rica: "The best book I've ever bought!"

This book is the best book I've ever bought! It has turned my life around! All of you out there, Sharon's tools make magnetizing your heart's desires easy, creative, and lots of fun. Best of all, your life will improve beyond belief! Reading this book will take you to new levels of wellbeing! This book is very positive, and fun to read, and most importantly, it will magnetize wonderful things into you life!

Ana Keith, Costa Rica

I love this book! It's absolutely exceptional!

Magnetizing Your Hearts Desire is a very positive, upbeat, inspirational, and humorous book. Interesting stories are also included. This book is now among my favorites. Well worth reading.

Diane, United States

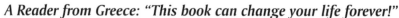

A Reader from Greece: "This book can change your life forever!"

Magnetizing Your Heart's Desire is a unique book that can change the way we think and create. I have many friends talking about positive thinking, but Sharon made me understand how it really works. I now know what to do to bring what I really desire into my life to be happier. Most amazing is how she managed from such a long distance and with such cultural differences between us, to make me understand me better!!! Do not buy this book if you want to be miserable and unhappy! It can change you, your thoughts and your life for good and forever!

Marina Angeletaki, Mykonos, Greece

AMAZING SHARON!

I ordered *Magnetizing Your Heart's Desire* two weeks ago and I wanted to savor each page by reading it slowly, instead of devouring it in one reading. The book is so delicious, uplifting and inspiring. Ms. Warren has such an incredible gift for expressing herself and for making the material very clear, simple and so yummy [which is now one of my favorite words]. I love the graphics and there are so many profound statements that most of my book is underlined and starred. I recommend this book to anyone who is serious about magnetizing your true heart's desire. If you don't like your present reality, it is time to magnetize a beautiful new reality by using the principles in this book. This book gives me the inspiration I needed to magnetize my heart's desires. I have already started to "play" with some of the projects. Ms. Warren's caring ways really shine through in her book. I feel like she is "co-creating" with me in magnetizing my heart's desires. A MUST READ FOR THOSE SEEKING TRUE JOY.

Jillian Mazzeo, Lynbrook, Ny

Become a magnet for miracles!

Sharon Warren has written a book that is unique, fun to read, full of brilliant ideas and powerful techniques: a book that really does help people deliberately create more and more of what they really want in life! I have been studying, applying and teaching the Abraham principals for over 10 years. This book, with its tiny but powerful magnets, has propelled my positive vibration into a whole new zone!

Linda Marie Sands, President & Co-Founder,
DreamQuest Intnl., Melbourne, FL

Spirituality Made JOYfull!

Sharon Warren has captured some very serious teachings with such clarity and depth, and the amazing part is how much FUN she makes the learning! So many of us take our spiritual soul searching too seriously. Life is supposed to be a JOYous journey and Sharon gives us many tools to make life fun and lighthearted. She truly is an "uplighter" and you will feel like you have your very own cheerleader encouraging you to grow, grow, grow, as you romp through the information-packed pages of this beautiful book. This book contains so many precious gifts, starting with the breathtaking cover design and rare-earth magnets, just waiting to enRICH and enLIGHTen the reader's life. Enjoy the JOYfull ride!

Germaine Cabe, Chandler, AZ.

Exciting Way to Grow and Play!

This book is sensational! Beautiful, appropriate, wondrous method of achieving your heart's desires! The accompanying set of magnets clearly demonstrates the principles of attraction Ms. Warren has presented. I have given this book as a gift to several of my friends, and we are all ecstatic about it. My cousin was so thrilled with the positive vibration that she actually slept with the book!

Joyous Lesperance, Fresno, Ca.

EXTRAORDINARY! EMPOWERING! ENLIGHTENING!

Many delicious, useful "hands-on" tools and heartwarming stories are available for one's own life-changing adventure. It is a "must read" for those seeking joyous spiritual expansion in their daily life. Sharon sets the stage, with encouragement, for creating new, fulfilling journeys in the readers' lives.

Carolyn Henderson, Ft. Wayne, IN.

Playful, Wise and Compelling Teachings!

Magnetizing Your Heart's Desire is more then a book. It is a delightfully wise, wonderful and practical guide for creating your life the way you want it to be. Sharon Warren weaves the complex into the simple, and the unknown into the obvious, as she shows us in a few simple steps how to bring more joy into our lives. Her sense of play, wisdom and compelling teachings will inspire today's reader and future generations.

Patricia Mulreany, Teacher/Artist, Fla.

Finally, a Self-Help Book that Truly Inspires!

Sharon's book, *Magnetizing Your Heart's Desire* is the first self-help book I've read in many, many years which truly got me excited and motivated to take action in making changes in my life. Fun, inspiring and empowering, her words, stories and exercises are sheer pleasure to read and live by! One is empowered to take charge, with the help of our generous and loving universe, rather than continue to let things "happen" to us, as if we were helpless victims of a prescribed fate. Throughout it all, I felt lifted by "wings" of encouragement, as if I had my own private cheerleader desiring the best in life for me. A wonderful book, which I have given as gifts and recommended to my dearest friends. Thank you, Sharon!

Karen, Cave Creek, AZ.

The world needs more books like this!

I want to tell you how marvelous your book is, which I am savoring with your beautiful sense of humor. The magnets are such a great focus and leave a strong impact. The graphics layout is wonderful with the bold print making key points. There is also a musical lilt to your words and they weave together a powerful message. Congratulations! The world needs more books like this!

Shirley Kussner, Michigan

A treasure!

Sharon Warren's book gives you the keys to unlock your own treasure chest of unlimited manifesting possibilities!

Gwenellen Marie, Phoenix, Az.

Most inspiring book I've ever read!

I "loooooved" this book! I found it to be the most inspiring and best motivational book I have ever read. It's fabulous!

Cella Weaver, OH

Laughing out loud!

Sharon Warren's humor kept me laughing out loud through the pages of this informative and detailed "how to" book, which is a must read for living a creative life.
  Patti Cordes, Mn.

Magically empowering!

I love this book! These are the true Keys of the Universe, written in a fun and understandable manner. I felt Sharon Warren's warm and inviting energy emanating from each page. These magically empowering steps to Deliberate Creation easily raise vibrations in a practical, down to earth way. The use of magnets is pure Genius!!"
  Karen Murphy, Chicago, Il.

A Masterpiece!

You have written a masterpiece. I can't put it down—I carry it everywhere! I am now accomplishing difficult tasks with joy, ease and gratitude. Thank you for writing this book!
  Joy Paige, Manager, Pacifica, Ca

An awesome blessing!

SO INSPIRING! Once I touched the book, and then read it, magic started to happen. Sharon brings very vivid, candid, clear, enlightened messages. Her approach teaches how to ignite and connect with our own inner magnetic attraction to produce wondrous life manifestations. What's the best part?! To partake of this feast immediately! A fun and light approach to a very complex subject. LUV'd it! What an awesome piece of work she has blessed us with!
  Cindy Hicks, Scottsdale, Az.

Amazing Grace!

Lovely, simply lovely. Your book glows and radiates with humor, life changing tools, yummy style, so much love and amazing grace. I am so happy for everyone who will read this book, especially me!
  Ann Kurchack, Az.

This wondrous book is filled with "do-able" techniques for those who wish to magnetize their heart's desires and align with their highest aspirations. I totally enjoy the bold graphics format, which bring the reader back again and again. I find this book captivating and the message sound and true! I enthusiastically recommend *Magnetizing Your Heart's Desire* to all of my clients. This book is a "must read" for anyone who desires support and inspired "know how" in moving from where they are to where they wish to be—beyond dreaming to actualizing.
  Mary Richards, M.A.
  Director, Master Your Mind

♥ ♥

The Aquarian Book Review, Kathryn Sargent, Editor

Books that discuss the principles of manifestation are not exactly rare, and many wonderful books along this line have been our mainstays for years. However, Sharon A. Warren, M.A., has a new and fresh outlook that breathes new life into this subject. In *Magnetizing Your Heart's Desire*, Warren presents a creative, dynamic approach to manifesting whatever your heart longs to attract. This book is just plain fun; it's like getting out your crayons and a fresh sketch pad and coloring to your heart's content. Or, like splashing acrylics all over a canvas-and yourself, in the bargain. Her techniques are irresistible for the Inner Child, trust me.

Magnetizing Your Heart's Desire comes complete with a tiny set of powerful magnets. Warren uses these to demonstrate how energy flows, or "The Law of Attraction." She compares the times when things are really popping in our lives, and we're bringing in all sorts of new friends and experiences, and attracting all kinds of yummy possibilities, to the positive attraction of magnets. The times in our lives when we are fearful and we aren't consciously choosing our reality are like the "de-magnetized" reaction when we try to hold the two negative poles of our magnets together. When the reader actually tries this with the magnets that accompany the book, it's rather stunning to see the magnets repel each other or smack together with great force, depending on which poles are placed near each other. It is an illustration that will really stay with you.

In the same way that the magnets can repel each other, we can repel the very things we want to attract into our lives with negative thinking. It's important to be congruent with the goals we want to achieve. If we're trying to attract more financial security-and who isn't?-and we are also feeling needy, we will begin to see the incongruity, Warren writes, of saying, "I can't afford" and upgrade it to "Well, I don't know how the Universe can create this although I believe it can." By changing the way we think it and say it, Warren writes that we will begin to see our energies flow in the right direction to magnetize our hearts' desires.

If you think, speak, and feel positively, "your vibrations summon your destiny," Warren teaches. She quotes Abraham, a channeled entity, who says, "You cannot improve your life by pushing against what you do not want. The more you are in conscious connection pulsating and resonating pure, positive energy with Source, the more vibrational matches you create and attract."

I can't emphasize enough that Warren makes learning these principles fun. She teaches you how to phrase affirmations in the most positive way, how to avoid sabotaging your creations, and really, how to change your whole outlook on life. She says she is a member of Virginia Satir's club called the I.I.A.F.F.I., which means, "If it ain't fun, forget it!" In a chapter titled, "Delicious Rituals," she offers many techniques for attracting—or magnetizing—our hearts' desires.

♥ ♥

Sharon captures the magic!

Sharon Ann Warren has captured the magic and wonder of how to manifest in a most beautiful way in her book, *MAGNETIZING YOUR HEART'S DESIRE*. Now everyone can learn this process easily and effortlessly from her book.

    Sharon Kay Warren, Author, *Angel Fingerprints*

This book provides all the tools you will ever need!

I loved the chapters on synchronicity and the law of attraction in action. There is so much guidance provided in Magnetizing Your Heart's Desire whenever we open ourselves through our awareness. This book provides all the tools one could ever need. I love it!

    Joanne Snow, Fort Wayne, IN

A Mystical Path for Practical Feet!

Magnetizing Your Heart's Desire is a groundbreaking book that clearly lays out the mystical path of manifesting at our practical feet. Sharon Warren has given us all a gift in this book that brings together the essential pieces for understanding how we create our world. Sharon is a master at magnetizing her heart's desires. I have watched her "walk this talk" for over 24 years. Now she gifts us with material that invites us all to join her. This book has the potential of changing your life. When I was at the "end of my rope," the techniques in these chapters guided me to transform my world! In only one month, I manifested the perfect job, healed a relationship and conceived a baby. Thank you, Sharon!

    Robin Mullen, M.A., Laguna Niguel, CA

This book is a winner!

Your book is incredible—very clear, very easy to read and very inviting! The magnets are really a marvelous and unique tool to accompany the book. It's a winner! Thank you!

    Shawn S., San Diego, CA.

Bravo!

I have just finished reading Magnetizing Your Heart's Desire. It is great!!! It is one of the most comprehensive, well-written, and incredibly informative spiritual books I have ever come across! BRAVO! Thank you!

    Marguerite Zaimes, Malvern, PA

Lots of heart!

In *Magnetizing Your Heart's Desire*, we all benefit from Sharon Warren's life-long learning in the magic of life. Her book is a walk in the park with a friend filled with ancient secrets, modern wisdom and lots of heart. With Sharon's wise words and techniques, we can all prosper and shine on and on!

Joanne Karl, author, OriginalTribe Handbook of Angels

Inner Words

Magnetizing Your Heart's Desire has a powerful set of lifechanging tools to create, activate, and magnetize more joy in every arena of your life. Warren is successful in providing us with so many insights that mirror how you 'magnetically' repel or attract your heart's desires with every thought and action. Having a set of rare-earth magnets for demonstrating the Law of Attraction is compelling and enlightening.

Ronney Aden, Publisher-Editor, *Inner Words Magazine*

Renewed Inspiration

Your book is magnificent! Even while many of us know these concepts, it is like a refresher course to take another look at our life and the way we are living it. It helped me to refocus and live more creatively—every hour of the day. Thank you for renewed inspiration. You have brightened my life.

John Hornecker (Retired Executive)

Truly a life-changing work!

"Truly a life-changer. This gem of information really works! It's easy and the results come in fast. I feel it should be taught to us as young children, so we could have a lifetime of this kind of power."

Toni Ambiel, Counselor, Odyssey Book Store, Reno Nevada

Miracle consciousness is alive and well!

Sharon Warren's book, Magnetizing Your Heart's Desire, is such a blessing to have in these times we are living in. It is inspiring on so many levels. Miracle consciousness is alive and well! This book is a living and breathing companion on the journey to manifestation. I have deep gratitude for bringing this book as a gift to us all.

Bali Guide Ken Ballard, Thailand, 1/2/04

Thank you, Thank you, Thank you!

Magnetizing Your Heart's Desire truly is a blessing and a life-changing book. Once I changed my thinking, I was also able to change my whole life for the better. And I mean each and every aspect of my life. I know now that I am the creator of my circumstances. How exciting! Magical experiences occurred whenever I am reading this book. In Chapter 11, while reading about "Lessons of the Geese," an entire flock of geese descended upon the parking lot at work. I have never seen that before, nor since! As a reminder of the universal law of attraction, I carry the magnets with me daily. Thank you, Thank you, Thank you!

Lee Ann Tassotti, 1/8/04

♥ Notes ♥

♥ Notes ♥